Kansas City's Commercial Club, meeting in the 1890s under decorations celebrating the city and its railroads.

BUSINESS
AND THE MAKING OF
Kansas City

Monroe Dodd

THE CHAMBER

Greater Kansas City Chamber of Commerce

125 YEARS

ROCKHILL
BOOKS

Rockhill Books
Kansas City, Missouri

Business and the Making of Kansas City
Copyright © 2012
by Greater Kansas City Chamber of Commerce.
All rights reserved.

Published by Rockhill Books,
an imprint of The Kansas City Star Co.
1729 Grand Blvd., Kansas City, Missouri 64108

ISBN: 978-1-61169-078-1

Library of Congress Control Number: 2012919516

Printed in the United States of America by
Walsworth Publishing Co. Inc.,
Marceline, Missouri

Page 1 photo: Members of the Commercial Club on a
promotional excursion in the early 1890s.

Main Street, looking north, late 1860s.

CONTENTS

The Downtown skyline in the late 1880s, marked most prominently in this engraving by the new Board of Trade Building, left center.

FOREWORD

The Greater Kansas City Chamber of Commerce is celebrating our 125th anniversary and, as we have from our 1887 beginnings, we're celebrating Kansas City as well.

This book is an anniversary gift from The Chamber to the businesses and people who make up our great community. Anniversaries are markers on the path, an opportunity to stop, step back, and look back, to realize and appreciate "whence we came."

The title, *Business and the Making of Kansas City*, is certainly appropriate because business built this city — and by "city" I mean the region, "Big KC."

We grew up on the Missouri River from a natural stone levee at what is now the foot of Grand Avenue. Goods unloaded there were taken overland to Westport to supply the covered wagons heading west and south. Our strength in transportation, freight, and freight-handling today is a result of that long-ago foundation.

Commerce drove development. We cut our streets through the bluffs on the south side of the river toward what is now downtown. When the railroads started pushing west, visionary business leaders organized the town's first chamber of commerce to bring the railroads through Kansas City. Opportunity came in the form of the first railroad bridge across the Missouri, and we know what happened next.

This book beautifully details our community's growth from frontier outpost to today's "Big KC." It is a story of enterprise and entrepreneurship, a story of both difficulties and bold leaps forward, a story of leadership.

Copies of *Business and the Making of Kansas City* will be placed in our Chamber archives, an early 21st century publication for readers in the future. Perhaps 125 years from now, someone will leaf through these pages just as we today look through the early documents in the archives.

We thank our partners in this venture — Monroe Dodd, Kathie Kerr, Doug Weaver and Jean Dodd, and the sponsors profiled beginning on page 188.

Enjoy — and happy anniversary!

[signature]

James A. Heeter
President and Chief Executive Officer
Greater Kansas City Chamber of Commerce

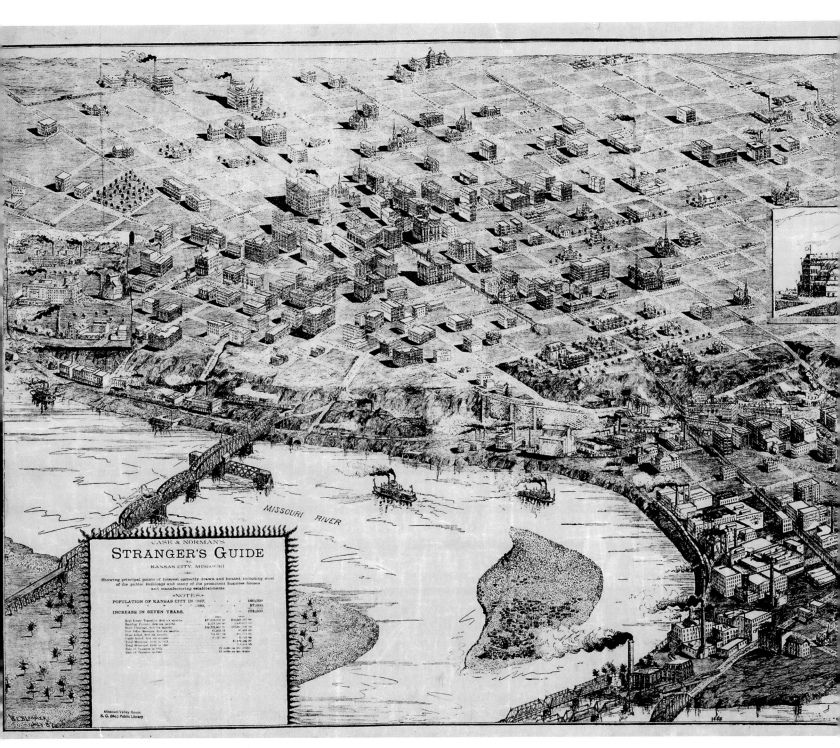

With lesser buildings and other obstructions removed, this 1887 bird's-eye view of Kansas City aimed to show off the city to its best advantage. The artist placed buildings in their proper locations, but rotated many so a viewer saw their best faces.

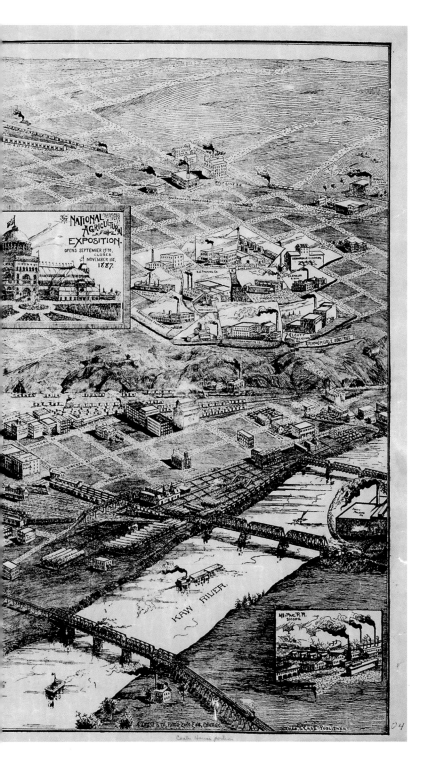

Boom Town

The year was 1887, and Kansas City could hardly contain itself.

Money flooded the city. Investors trolled for parcels to snap up and then promptly sell at a fine profit. Out-of-town insurance companies and old-family fortunes from the East looked for big gains and found them in Kansas City. Real estate turned over with lightning speed and astounding increases in value. Two years before, transactions exceeded $11 million. One year before, they hit $39 million. This year, 1887, they topped $88 million.

Boston money was at work at the northeast corner of Ninth and Wyandotte streets. There, stonemasons, carpenters and laborers toiled to build the top floors of the New England Building. The distinctive corner oriel was ready to bear the seals of all the New England states courtesy of its Boston architects and its owner and chief occupant, the New England Life Insurance Company. Also signed up to rent space: the New England Safe Deposit and Trust Company and the New England National Bank.

Just down the hill to the east on Ninth street, New York capital was putting up its own monument, a 10-story, H-shaped structure at the foot of Baltimore Avenue. The New York Life Building would rise to 10 stories once it was finished and become for awhile the largest and tallest office building in the budding city.

More than 5,400 structures, big and small and worth a total of $15 million, would be erected in the year 1887. Only recently, Kansas City, Missouri, had annexed eight square miles to the east and south, stretching the city from the Missouri River south to 31st Street.

Kansas City's money men stayed busy, too, only they didn't have quite as much to work with as the Easterners. The city's old money was no older than a couple of decades, not enough time to accumulate the kind of fortunes that a century's effort in the exchanges and in international trade had bought East Coast interests. Some of Kansas City's oldest families represented East Coast money, anyway. Perhaps the city's most respected and prominent resident in its early decades, Kersey Coates, builder of the Coates Opera House and the Coates House hotel, himself had come to Kansas City before the Civil War on behalf of investors from Pennsylvania.

Most of Kansas City's own, younger fortunes were being made in pursuits that formed the foundation of the local economy. The greater part of that was the prosaic world of wholesaling. That was a natural pursuit in a city where scores of trains on 11 railroads came and went each day. The rails brought goods to the city's staging area, the bottomland where the Kansas River met the Missouri River.

At warehouses there, wholesalers marked up products and resold them to retailers in hundreds of little towns going up across the Great Plains. In came hardware, farm implements, harness, work clothes, shoes, construction materials, groceries, furniture and drugs. Out they went again. Back came profits. Wholesaling lacked the permanence and renown of constructing

Below:The stockyards, somewhat idealized, in the 1880s. Merchants advertised buggies, plows, windmills and, of course, real estate. Facing page: Inside the Crystal Palace on the city's east side.

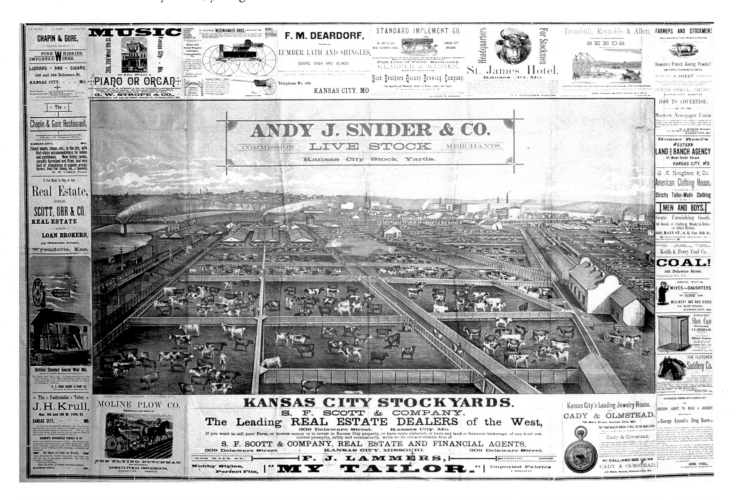

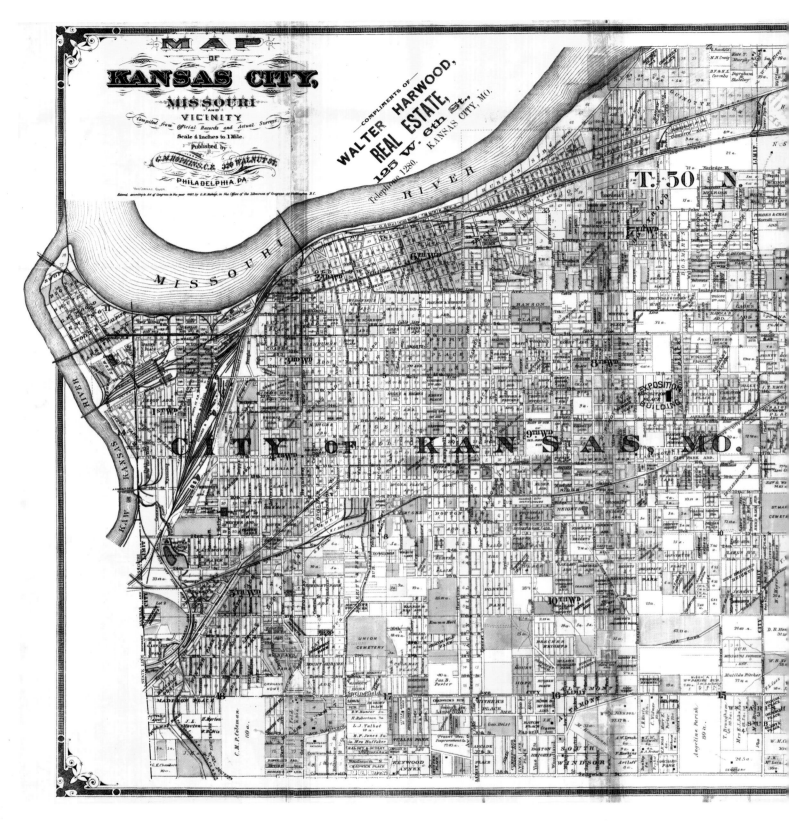

The matrix: Additions and subdivisions formed a pastel quilt on this 1887 map of Kansas City. The city limits contained a little more than 13 square miles.

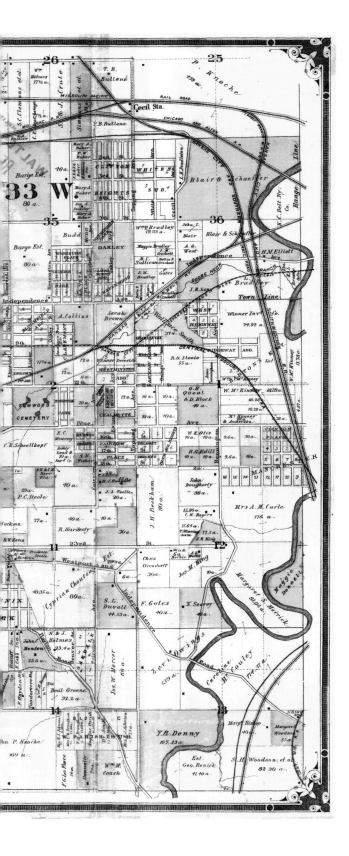

WE HAVE UNFURLED

OUR FLAG

In Honor of Kansas City's

Greatest Day!

It is apparent that

THE BOOM!

Continues with unusual vigor and with legitimate increase ir values of

REAL ESTATE!

We have large lists of

IMPROVED AND VACANT

Property to show to our friends and strangers visiting us. We shall pay careful attention to any inquiries. Call and see us.

———

H. J. LATSHAW & SON,

805 Delaware Street,

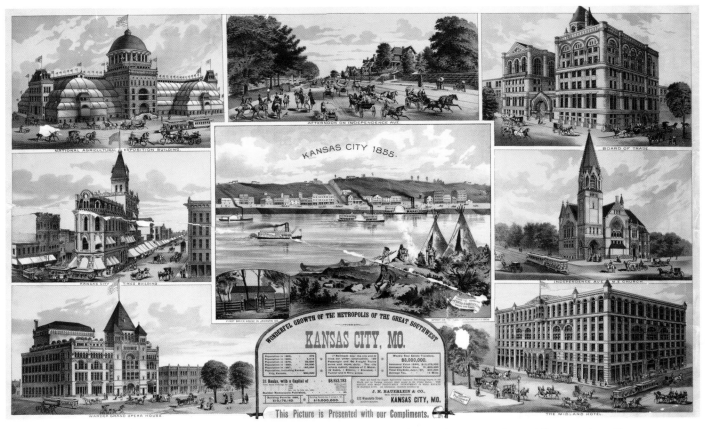

An artist assembled scenes around Kansas City, including hotels, churches and opera houses. In the middle was a bit of history.

skyscrapers or the romance of the cattle trade, but it formed Kansas City's most lucrative commercial activity.

As for the cattle trade, beeves rolled in from the west and southwest along with hogs and sheep. Sometimes the product of one ranch filled several railcars, their human handlers hitching a free ride to the city from Kansas, Texas or from Indian Territory in between. Those cowhands and hog farmers found themselves amid acres of stock pens, smelly and noisy and profitable night and day. The stockyards were financed by more New Englanders, the Adams family of Boston, heirs to two presidents.

From the stockyards, the newly arrived cowhands could look north and west and see the smokestacks of six packing plants, where thousands of workers conducted the messy work of slaughter. The packinghouses were built by the Armours of Chicago and Milwaukee, and Fowler Brothers of Chicago, and others. Looking east, they saw a line of bluffs, where ramshackle homes of

slaughterhouse workers dotted the steep sides and homes of the rich peeked over the crests. A block or two beyond those homes stood Downtown Kansas City — the one in Missouri, where skyscrapers were going up on Ninth Street.

To the west, the view across the stockyards and the Kansas River took in a brand-new Kansas City, the one in Kansas. That town, only one year old in 1887, was the work of a city named Wyandotte and of neighboring communities that bundled themselves together to improve their own prospects. Investors, they hoped, would look for easy money in anything named Kansas City, no matter which state.

Whether the money came in from the coast, or from Chicago and the older parts of the Midwest, or even locally, the stuff circulated madly. In mid-1885, Kansas City's bank clearings surpassed $200 million. In 1887, as of the fiscal year just ended in June, clearings exceeded $350 million, promoting Kansas City into 10th place in the country.

Scarcely two decades before, only a few thousand people lived and worked here at the great bend of the Missouri River. In 1880, the population reached 56,000. When the census-takers made their rounds in 1890, they would find almost 133,000, a healthy increase of 138 percent in a single decade.

In 1887, the city decided it was time to lasso this progress, and also to celebrate it.

On a hot afternoon that July, civic leaders gathered at the Alamo Building at the northwest corner of Seventh and Delaware streets to form a business leadership and promotional organization. They had tried something like it eight years before, but the idea was put aside. Now, the project took hold and so was born the Commercial Club of Kansas City. Its aims were to attract even more businesses to Kansas City, to exchange views, to influence legislation and to prevent litigation among its members.

The Club's first president was William B. Grimes, who had come to Kansas City a decade before, having made his money in the cattle business. Grimes opened a dry-goods wholesale operation on Delaware Street, founded a bank and accumulated property. Along the way, he joined the Board of Trade and the Mercantile Exchange. Mixing with other businessmen came easily to him, as did a sense of having a stake in the city's future.

The new Commercial Club, one member told a reporter, "will be a fit representative of the glory and prosperity of Kansas City as a commercial Center. Just remember that, please."

The Evening Star editorialized: "Success to the Kansas City Commercial Club! May it have many anniversaries and frequent notable banquets."

The leaders of the new club could not have chosen a more advantageous year to begin. In addition to the

New England was written all over the New England building at Ninth and Wyandotte, even to the seals of Yankee states that would grace its oriel.

business boom — and what the city experienced then was nothing less than a Capital "B" Boom — everything was aligned in 1887 for the greatest celebration in the history of this young western town.

Since 1871, Kansas City had staged an annual exposition to show off wares, its own and those of other cities. This year's extravaganza, scheduled to begin in mid-September, would center on a new and impressive hall for exhibitors, covered in glass and popularly called the Crystal Palace after the one in London. Also, in early October there would be three nighttime parades on three consecutive nights, each with a different theme. The last would be the rather mystical Priests of Pallas event, run by businessmen. That parade was a bow partly to whimsy, partly to myth, and partly to St. Louis' Veiled Prophet and New Orleans' King Carnival. Kansas Citians devised their own Pallas Athena, who would "preside" over legions of priests and supplicants.

In the midst of that heavy schedule, the president of the United States was coming to town. Grover Cleveland had accepted Kansas City's invitation to pay a visit as part of his monthlong tour of the United States by train. The president was going to bring along the person who had captured America's interest, his 23-year-old bride, Frances Cleveland. He would be only the second president to visit Kansas City, and the first to make speeches and spend the night.

To Cleveland or any other outsider, it must have seemed that Kansas City sprang full-blown out of nothing. But, the city's fortune in 1887 was the product of years of dreaming and scheming and planning and promoting. The grand celebration was the exuberant, explosive culmination of nearly a half-century's work.

Trailhead

KANZAS CITY.

Riverfront buildings in the early 1850s.

o Trading Center

Looking to make a living in the new and sparsely inhabited western part of Missouri, English-speaking settlers began arriving in force in the 1820s. This was the Far West. The organized United States ended here. Beyond Missouri's boundary lay unorganized territory, simply part of the Louisiana Purchase, without counties or property boundaries and without laws, judges, lawyers or lawmen. Far beyond lay territory claimed by Mexico and beyond that the Pacific Ocean.

The English-speakers were not the first people to arrive at the bend of the Missouri. Native Americans had preceded them, as had French-speaking trappers and fur-traders under the leadership of a couple named Francois and Berenice Chouteau. But these newest English-speaking people — French-speakers referred to them simply as "Americans" — established a lasting community. They reckoned they'd have the chance to start life in a new place.

Trading with the tribes

There were ways to do that. As the 1830s began, the U.S. government was moving Shawnee and Delaware Indians to that vacant prairie just west of Missouri, by now entitled Indian Territory. In return for displacing those tribes and others from the East, the government gave them annuities, often in substantial amounts. The native Americans would need some place to spend that money and white merchants moved in to help them do it. In the middle 1830s, the trading town of Westport sprang up about four miles south of the Missouri River and a mile east of its border with Indian Territory. Westport merchants bought supplies from St. Louis and traded directly with Indians. A local economy developed.

Meanwhile, western Missouri became a trailhead for traders bound for Santa Fe and emigrants headed for Oregon and California. In Independence and Westport outfitters provided livestock, wagons, gear and food. Landlocked Westport found a handy place for suppliers to dock at a rock ledge along the Missouri River. There, on land rising to a line of bluffs, warehouses opened to store goods made in the East. In turn, Santa Fe traders hauled those goods overland in the spring and summer to sell in the Southwest and Mexico. Returning in late summer and autumn, they brought not only cash but also different goods — silver and mules among them.

A crude port sprang to life at that rock on the river's edge. Small merchants and warehousemen built wooden structures nearby in the 1830s and 1840s. They had no way to know it, but they were the advance guard of the area's business future.

Early business leaders Kersey Coates, left, and Charles E. Kearney.

The Town of Kansas

In 1838, 14 businessmen seeking to organize and profit from the busy landing pooled their money to buy a 257-acre farm originally owned by a French-speaker, Gabriel Prudhomme. His property began at the river bank and continued southward up the bluffs. The 14 investors named their riverside commercial development the Town of Kansas, after the river that flowed into the Missouri River nearby. Often, the hamlet was called simply "Kansas."

As commercial developments go, this one started slowly — a warehouse here, a store there. In 1844 the Missouri River flooded, carrying away all but one warehouse. The community started over. By the late 1840s, things picked up. Property began changing hands, and a row of buildings arose, facing the river. By 1850 the development had progressed to the point that it was organized into a town of sorts under Jackson County law. In 1853, things became official. The City of Kansas was chartered by the state of Missouri, joining Westport and Independence as the prime communities of Jackson County, if still only tiny ones.

As late as the 1850s the Santa Fe trade carried on using ox-drawn wagons, and it still fueled the economy of the young town. From Kansas City, the best transportation from the East was by river steamer. Packets from St. Louis hauled in people and goods, but not in large enough quantities to build cities.

Change was coming. In the Capitol in Washington, the talk was of building railroads across the continent, connecting the East with a newly minted state in the West — California, acquired from Mexico. The railroads, businessmen and politicians said, would link the country from sea to sea. To clear the way for the railroads, Congress began organizing the western land into territories. A new Nebraska territory was created, and then in 1854 it was divided in two. The northern part kept the name Nebraska. The southern one lay at the doorstep of the City of Kansas and its businesses. It would be called Kansas Territory.

Pining for a railroad

Immigrants to the new Kansas Territory surely would enhance Kansas City's trade right away, but trade would go through the roof if only a railroad came along. Unlike bumpy western trails or slow travel on the rivers, railroads could carry almost anything quickly and

The Pacific Railroad, later renamed the Missouri Pacific, entered Kansas City from the east and laid track along the riverfront.

smoothly. In communities up and down the Missouri River, business interests fought to lure this railroad or that. If a road was building westward, they said, then build it through our town!

Atchison, St. Joseph and Leavenworth made their cases. So did Kansas Citians. Landowners, warehousemen, merchants — in fact, most of the little town's business interests — pined for a railroad. A few local roads were created, but only on paper.

Business leaders organized a Chamber of Commerce; promoting a railroad — or railroads — was this body's primary task. It became an obsession. Leading the charge were Kersey Coates, a Quaker from Pennsylvania, who busied himself acquiring property, and Johnston Lykins, a former missionary to the Indians. They were joined later by Charles Kearney, a renowned dealmaker, and lawyer John W. Reid. Speaking most often for the group was Robert Van Horn, who had

been recruited to run the local newspaper, first named *Enterprise* and then *Journal of Commerce*.

Of the group, Coates was the leader. He had come to town in 1854 as an agent for a Pennsylvania syndicate looking to buy land. Among Coates' early investments was property in the West Bottoms. When troubles cropped up, the Pennsylvania syndicate got cold feet and Coates took the land off its hands. He also developed a neighborhood for the well-to-do on high ground that would be called Quality Hill.

The businessmen of that early Chamber of Commerce soon found that attracting railroads could be a messy business. The Pacific Railroad was supposed to be building across Missouri, but would it simply take a direct route due west from Jefferson City and bypass Kansas City? What would it be worth to Kansas City to cause the road to redirect its tracks northwest a bit? For the railroads, huckstering was common as they built west;

This detailed lithograph of the Kansas City riverfront was printed in Boston in 1855. The scene was cleaned up, possibly to encourage free-soil immigrants. Four years later, new arrival Theodore Case would say of the hotel at right that it was "miserably kept."

if they were going to lay tracks to this city or that, they usually wanted to extract something in advance.

Kansas City made the arrangements. By 1858 the Pacific aimed its tracks at the little town. But events would postpone the effort, because railroads were not the only obsession of the day. There was the matter of slavery.

When Congress carved out the new Kansas Territory, it let locals decide whether their new state would be slave or free. The result would affect the power of either slave or free states in the U.S. Senate, and the debate over the future of Kansas Territory grew briefly into the most heated argument in American life. Because Congress established no clear mechanism for the locals to make their decision, the lines were drawn not only in speaking and balloting and politicking, but also in armed combat. Neighbors disagreed with neighbors. Kersey Coates, the Quaker, was fiercely anti-slavery. Business compatriots like John W. Reid were just as fiercely pro-slavery.

Arms would decide the issue

Things roared along that way for the City of Kansas and for the region until the outbreak of the country's great cathartic — the Civil War. That year, 1861, Kansas entered the Union as a free state, aligned with the Union. Missouri remained open to slavery, but the state stayed in the Union, courtesy of Union sympathizers and a contingent of Union troops in the largest city, St. Louis.

> *Kansas City's sentiments were split fairly evenly, but a Union detachment kept the peace and the Union flag was flown.*

Kansas City's sentiments were split fairly evenly, but a Union detachment kept the peace and the Union flag flew. That was inside town; the approaches to Kansas City and the land beyond lay in contested countryside.

Commerce dwindled to nearly nothing. Kansas City hunkered down for the duration, and the railroad question languished.

Most of the war played out to the east, but in late summer and fall 1864, Confederate forces raided Missouri. They entered the state in the southeast, bypassed Union-controlled St. Louis, made a feint at Jefferson City and headed west. In late October, the Confederate forces engaged Union troops in northern Jackson County, surging briefly near Brush Creek south of Westport, but were turned back and fled to the South.

After that, things began to settle down in western Missouri and eastern Kansas, and by the next April the war was over. The outcome solved the slavery question, but the railroad question remained open.

Once more, the fever boiled up. Rails were laid west from Wyandotte, the Kansas town across the Kansas River valley from Kansas City. By September 1865, the Pacific Railroad arrived from the east, linking Kansas City with St. Louis. That was as far as the rails went; no bridge yet crossed the Mississippi River at St. Louis — nor would one until 1874.

But there was another way to access the great markets of the east, through Chicago. By 1865, northern

Missouri was crossed by a railroad linking Hannibal on the Mississippi with St. Joseph on the Missouri. A bridge over the Mississippi was in the works north of Hannibal at Quincy, Illinois. Soon, Chicago goods could travel by rail across Missouri to some place on the Missouri River and from there into the new markets of the West and Southwest.

But where would it cross the Missouri River?

Oh, for a bridge

Boosters in St. Joseph and Atchison made bids. Leavenworth, the largest city on either side of the Missouri River, entered a strong one, too. But so did Kansas City, which probably had less than one-third of St. Joseph or Leavenworth's population, and fewer residents than Atchison.

Robert Van Horn, editor of the Journal of Commerce *and spokesman for the city's business interests.*

Clearly, the winner would prosper, because railroads brought business wherever they went and this railroad would bring a lode of business.

For various reasons St. Joseph and Atchison fell by the wayside. As the largest and busiest of the Missouri River towns, Leavenworth's case probably was the strongest, but it was hobbled by division among its business community.

Kansas City's boosters spoke with a single voice and acted boldly. Through middleman Theodore S. Case, Kersey Coates and other businessmen made acreage in the West Bottoms available to a key figure in the process. This individual, James F. Joy of Detroit, became the principal stockholder in the West Kansas Land Company (The name referred to the former name of the West Bottoms, not to the new state of Kansas.). That land, it was obvious,

Theodore S. Case

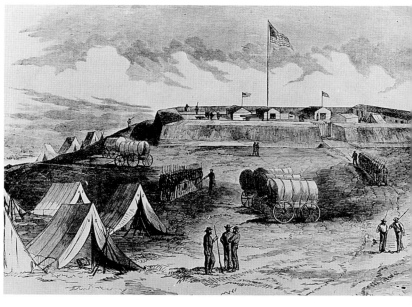

Camp, or Fort, Union at 10th and Central Streets, where a federal outpost kept the Union flag flying. According to other evidence, the artist enhanced the looks of the installation.

would skyrocket in value once the railroad arrived — if it arrived in Kansas City.

Joy was president of the Chicago, Burlington & Quincy railroad, which controlled the cross-state Hannibal & St. Joseph railroad. From the Hannibal & St. Joe's track near Cameron, Missouri, a 30-mile extension would reach the north bank of the Missouri River at Kansas City.

Eventually, Joy advised the directors of the Burlington where he thought the Missouri River ought to be bridged. That place was Kansas City.

Robert Van Horn, now in Congress, maneuvered through legislation supporting the bridge in Kansas City, along with one at Quincy. As an incentive, the bill also called for a railroad to the South, making the package irresistible to Joy's compatriots in the CB&Q.

In 1866 came the news: Kansas City would get the railroad and its bridge across the Missouri. That meant the products of the Southwest — the corn and grain and livestock sure to be produced once the land was

Following pages: Two years after the end of the Civil War and two years before the railroad bridge was completed across the Missouri River, Main Street looked like this. The 1867 view was south from Third Street.

Hundreds of Kansas Citians perched on the railings of the new bridge and hundreds more sat and stood on the bluffs to watch the first locomotive chuff across the Missouri River. The day was July 3, 1869.

settled — would most easily funnel through Kansas City. The products of the East — farm implements, building materials, liquor — would move to and through Kansas City to the newly organized lands beyond.

Scores of new businesses flocked to town, entrepreneurs drawn by the promise of a boom. Some came downriver from the once-ascendant Leavenworth, consigned now to a lower status than its rival city.

In Kansas City, contractors set to work replacing wooden structures with brick, carving streets out of the earthen bluffs, and building more offices and homes. People by the tens of thousands came to town, looking for jobs and a living in the burgeoning city.

Considering its work of railroad promotion done, the first Chamber of Commerce shut down in 1866. Three years later a new body, the Board of Trade, took upon itself promotion of local business, although over time its efforts would narrow into the grain trade. Later, a Merchants Exchange formed but never found a footing. With growth came diverse business interests. No single cause as obvious as attracting railroads showed itself,

and for a while the business community did not coalesce around a new one.

The longed-for bridge — itself something of a marvel of construction over the tricky Missouri River — opened in 1869. It was a quarter-mile long. The first train steamed in from the north on July 3, and people flocked to the bluffs to watch it cross the river. Kansas City threw a great celebration with a balloon ascent, a parade, a grand feast with appropriate toasts and fireworks. Kansas City's future was pronounced bright — just as had been forecast for so long by the railroad boosters.

They were right. In the first year after completion of the bridge, 70,000 people traveled into and out of town by train. The city's population, which probably numbered only a few thousand at the close of the war in 1865, reached 20,000 to 25,000 in 1870. (The official number, 32,268, was thought to have been padded at the urging of businessmen trying to meet a Missouri threshold for issuing certain railroad bonds).

The railroad enabled Kansas City to grow, and so did the new markets to the west. Across Kansas and Nebraska

Since its establishment in 1857, the City Market was the hub of Kansas City's retail trade. It also had a public well, so people could drink something better than creek water. In years to come, the commercial hub would move south.

and into Colorado and New Mexico, settlers used the Homestead Act to acquire land. Five years after settling it, the land could become theirs. To serve them, new towns sprang up hundreds of miles from Kansas City. The towns with a railroad running past became going concerns. Their merchants depended on Kansas City for supplies that they couldn't make or grow themselves.

Clearinghouse for the Great Plains

The task of receiving, storing and shipping goods to serve those new cities kept Kansas City humming. From the east came boxcars full of plows and harness, reapers and harvesting machinery. Wholesalers resold them to merchants in Ottawa, Abilene, Emporia, Newton, Salina, Great Bend and Dodge City — wherever the railroads ran and wherever farmers needed equipment. From those towns, money flowed back to Kansas City. Likewise, into Kansas City and out again went groceries, lumber, hardware, tools, clothing, drugs, furniture, stoves and cooking utensils, plates and dishes and liquor.

Spun off from this activity were jobs – from

> *Retailers proliferated, selling the necessities and a few luxuries of life to legions of new customers.*

warehouses to railroads to construction. There were plenty of jobs, too, for hoteliers and restaurateurs, lawyers and doctors.

Retailers proliferated, selling the necessities and a few luxuries of life to legions of new customers. At the hub of the retail trade was the City Market. By the early 1870s, the market was jammed with wagons of area farmers, selling produce and meat animals. It was lined on four sides by restaurants, entertainment halls and stores. Streetcars drawn by horses and mules linked the City Market to city additions that had grown to the south and east, and to the West Bottoms. Local government found a home at the City Market, too. City Hall and a police

The first livestock exchange building in the early 1870s was a simple, wooden affair. Later ones would be built on a grander scale.

station arose at one corner and a second Jackson County Courthouse — the original was still in Independence — went up a block north.

Kansas City's big money machine was in the West Bottoms. There, the railroads chose grounds for their basic operations of shipping and delivering, switching and repair. Trains crossing the new bridge from the north reached the south bank of the river and then curved gently west along a slender route called the Gooseneck between the river and the bluffs. As the tracks entered the open flats formed by the bottomland of the Missouri and Kansas rivers, they multiplied into siding after siding.

Along the way rose multi-story brick buildings where the city's wholesale trade could offload merchandise for storage. Deere, Mansur & Company erected a new building to house farm implements, and added to it as years passed. By 1887, Deere and 26 other companies would be engaged in the agricultural implements trade in Kansas City. Ridenour and Baker's three-story brick grocery warehouse stocked sugar, coffee, box goods, teas, cigars, vinegar, syrup. They and others shipped those goods to countless merchants across the west. Back came money.

Now, too, increasing amounts of livestock and grain were arriving.

Money on the hoof

Along the Missouri-Kansas line, stockyards spread out and commission merchants fanned out to meet the animals and their owners. Cattle, pigs and sheep tramped down ramps and into the growing labyrinth of

fences and chutes. Some animals headed on east. Others were dispatched for fattening. Some went directly to packinghouses.

Meatpackers erected massive operations in the Bottoms, employed more than 6,000 people and devoured much of the pork and beef that could be imported from the hinterlands. At first the meat was canned but with the development of refrigerated boxcars in 1875, fresh dressed beef could be shipped east, too.

In the early 1870s, a new strain of wheat that could survive the dry weather and hot summer in the plains was introduced by Russian immigrants in Kansas and Nebraska. Turkey Red wheat soon became the dominant crop; yields grew and so did shipments of grain to Kansas City. Here, trains were unloaded at new elevators. Once milled, the grain was moved to bakeries and turned into

Great granddaddy of the Herefords that transformed America's taste in beef was Anxiety IV, a bull raised in Independence.

The Kansas Pacific Railway left no doubt in 1873 of its route — through the buffalo grazing lands of Kansas and Colorado. Its Kansas City office faced Broadway. Across the state line in Armstrong, below, the locomotive roster lined up.

In 1871, the city's commercial interests led by Kersey Coates instituted an annual Industrial Exposition, a mercantile fair aimed at advertising the city's wares to residents and — more important — visitors. The fair took place first in McClure's addition near 20th Street and Grand Avenue, and then moved to grounds near Westport, and finally settled in the eastern part of town.

Speculation and real-estate frenzy

In 1880, Kansas City's population reached 56,000 and kept soaring upward. Real-estate speculators matched the pace of the population. Properties in downtown Kansas City turned over and over, each time bringing a higher price. The Goodrich Addition was a fine example. The parcel, stretching from Baltimore Avenue to Broadway and from 17th to 21st streets, was bought in the 1880s by a syndicate for $800,000. A year later, it sold for $1.8 million and the syndicate divided up a $1 million profit.

Investors from the East Coast and Europe made the big deals, but real estate turned into a public mania. Even clerks and mechanics bought land on monthly payments and hoped for the best. Farmers sold prairies south of town and saw their expansive farms divided into lots.

The real-estate frenzy was marked by the extension of streetcar routes — led by cablecar technology, which arrived in 1885 and moved more people faster than had been possible by horsecar. The new routes often ended in new parks, established by the very business people who developed the subdivisions around those parks. To the south there was Troost Lake, to the east Washington Park, and to the west Chelsea Park in Kansas City, Kansas. All were streetcar parks, planned by people in hopes that buyers would visit the park, look around at the subdivisions and end up buying land and building a house. Home, after all, would lie conveniently close to a streetcar line.

bread, crackers and cookies.

On through the 1870s more rail sidings were laid as businessmen demanded more space and better access to transportation. Late in the decade, the railroads built a Union Depot in the opulent Second Empire style then prevalent. Streetcar tracks descended from the city to the station. Mules and horses kept the cars in continual motion.

Atop the bluffs, the city expanded as the decade of the 1870s wore on. The center of activity moved south from the City Market to a newer nexus at the intersection of Delaware, Main and Ninth Streets, which came to be called the Junction. In the 1880s the business center moved farther south toward 11th Street.

Delaware and Main streets angled in from the north at Ninth Street, creating the parcel on which was built Vaughan's Diamond, a flatiron structure. This area, where streets and cablecar tracks crossed from most directions, was called The Junction.

The newly finished Crystal Palace formed the centerpiece of Kansas City's 1887 Exposition. It ran from mid-September through October that year.

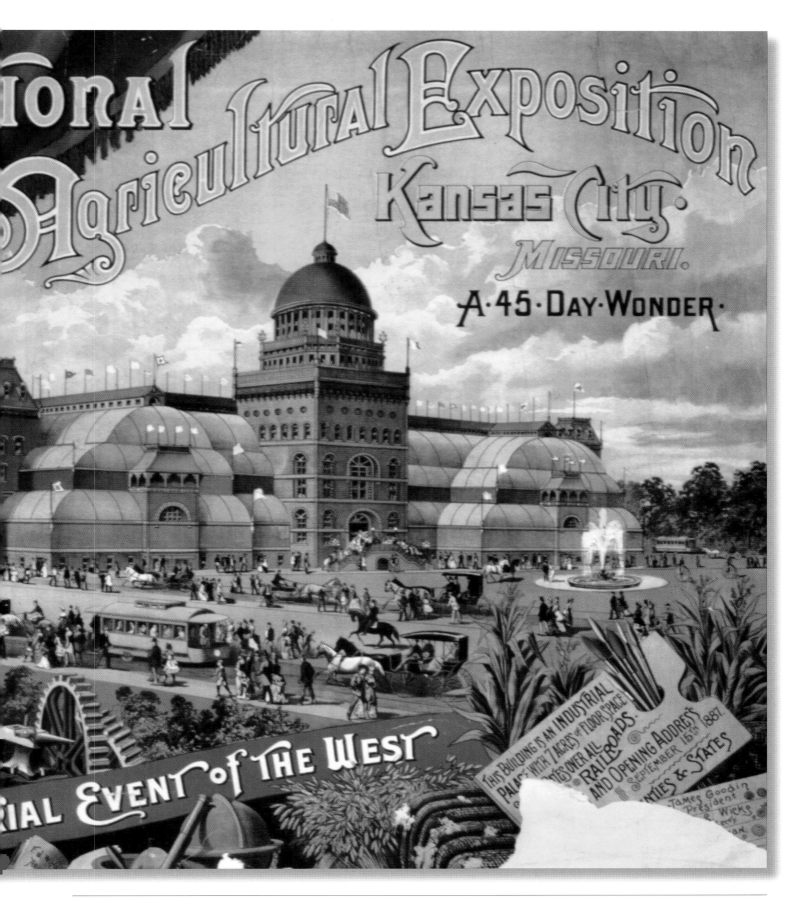

Full-color engravings depicted the fanciful floats that rolled up Main Street in the city's first Priest of Pallas parade in 1887. The parade was organized by an imaginative official of the Commercial Club. Below: Scenes from the manufacturers' parade a day earlier.

Land values rocketed to unheard-of levels. Fortunes were made in real estate and also a few lost. Naturally, unscrupulous operators flocked to the city, too.

The city boasted four newspapers, where real-estate people loved to advertise. *The Journal of Commerce* continued as it had since pre-Civil War days as the voice of the city's business establishment with a Republican bent. *The Times* entered the field in the late 1860s with a point of view that was politically Democratic — in fact, unreconstructed Confederate — and mighty favorable to real-estate propositions. By the middle 1870s, the *Journal* and *Times* were joined by *The Mail*. In 1880, two businessmen from Indiana, William Rockhill Nelson and Samuel Morss, moved to town and began *The Evening Star*. The four-page sheet, issued in the afternoon, professed alliance to no party but a determination to mix it up in local affairs.

The Commercial Club is born

The city was bursting at the seams with the combined forces of money, energy and promotion. Thus, it was the time to celebrate — and to invite the President to town. On July 27, Grover Cleveland accepted. Two days later, after planning committees had met earlier in the month, the Commercial Club formally organized itself.

The club's first membership roster numbered 35 firms. Eligible for membership were wholesalers, manufacturers, bankers and no more than 10 retailers. Real-estate operators were not accepted. Their vocation, the club decided, was "not a commercial pursuit." Also excluded were lawyers and other professionals.

One of its first orders of business would be to carve out time to meet the President. The club's first vice president, L.E. Irwin, a crockery and glassware wholesaler, would have his own special role — head of the Parade Association. He would become the driving force behind the Priests of Pallas.

Parades there would be aplenty, along with much more hoopla.

The festivities would culminate the second week of October. Out at the fairgrounds, between 12th and 15th streets on Kansas Avenue, the annual Exposition was in full swing. It would continue until mid-November. The newly opened Crystal Palace covered seven acres and its managers boasted that it contained "the greatest display of products, industries, machinery, manufactures and art ever seen in the West." Entertainment that week was provided by the Dodge City Cowboy Band.

The night of October 11, a military and civic parade moved north along Grand Avenue and Main Street, drawing crowds that overflowed the curbs to see seven bands, a drum corps and the fire department towing an old hand engine. The police department unit towed a Gatling gun that was fired at several points along the parade route — with no injuries — and the Flambeau Club's members shot off fireworks the whole way. Best received was the Traveling Man's Protective Association, salesmen or "drummers," who marched and joked 200 strong, carrying signs reading, "Grand Army Rustlers" and "Trade falls before the beat of our drummers."

The next evening, streets were blocked for a Pageant of the Trades parade. All along the way were horse-drawn floats — 30 in all — drumming the work of the city's merchants. The Manhattan Clothing Company display was topped by a giant globe with the motto, "We clothe the earth & planets." Richards & Conover, hardware merchants, showed samples of their wares — hoes, rakes, shovels, wagon wheels, anvils, bellows, scales, barbed wire, horseshoes, circular saws, straight saws, grindstones and atop it all a safe, on which sat a two-foot-high lock. Long Brothers, wholesale grocers, showed three sailboats with hulls like cigars, advertising their "Leader" smoke. Martin, Perrin & Company, liquor merchants, mounted a steamship lookalike on their float. Its deck was stacked with barrels labeled "Old Bourbon" and "Rye" and at the top, one labeled "Liquors for Kansas" and one labeled "Kansas Malt," pulling the leg of the now-dry state. The float, it was reported, met with loud applause.

One wing of the Board of Trade was under construction at Eighth and Wyandotte.

Hail to the chief and the First Lady

As the parade was on the march, President Cleveland and his wife arrived at Union Depot, stepped into their carriage and rode it from the Bottoms around to Broadway, then uphill to the Coates House at 10th Street. The streets were jammed with onlookers. Plans called for 300 people to attend a reception inside the hotel, but many of those 300 evidently invited friends and relatives, and the number at the reception tripled. By 10 p.m. the first couple retired.

They awakened the next morning for a carriage tour

Ogled from all sides, President Grover Cleveland and his new bride, Frances Cleveland, stopped long enough in their tour of Kansas City for this photograph to be taken. The First Couple sat in the carriage, under a parasol. Below, the throng at the Federal Courthouse.

of the city, once more accompanied by crowds all the way. At a bluff atop Quality Hill, Cleveland and his wife looked out over the busy West Bottoms and, on signal, whistles on scores of locomotives and on packinghouses were sounded in salute. Heading east, the President's procession passed the Exposition grounds but did not stop, and then proceeded to the new YMCA building, which was under construction at the northeast corner of Ninth and Locust streets. The President participated in a cornerstone-laying ceremony. Then it was back to the Coates House for lunch, and then on to Ninth and Walnut streets for a speech at the "custom house," the twin-towered federal building. Praising the growth of Kansas City, he remarked on "the new, fresh and astounding growth of this new west." Thousands of dignitaries and onlookers then passed by the President and First Lady; the crowds were mostly prohibited from handshaking but nothing stopped them from gawking.

That evening's Priests of Pallas parade, the third Downtown in three days, was a wonder. Participants passed under three temporary arches erected along Main Street, one of which bore the words, "Welcome to Kansas City." Leading off the parade was mounted cavalry, and then came the Flambeau Club once again and the High Priest of Pallas and his ministers, all dressed in the style of ancient Greeks. They were followed by floats representing a pageant mixing myth, history and fable. Finally, after a grand float on which perched Pallas Athena, the cortege wound down on a surprisingly silly note. One float in the last section depicted royalty of various countries humbled and hard at work tending bar or doing wash in the century to come. Afterward the Priests and their followers danced the night away at a temporary ballroom built at Seventh and Lydia streets.

Although places were set for the Clevelands to review the Priests of Pallas parade at the Junction, the First Couple missed the festivities. Reportedly, their absence was caused by a concern about their security. Instead, the President and his wife attended one more banquet and then reboarded their train and left Kansas City, headed south. Their hotel room, Number 216, was stripped of its presidential decorations. Only the Coates

Cycloramas, giant 360-degree paintings of scenes from history with three-dimensional foregrounds, were popular entertainment spectacles in the late 1880s. Kansas City's version, at Eighth Street and Broadway behind the rising Midland Hotel, showed a scene from the Battle of Missionary Ridge in Tennessee. The panorama was created in Germany. It remained on display in Kansas City until 1890, when it was moved to Chattanooga.

House's stock furniture and carpet remained.

Sadly, the hotel's namesake and former owner was not around to show the president the city to which he had contributed so much. Kersey Coates, the Pennsylvania Quaker and the solidest of Kansas City's early solid citizens, had died in April at 62 years of age. In his three decades in Kansas City, Coates had assembled the property that helped lure the railroads to Kansas City, built the Coates Opera House and the Coates Hotel, and started the Industrial Exposition in 1871. Before the Civil War, he helped found the first Chamber of Commerce.

As the early giants of Kansas City passed from the scene the exuberant young city passed into adulthood, with all the triumphs and trials that would involve.

Following pages: The West Bottoms, crowded with tracks, business and humble residences and getting more so as the 1800s wore on.

In this 1895 bird's eye view, Union Depot stood at lower left, barely noticeable because of the perspective. Packing houses dominated the right side of the scene, stockyards the upper left and railroad tracks and warehouses all the rest.

Boom to Bust... and Back

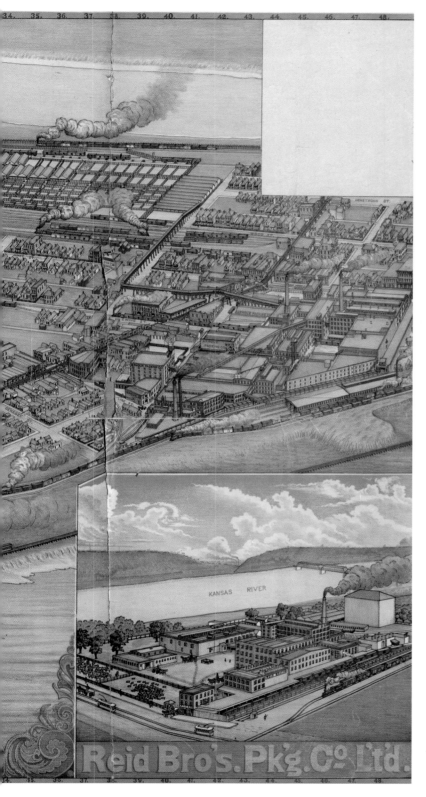

Cities have peaks and valleys, and 1887 marked one of Kansas City's peaks. Then things went downhill. About the time the big festivities of that autumn ended, the real estate boom was turning to ashes. Land prices had reached the point that buyers balked. Sales slowed and soon property hardly sold at all.

Stuck with big mortgages based on inflated prices, speculators and agents pulled back or fled the market. Investors from the East who had superheated the Kansas City real-estate boom began looking for action anywhere else.

As if fatigued by too many years of hyperactivity, the business of the city slowed down.

Construction activity, lively in the late 1880s, paused. By 1890, the New England building, the New York Life building, the Crystal Palace, the new Board of Trade building at Eighth and Wyandotte streets, the giant department store of Bullene, Moores and Emery on 11th Street between Walnut Street and Grand Avenue — all were completed. Through the rest of the decade, few notable structures were built with private money. Kansas City's real-estate market would not regain its health until after the turn of the century.

In the city's trade territory west and southwest, things also looked grim. A poor corn crop in 1886 led to panic selling of cattle, depressing the Kansas City market.

The New York firm of Schwarszchild and Sulzberger took over an Armourdale packinghouse in 1893 and enlarged it. The company was sold to Wilson & Company in 1916.

In 1887, a second straight hard winter damaged herds. Bad times on the range led to diminished farm lending. Kansas City's wholesalers stayed busy shipping groceries, dry goods and hardware until 1891, when the slowdown caught up with them, too.

Before the city could recover, financial panic broke out across the country in 1893, carrying many businesses down with it. Prices dropped and stayed low for five years.

The city and its business establishment faced the question: Where to now?

Creating competition

Certainly, attracting railroads was no longer the solution. Kansas City had plenty of them. Instead, railroads had become part of the problem.

By 1887, the city was served by 11 railroads. Kansas City's wholesalers and manufacturers could reach both coasts, the Canadian border and the Southeast — if

they could afford the shipping rates. The problem wasn't access, but cost.

Rates to St. Louis, Kansas City interests cried, were exorbitant. They complained that St. Louis and Chicago wholesalers were aiming to capture Kansas City's markets without having to ship goods through Kansas City, and so had influenced the railroads to maintain high rates across Missouri. In March 1889 the Commercial Club reported that the Santa Fe charged half as much to ship goods to Mexico City from Denver as it charged to ship them to

Standing atop the bluff looking west toward Kansas City, Kansas, a photographer captured the gritty reality of business in the Bottoms.

the same place from Kansas City.

Grain farmers and cattle ranchers in the countryside faced the same problem as wholesale houses and packinghouses in the West Bottoms: Shipping rates had risen too far, they said, and the railroads were colluding to keep them that way. In the second year of its existence, the Commercial Club found a new focus: Create competition for the railroads.

The club instituted a Transportation Bureau, which gathered support for turning to an old source of transportation in these parts, the Missouri River. In April 1890 the Kansas City and Missouri River Transportation Company began operations with three riverboats. Upriver from St. Louis, the boats carried dry goods, hardware, canned products and general merchandise. Downriver from Kansas City they hauled grain.

For a while, the scheme worked. The railroads lowered their charges. But then the riverboats lost traffic. Also, they couldn't carry as much tonnage as trains and the boats had to shut down in winter, when the river turned icy. By 1893, the Commercial Club ended this first river experiment. There would be more in years to come.

Holding their own

Through it all, and in spite of dips in the economy, Kansas City most notable raw materials —livestock and grain — still made money. The city's location in the middle of a good grass and corn region made it by the 1880s the leading market for stocker and feeder cattle. Early that decade, the Kansas City Fat Stock Association was formed and sponsored annual exhibitions aimed at keeping the quality of beef high. As for hogs, by the early 1880s Kansas City trailed only St. Louis in animals received. The Kansas City Live Stock Exchange, which standardized inspection and pricing of meat animals, was formed in 1886.

By 1881, Kansas City had passed St. Louis and Cincinnati in pork packing, the work of the Fowler Brothers and Jacob Dold & Son packinghouses. The Armour house began packing mutton by the early 1890s. Swift and Company arrived in the late 1880s and Cudahy in 1899.

The grain market had been up and down since the Civil War, up with building of grain elevators in the early 1870s and down with the locust plague of 1874, up with more elevator capacity by 1880 and so continuing until the mid-1880s,when bad weather and high freight rates

Drug wholesaler Frank Faxon, standing, with Commercial Club colleagues — hardware wholesaler John F. Richards, right, and George W. Fuller, financier and former implement dealer.

dampened the trade in wheat and corn. The market went up when railroads eased their shipping rules and elevator capacity increased, and then down with the failure of the Kansas wheat crop in 1895.

In 1889, the Commercial Club appointed a committee to promote milling in Kansas City. By the end of 1893, seven companies were milling corn, which dominated production until after the turn of the century, when wheat took over first place.

For much of its history, Kansas City businesses had supplied products made by others. Now Kansas City was making its own products, and not only from livestock and grain.

In the city of Argentine in Wyandotte County, the Argentine smelter, one of the largest in the country, employed hundreds. In the Blue River Valley in Jackson County, nine iron products companies had on the payroll more than a thousand workers in the late 1880s. Other plants made overalls, leather products, soap, paints and novelties. Also: baby carriages, office fixtures, bottled vinegar, cleaning powder, clay pipe and steel roofing. By 1897, seven shirt factories were in operation. Some manufacturers started here. Others moved in from Illinois and Iowa and still others from Wichita and Kansas City's long-ago rival, Leavenworth.

Despite the occasional economic rough patches, Kansas City was proving a fine place to do business and make money. But was that enough?

Toward a better way of life

Perhaps an answer lay in a Commercial Club motto, devised by drug wholesaler Frank Faxon, who was the club's third president in 1889-1890. It was simple:

"Make Kansas City a good place to live in."

To 21st-century ears, that sounds tepid or, perhaps obvious. Hardly is it a stirring call to action. Turned on its head, however, Faxon's slogan acknowledged a sad fact:

Nineteenth-century Kansas City was, in fact, a *poor* place to live.

Most streets were roughly paved — if they were paved at all. Smoke and soot from railroad locomotives and packing plants blanketed the bottoms and reached Downtown, along with the stench of the stockyards. The working class lived in crowded housing, the poor lived in hovels and no area was zoned. From one block to another, Kansas City was a hodgepodge of businesses and residences. On certain infamous streets, bars and joints operated with minimal interference from police. In most wards, politicians largely answered to one neighborhood boss or another.

If Faxon could have seen a century and a quarter into the future, he would have found civic leaders still concerned about providing amenities to attract intelligent and skilled workers and residents. In the 21st century, those amenities would include good schools, fine restaurants, an exciting arts scene, recreational opportunities and lively entertainment. In the late 19th century, too many Kansas Citians lacked even decent sanitation.

August Meyer

Thirty-nine years old when the Commercial Club was founded in 1887, Faxon represented a younger group of business people who believed that a better city for living would attract more visitors and more residents and, in the end, more businesses.

The star of the group was younger yet. August Meyer, born in St. Louis in 1851 and educated as an engineer in Germany, had started his career in Colorado as a government assayer. Within a few

years he became head of a mining company in Leadville, a city he helped lay out. In 1881, Meyer arrived in Kansas City and bought a smelting plant that had been built the year before in Argentine in the Kansas River bottoms. The plant melted silver and lead from ore shipped in from the Rocky Mountains.

He joined the Commercial Club, served as a director and would become its president in 1895. In February 1892 he gave a speech, "How to Build a City," that proposed various reforms, including a non-partisan government and a sustained public works program. In the best-remembered passages, however, Meyer proposed that the city needed a physical makeover. Make the city beautiful, he said, and people would come.

Parks and Boulevards

Before the year was out, the mayor had appointed a board to create parks and boulevards in Kansas City, Missouri. Meyer was elected president. Arm in arm with William Rockhill Nelson of *The Star*, Meyer inspired a movement that would create miles of beautiful streets and acres of recreation grounds for Kansas Citians. Meyer hired a landscape architect, George Kessler, who by 1893 had produced a plan that Meyer's parks board presented to the city.

Nelson, meanwhile, banged the publicity drum. Give Kansas Citians open places with trees and greenswards where they could stroll and play and breathe fresh air, his *Star* said, and life would be better all around. Now, connect those parks with wide, handsome boulevards. Neighborhoods would improve and property values would stabilize and probably rise. Early proponents even argued that parks and boulevards would reduce the city's tendency to gobble up land — to sprawl.

The movement captured the imagination of many Kansas Citians, but its proponents had to fight objections from landowners who balked at paying the taxes necessary for construction. Even Thomas Swope, who had donated 1,300 acres outside the city limit for a city park in 1896, helped form a Taxpayer's League of objectors. Swope still owned plenty of property inside the city and thus would be subject to new taxes.

Nelson's *Star* called the opponents "mossbacks"

Left: Not all was smoothed out in 1890s Kansas City. Here, a new federal courthouse would rise at Eighth Street and Grand Avenue.

The Star's caricature of Thomas Swope exhorting parks naysayers.

William Rockhill Nelson

and lampooned Swope in a front-page editorial cartoon showing a character that resembled the bachelor millionaire, who was known for pinching pennies. The paper quoted this character addressing his fellow parks opponents:

"What use have I for parks? I have neither children to play under the trees nor carriages and horses to display on the boulevards and never will because carriages must be bought….Let us stand forever in one place like we have always stood and refuse to move on jot or tittle, one iota or one cent!"

In the end, the constant campaigning by parks

Following pages: *Wags called this section of the city "Baltimore Canyon." Although the impressive New York Life Building had risen at the end of the street, truncated hills stood along its edges in 1890.*

The landmark Bullene, Moores and Emery store opened in 1890 at the northeast corner of 11th and Walnut streets. Later, it would become Emery, Bird, Thayer.

Below: Advertising the route of the new Kansas City, Pittsburg and Gulf railroad, the city's link to the Gulf and beyond.

advocates succeeded. After years of struggle and losses in court, Swope and other opponents gave up. By 1900, construction of the system was under way.

August Meyer, meanwhile, moved from his home in Argentine to a mansion in a new and upscale neighborhood along the fringes of Westport. Across the street sat the home of his collaborator in the City Beautiful movement, William Rockhill Nelson.

Upward once more

Toward the turn of the century, Kansas City business began to recover from its malaise, spurred in part by the opening in 1897 of the Kansas City, Pittsburg & Gulf railroad to the Gulf of Mexico. The north-south route was the brainchild of Arthur E. Stilwell, only 38 when his railroad made its first run from Kansas City to the seaport he named for himself, Port Arthur, Texas. Now, markets for Kansas City-distributed products opened from southwest Missouri through Arkansas — both of which had long been dominated by St. Louis interests. The tracks traveled on through Louisiana and Texas to the sea. Three years after its completion, the railroad was

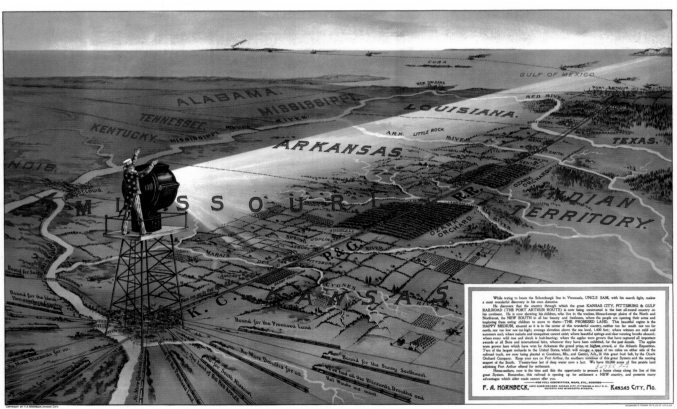

UNCLE SAM AND HIS SEARCH LIGHT.
LOOKING OVER THE "PORT ARTHUR ROUTE".

Pride and joy of the city in 1899: Convention Hall, constructed with masonry, metal and wood.

renamed Kansas City Southern Railway Company.

Kansas City began another long era of growth, this one to last a decade and a half.

At the close of the 20th century, Kansas City's business leaders turned their attention to the meeting and event trade. The Commercial Club took the lead, making its pet project construction of a big, new arena that would house not only market shows but also entertainments.

The work of raising money began in June 1897 at a special meeting of the Club. From an estimated 250 people in attendance, $23,400 was raised. Arthur Stilwell promptly chipped in $5,000. Hugh McGowan, head of an asphalt company and a local natural gas utility, pledged $2,500. A committee of 15 was appointed to raise more. Subscribers would receive one share in the hall for each dollar contributed. Directors thanked Kirkland Armour of the meatpacking family for his donation of a Hereford heifer of such good breeding that it wound up adding tens of thousands of dollars to the fund.

The Club invited downtown landowners to propose a site, and 13th Street and Central Avenue was decided upon. The contractor broke ground in late May 1898 and a little more than seven months later the nearly finished hall was thrown open for a concert. On February 22, 1899, the hall — made of steel, brick, stone and wood — formally opened. Its final cost: $250,000. To mark the occasion, little speechmaking was done, but John Phillip Sousa and his band played an afternoon and an evening concert and then stuck around to play for a dance.

The business community had big plans for the structure, a showplace without rival in the West. No plan was bigger than wooing the national convention of a political party, and local boosters went after the Democrats with boasts about the brand new hall, not to mention a $50,000 deposit. On February 22, 1900, the party's national committee meeting in Washington decided on Kansas City. The nominating convention was scheduled to begin July 4, 1900.

Kansas City would return to the national spotlight — although not in quite the way civic boosters intended.

Ruins of Convention Hall, Kansas City,

Rising to the Occasion

From the earliest days of settlement, Kansas City's waves of success and high hopes inevitably were interrupted by **floods or storms,** war or economic crisis. In 1900, fire crashed the city's party.

At 1 p.m. on April 4 that year, passersby saw smoke and then flames appear at the northeast corner of Convention Hall. Within a quarter-hour, a fire engulfed the building, and before an hour was gone the roof of the hall collapsed. Brick columns surrounding the loggia swayed and then fell outward to the sidewalk. In no time, the hall was reduced to its masonry walls. A brisk southeast breeze blew embers across the street, setting fire to the Lathrop School and the Second Presbyterian Church.

Inside the charred stone walls there remained only ashes and steel I-beams, twisted into fantastic shapes by the heat. There were suspicions of arson, or poor wiring, or a neglected stove, or careless workmen, but no cause was ever determined.

Only 90 days remained before the Democratic National Convention was to begin. Could the thing be put back together in time? If not, officials in Cincinnati and Milwaukee were knocking on the party's door, offering their cities and their facilities as a replacement.

Leaders of the Commercial Club, witnessing their pride and joy ruined scarcely a year after it opened,

The city's 90-day wonder, showing a temporary wood balustrade around the roof and other spots where construction was unfinished, welcomed its first occupants in July 1900. This time, more metal and masonry and less wood were used.

summoned their resolve. Even as the Convention Hall burned, Club President U.S. Epperson started a public subscription. As for supplies, replacement lumber could be had in 10 days, but contractors and architects thought new steel would be impossible to acquire in time. Club Secretary E.M. Clendening wired the steelmaker anyway.

The Kansas City spirit

Within hours, the Convention Hall directors met at the Commercial Club, and decided to try to rebuild. Contributions already were coming in — $5,000 each from the estate of Kersey Coates and *The Kansas City Star*, $1,000 each from the Jones Brothers Dry Goods Company and the Heim Brewery, and smaller donations not only from other businesses but also from everyday folks.

Within four days, the city raised $60,000, worth roughly $1.5 million in 21st-century money. Steel, it turned out, could be had — for a premium price.

U.S. Epperson

Local trade unions agreed to let non-union steelworkers do the job in return for promises that all other work would go to union men. National Democratic Party officials stuck with Kansas City.

An astonishingly brief 90 days after the fire, a rebuilt and fireproofed hall reopened, blessedly in the nick of time. The original construction had taken nine months. The new hall cost $400,000, far more than the first one because organizers had to pay extra for rush-ordered materials and for night-time and weekend overtime labor. As the nominating convention began, blemishes and unfinished sections remained, but they were obscured by liberal use of bunting.

The visiting press reported pleasure and perhaps some surprise.

One New York reporter, though complaining of the July heat, wrote of Kansas City, "There is no getting away from the fact that its citizens have risen to the occasion."

The city turned its calamity into a rallying point.

New Year's Eve 1900 brought the well-to-do and well-dressed to Convention Hall to mark the arrival of 1901 and the 20th century.

Rebuilding of the hall was the result, leaders said, of "The Kansas City Spirit." Spirit is an indefinite thing and certainly not unique to a single city. Yet something positive had animated business leaders and workers to engage in big deeds that spring and summer of 1900. "Spirit" probably fit as well as any word.

Deservedly pleased with themselves, the city's business elite gathered at year's end to celebrate. On December 31, 1900, on the eve of the new century, the restored Convention Hall played host to a grand evening of dancing and entertainment, The Century Ball. The idea had been suggested in *The Kansas City Journal* and adopted by Convention Hall directors.

Ten carloads of evergreens strung in garlands decorated the newly restored hall, along with red and white electric lights. Thousands of attendees paid $10 each — more than $200 in today's money — to dance to a band playing two-steps and waltzes, or to watch others do so. At 11:30 p.m., more than a hundred men and women costumed in the style of a century before performed the minuet.

High above, at the north end of the hall, a giant panel of electric lights in an hourglass shape counted down the minutes until the new year of 1901 — and the 20th century— began.

The box seats were filled with business leaders, their associates and family members. They represented a panorama of Kansas City's business pursuits, and in some of them were names that would be recognizable a century later.

The Kansas City stockyards in wide-angle view, captured in 1907 by a camera mounted in a balloon. At left is the Kansas River and beyond it Armourdale, a part of Kansas City, Kansas.

In Box 46 sat Kirkland B. Armour, who with his brother, Charles, had come to Kansas City from Chicago in about 1870 to work at the family packing plant with their uncle, Simeon B. Armour. Kirkland Armour now was president and general manager of the operation, the biggest among local meatpackers.

Kirkland B. Armour

Because of Armour, Swift and other packinghouses that lined the Kansas River, and because of the vast stockyards where cattle, pigs, sheep and mules were moved in and out by the thousands, Kansas City had gained the reputation of a cowtown. The numbers showed it was now the second-largest livestock processor in the country.

It was clear why Kansas City now played host to The National Hereford Cattle Show, an annual affair invented by cattle breeders housed under a tent in the West Bottoms. In 1901, *The Drovers Daily Telegram* would suggest that the event be named after the British Royal livestock show, and so Kansas City's show was renamed the American Royal. In later years, the Royal would move up to Convention Hall and later to an amusement park, and finally would settle back in the West Bottoms for good in 1922.

The cowtown was a grain town, too, taking on shipment after shipment from the Great Plains, and

then milling and baking the stuff into crackers and biscuits and bread. One of the city's coterie of grain merchants was watching the Century Ball celebration from Box 59. He was William T. Kemper, at 34 the youngest president of the Kansas City Board of Trade. Before coming to Kansas City in 1893, Kemper had been partner in a Valley Falls, Kansas, bank with Rufus Crosby. Crosby's daughter, now Kemper's wife, sat with him on this festive evening. In years to come, Kemper would return to banking, eventually handing the reins to descendants.

On the dance floor that night was another grain trader, E.W. Shields, and his wife. In only a few years, Shields, along with fellow trader Herbert Hall, would become early financial backers of a young developer named J.C. Nichols.

Jacob and Ella Loose, meanwhile, shared a Century

Hall box with the Armours. In 1882, Jacob Loose and his brother, Joseph, bought the Corle Cracker and Candy Company and renamed it the Loose Brothers Manufacturing Company. In 1890 Jacob Loose organized the American Biscuit Company and moved to Chicago. When he stepped down in the late 1890s because of ill health, American Biscuit was absorbed, over Loose's objections, into the new National Biscuit Company.

Back in town on this night for the Century Ball, Loose was already planning to go head to head with National Biscuit. Two years later, Loose and his brother would begin the Loose-Wiles Cracker and Candy Company at Eighth and Santa Fe streets in the West Bottoms. That would become Sunshine Biscuits. In the 1920s, after Jacob's death, Ella Loose would purchase the former site of the Kansas City Country Club south of the Plaza and give it to Kansas City, which would rename the acreage Loose Park.

Among the city's wholesalers, in Box 40 sat James K. Burnham, A. H. Munger and their wives. The two had arrived in Kansas City at the peak of the real-estate boom in 1887 and bought a wholesale dry-goods firm. Surviving the real-estate crash and the dismal times that came afterward, Burnham-Hanna-Munger became a leading supplier of denim overalls and other work clothes to the farms and ranches of the West and Southwest. By the time of the Century Ball, Burnham and Munger were planning to move their operation to a grand new brick building at the corner of Broadway and Eighth streets, in a growing garment district.

The end of the 19th century saw wholesaling reach a plateau in Kansas City. Even with inroads by other cities in their trade area — Denver, Fort Worth, Dallas and Oklahoma City — Kansas City's wholesalers held their own well into the 20th century.

Retailers were represented, too, at the ball. In Box 10 sat Mr. and Mrs. J. Logan Jones Jr. Since 1895 Jones had owned the Jones Dry Goods Company.

The flood of 1903 twisted the tracks of the elevated street railway that crossed the West Bottoms.

A year before the Convention Hall disaster, fire took his store at Sixth and Main streets; Jones was operating out of a small brick building next door until work could be finished on his new building at 12th and Main. The Jones Store remained for years a Kansas City institution at that same address.

Jones' market, like those of other big retailers, kept getting bigger. Although the 1890s had been nothing like the booming 1880s, the combined population of Kansas City, Missouri, and Kansas City, Kansas, had still risen by more than 25 percent. Together, the two cities counted more than 215,000 residents and the five counties numbered more than 320,000. Kansas City, Missouri, had doubled its square miles in 1897, when it annexed Westport to the south and more to the east.

The gains in people and land would be even bigger over the first decade of the new century. Kansas City was riding high, and even natural calamity would be only a temporary setback.

The waters rise

The next disaster came not from fire but flood. A stormy April and May 1903 in Kansas pushed the Kansas River out of its banks, first in Topeka and then in Lawrence and finally, on May 31, in the two Kansas Citys. The Missouri topped its banks, too. Water spread across the stockyards, and flooded packing plants, grain elevators and wholesale warehouses. In Armourdale, it

Cold storage, dry goods warehouses, varnish companies and ice houses — all were inundated by the flood of 1903.

stood 20 feet deep. Union Avenue in the West Bottoms became a river and Union Depot was put out of service. The flood shut down the electric plant and therefore electric streetcar service through the city. Fifteen bridges across the Kansas River were destroyed, including the ones that carried Kansas City's municipal water supply from its sources along the Missouri River in Quindaro and at Kaw Point, where the Kansas River entered the Missouri. The water outage lasted 12 days. Twenty thousand people were made homeless. The Commercial Club arranged for some to be housed in Convention Hall.

Railroad shipping, the key to commerce in the metropolitan area, came to a standstill. In the country towns of the city's trade area, merchants turned elsewhere for goods to stock their shelves. Kansas City's hold on the wholesale trade of the west and southwest was interrupted.

Once the waters receded and the lowlands by the Kansas and Missouri rivers were cleared of debris and the

mud washed away, the railroads repaired their damaged tracks and facilities. Levees were built to hinder future floods.

As rail traffic was restored, Kansas City distributors resumed their work — but with second thoughts about their location in the West Bottoms. The flood hastened the move of wholesalers up to the new wholesale district along Broadway. It also helped determine the fate of Union Depot, long in need of a replacement.

The Commercial Club went to work to recoup the city's share of the market of the hinterlands. It sponsored semiannual buyers' trips with subsidized rail fares that brought business people to town from Kansas, Missouri, Oklahoma Territory, Nebraska, Arkansas, Colorado, New Mexico and Texas.

Luckily for Kansas City's effort to get back on its feet, agriculture in the Midwest and Plains prospered through the early 1900s. Farmers and small-town residents produced more products, and shipped more of them

Kansas City millionaire R.A. Long made his fortune selling lumber. With some of the proceeds, he erected the R.A. Long building at the northwest corner of 10th Street and Grand Avenue. In the northeast part of the city, along Gladstone Boulevard, Long built a grand home.

through Kansas City. They also visited and shopped in the big stores and hotels of the region's biggest city.

High among products shipped to those farms and towns in Kansas City's trade region was lumber, still scarce on the prairies. Greatest among the city's lumber barons — and one of the biggest in the country — was Kansas City's R. A. Long. His Long-Bell Lumber Company began with a small lumber yard in southeast Kansas, expanded and now stood at the apex of a nationwide supply empire.

Demonstrating the strength of his company and adding to Kansas City's still unimposing skyline, Long built a 14-story, steel-framed skyscraper — the city's first — as company headquarters. The R. A. Long building at the northwest corner of 10th Street and Grand Avenue soared above the tallest structure of the 1880s boom, the New York Life building. It opened in 1907. Along Gladstone Boulevard, Long built one of the city's biggest residences, which he named Corinthian Hall. The ornate house and grounds, which featured a stable for his daughter's horses, occupied an entire city block.

Now, as if in salute to the new century's prosperity, the skyscraper built by Long and his new money was

Classical to practical, the architecture of the early 1900s fit the styles of its occupants. Along Baltimore stood the First National Bank, left, at 10th Street and the Hotel Baltimore, above, between 11th and 12th. Wholly utilitarian was the Standard Oil Refinery in Sugar Creek, above left.

joined by one built by old money. The Scarritt building, an 11-story structure, rose one block north of Long's building on Grand. The new building boasted an opulent interior, and was connected by a tunnel to an arcade facing Walnut Street. The project was built by the offspring of Nathan Scarritt, a pioneer preacher and educator who had accumulated property in the area with considerable acumen. He left a fortune to his heirs. The children were prominent in their own right, particularly lawyer William Chick Scarritt, whose middle name reflected the side of the family that reached back to a pioneer wholesaler of the 1840s.

Old or new money, business relationships were close and often familial. In 1908, one year after the Long and Scarritt buildings opened, the National Bank of Commerce Bank moved into its own building, a 15-story structure at 10th and Walnut streets. The bank was successor to the Kansas City Savings Association, formed at the end of the Civil War by a group led by R.A. Long's uncle and early financial backer, Francis R. Long. In 1881, William S. Woods bought a controlling interest and renamed the institution National Bank of Commerce. By 1900, it had become the largest bank west of Chicago.

The bank's new 1908 home also housed the

Farmers came from miles around and the customers flocked to peruse the goods at the City Market in 1906. The masonry structure was erected in the late 1880s and stood until the late 1930s.

Commerce Trust Company, another of Woods' projects. As president of that affiliate, Woods named William T. Kemper, the former Kansas banker and later Kansas City grain merchant who had been president of the Board of Trade at the turn of the century. After a succession of owners, mergers and renamings, the National Bank of Commerce and the Commerce Trust Company would join in 1921 under the latter's name. His son, James Kemper, was named president in 1925. William T. Kemper sold his stock in the bank in the early 1920s, and remained an influential figure in business and politics.

In the early 1900s, the First National Bank opened its imposing neo-Classical structure at the northeast corner of 10th Street and Baltimore Avenue. The building stood in the heart of what had become a Kansas City financial district that lined Ninth and 10th streets.

A new look for the city

As Long hoped with his building, the new skyscrapers not only helped develop a distinctive skyline but also symbolized the advent of new engineering technology. Yet they represented only a part of the surge

Manufacturing and distributing: A look inside

In 1902 Burnham-Hanna-Munger Dry Goods produced a brochure showing off its operations in its new headquarters at Eighth Street and Broadway. When the building opened, it ranked as the second largest in Kansas City, containing about six acres of floor space. President James K. Burnham involved himself in civic affairs, serving on the board of the Commercial Club and as a parks commissioner.

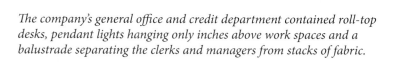

The company's general office and credit department contained roll-top desks, pendant lights hanging only inches above work spaces and a balustrade separating the clerks and managers from stacks of fabric.

Above: Workers neatly stacked bolt after bolt of fabric across the vast floor of the print and wash goods department.

Left: In the shirt department on the second floor, row after row of seamstresses sewed their way through piles of fabric. Traditionally a wholesaler of uniforms, overalls and other clothing, the company added manufacturing departments when it moved to the new building.

Railroads, store-fixture companies, printers and wholesalers advertised their goods and services in the 1901 city directory.

was planning a move south on Grand Avenue from 11th Street to a new and larger brick structure at 18th Street. The Star Company completed the move in 1911.

The same year the Kansas City Livestock Exchange built a new, brick high-rise at 16th and Gennessee streets in the West Bottoms.

By comparison, an architecturally inelegant but economically vital structure was built in 1904 in Sugar Creek near Independence. The Standard Oil refinery processed oil from new fields in southeast and south central Kansas, and the cheap fuel it produced spurred growth of industry along the valley of the Blue River. According to one count, 36 manufacturing companies began operating in that industrial district in the half-decade after the refinery opened. Also, Kansas City began making and distributing equipment for the oil fields that sent raw material to Sugar Creek.

And with a refinery nearby, what industry was more compatible than automobile manufacturing? In 1911, Henry Ford established his first assembly plant outside Detroit in Kansas City, in the northeast part of town at 1025 Winchester Avenue. The plant aimed to serve the growing population west of the Mississippi River from a closer shipping point than Detroit. Throughout the Great Plains, counties and states were improving roads and Ford foresaw big demand for motor vehicles from farmers and other rural residents.

In those early days of the motor car's popularity Ford could ship only three fully assembled automobiles on a railroad freight car. He soon learned that the same freight car could carry parts for 20 or more automobiles if they were packed efficiently. Assemble those parts in some place closer to new markets — some place like Kansas City — and Ford could reduce his shipping costs

in commercial construction that marked the early 20th century in Kansas City.

There was J. Logan Jones' new store building at 12th and Main streets, which he soon expanded because of the thriving business at the site in the heart of downtown traffic. The Baltimore Hotel, built in the late 1890s, added expansions throughout the first decade of the century until by 1908 it extended the full block on the east side of Baltimore between 11th and 12th streets. Catercornered across the intersection of 12th and Baltimore, a competitor would rise in 1915, when brewer George Muehlebach opened his Hotel Muehlebach.

Having surpassed its competitors in circulation and revenue, *The Kansas City Star* began the new century by purchasing the struggling morning *Kansas City Times* and printing two editions a day. By the end of the decade, it

Convention Hall was decked out for a horse show in 1905, right, and an automobile show in 1907, below. Car salesman hopped into their company's vehicles to be photographed. Packard, Peerless and Stevens-Duryea were among the models on display.

Automobile Show March 4th 1907

Members of a Commercial Club promotional trip lined up beside and on top of their train's locomotive about 1910.

dramatically. Production of Ford's popular Model T, a car that was light, useful and simple to operate and maintain, began in 1912. By 1914 the Kansas City assembly plant was turning out a thousand automobiles a day.

Not far from Ford in the Blue River Valley was the Kansas City Bolt & Nut Company, situated in an area named Sheffield. The Britishism was no accident. In the 1880s English investors employed agents to buy up land in the vicinity to convert into industrial sites. Those became the Sheffield and Manchester districts. A later district would take the name Leeds. As for Sheffield, in the 1920s it would lend its name to Kansas City Bolt & Nut. Eventually, the plant would become Armco Steel.

The steel plant found a customer next door, a

Preceding pages: Horse-drawn vehicles still traveled Main Street in 1909, along with streetcars and crowds of pedestrians. The view is north from 12th Street.

company that made farm equipment and buildings out of metal, Butler Manufacturing. Like many Kansas City businesses, the company was born of an idea hatched in a small town, Clay Center, Kansas. There, a 20-something named Emanuel Norquist set out to improve the quality of livestock watering tanks. Metal watering tanks were nothing new, but Norquist's idea was: Make them of copper-bearing galvanized steel, engineered carefully so they wouldn't leak and transportable in one piece. In 1901, Charles Butler, a salesman for Fairbanks Morse, made a business trip to Clay Center. There he saw Norquist's new watering tank. Norquist, the designer, and Butler, the entrepreneur, formed a partnership.

They moved to Kansas City and, with seed money from Butler's brother, started manufacturing the tanks. In 1902 they incorporated as Butler Manufacturing Company in the West Bottoms. Surviving the flood of 1903 and a recession in 1907, they devised in 1909 an all-steel garage,

Once railroads established their presence in Kansas City, the importance of river transportation diminished. From time to time, however, merchants annoyed by railroad shipping rates pushed to renew river traffic to create competition. In 1911, the Kansas City, Missouri River Navigation Company began sending these steamboats downriver with cargo. The operation lasted until 1917. In the end, investors lost their money.

the first Butler building. A couple of years later, Butler moved to Eastern Avenue in the Blue River Valley.

Coming to town

At the turn of the century, Kansas City was a magnet for visitors and aspiring business people alike. In the early 1900s, there was no place as big between Chicago and San Francisco.

"Oklahoma," the hit musical and later movie set in turn-of-the-century Oklahoma Territory, featured a number called "Kansas City," containing the memorable line, "Everthin's up to date in Kansas City."

In the show, the song is sung by a young Oklahoman returned to the territory from a brief trip north to the big city in the early 1900s. He reports on the wonders he saw, among them "twenty gas buggies goin' by theirsel's," Putting a newfangled telephone to his ear, he recalled, "a strange woman started in to talk." That would have been the operator. As his listeners marveled, he continued by describing a skyscraper seven stories high, and a burlesque show.

The song was fictional but the experience was true for thousands of visitors from smaller places in the early

1900s. Kansas City's motor cars, telephones, bright lights, big buildings and booming businesses became a powerful magnet.

In 1910, a 19-year-old salesman from Norfolk, Nebraska, came to town and rented a room at the YMCA. From there, he sold postcards to local shops, starting with cards he had brought in shoeboxes from Nebraska. He mailed sets of cards each month to one store in each town of more than 1,000 people but smaller than 10,000. His idea was to hit the stores that traveling salesman would skip. The stores could buy the cards or send them back.

This young man had considered heading to Omaha, which was closer, but a traveling cigar salesman told him the story of Convention Hall and the Kansas City spirit. So Joyce Hall was sold on Kansas City.

When the YMCA objected to his operating a business on its premises, Hall rented an office. Also, he enrolled at Spalding's Commercial College to learn more about the world of business. In 1911, Hall hired his brother Rollie Hall and three other people and in 1912 entered the greeting-card business in Kansas City as Hall Brothers. By 1915, they were printing their own greeting cards, which one day would carry a distinctive brand — Hallmark.

As visitors swarmed in, the city continued to spread out. Two packinghouses, Armour and Swift, along with the Burlington railroad got together in 1908 to begin building a new bridge north across the Missouri River. The bridge would lead to an industrial town just then on the drawing boards, North Kansas City. The ASB Bridge could carry motor vehicles and an electric interurban streetcar line on one deck and heavy railroad traffic on another. A section lifted to allow river traffic to pass.

On the south edge of downtown, along tracks of the Kansas City Suburban Belt Railway, the mail-order giant Montgomery Ward put up a nine-story general merchandise warehouse. The structure at 19th and Campbell streets was built in two phases, beginning in 1908 and finishing in 1910. It covered half a city block, and sat on the tracks that served many of the major railroads. When the catalog retailer moved to an even larger building in 1915, the building was rented out. One new tenant was the Berkowitz Envelope Corporation, later Tension Envelope, which eventually occupied the entire structure.

The Suburban Belt Railway served many of the trunk railroads that entered the city. Using the Belt Railway, a company could ship goods in any direction. Refurbished as the Kansas City Terminal Railway, the same line would serve Kansas City's grandest building of the new century.

On the north bank of the Missouri River, men and boys set out nets to catch fish about 1910. In the background, the Armour-Swift-Burlington bridge was taking shape. It opened in 1911.

People thronged the plaza in front of the new Union Station at its opening in late October 1914. The station, third largest in the country when it was built, replaced the deteriorating and flood-prone Union Depot in the West Bottoms.

The city beautiful

The 1903 flood had put doubts in the minds of some railroads and of the city that the West Bottoms was a reliable site for a passenger station. After more than a quarter century of hard use by a population far larger than the one for which it was built, Union Depot showed its age — crowded, dirty and dilapidated. To overcome the reluctance of a few railroads to leave the Bottoms, the Commercial Club formed a committee to lobby for a site on higher, drier ground. After dallying with a northside property near the Missouri River, six of the railroads entering Kansas City decided in 1906 on land along OK Creek, roughly along the path of the Suburban Belt Railway. By mid-1906 six other railroads joined them.

Together the dozen rail companies formed the Kansas City Terminal Railway Company, which chose a Chicago architect, Jarvis Hunt, to design a new station. The enormous new structure built by the consortium opened in autumn 1914. Its main building was the third largest passenger edifice in the United States, designed to serve an increasing cross-country passenger load and a city projected to grow to two million people.

Two million was five times the population of the Kansas City metropolitan area in 1914, and stood as a clear statement that the railroads were betting not only on their own future — rail passenger traffic — but also on the future of greater Kansas City.

During the opening ceremonies, several city leaders rhapsodized about the glories of the new building. When it came his turn, Mayor Henry Jost rather sourly reminded the audience that the railroads weren't making a grand gift to the city. They were seeking "profit — the same as the builders of the Muehlebach Hotel."

Naturally they were yet, no matter what the reasons for the building's construction, privately owned Union Station would become the city's major civic monument.

In the Kansas City of the early 1900s businesses of many kinds were going strong and money was turning over in the economy. Meanwhile, the dream of a prettier, more pleasant city was beginning to come true. What had been a rough-looking town as late as the 1890s now sat still for a shave and a haircut.

Once finished with its legal challenges, the parks and boulevards campaign in the early 1900s went into full

Jewel of Kansas City's boulevards was the Paseo, where symmetrical gardens were planted at 12th Street. Below, a postcard showed the view of the same area from the north.

swing. By 1913, the system was substantially complete. From Swope Park in the south to Cliff Drive overlooking the Missouri River on the north, to West Terrace Park with its spectacular views on the west, the city was flanked by big open spaces and dotted by smaller ones. Connecting most of the parks were wide, tree-lined boulevards, some of them with medians containing fountains, floral plantings and pergolas.

Kansas City's parks and boulevards became another civic monument. The businessmen who promoted them had much to be satisfied about.

By the middle 1910s, the lions of the last century were beginning to disappear from the scene. August Meyer died in 1905. Frank Faxon, inventor of the "Better Place to Live In" slogan as president of the Commercial Club and later member of the School Board, died in 1913. William Rockhill Nelson, having used his newspaper's firepower to successfully promote the City Beautiful, died in 1915.

Yet the idea continued in the minds of local businessmen. One of them would hire the parks' designer, George Kessler, to lift private residential development to a new level. J.C. Nichols, who had grown up in Olathe and begun developing property with the backing of some fraternity brothers, would continue the City Beautiful

movement in his own way. Nichols would prove not only visionary but also influential, putting his stamp on a big swath of Kansas City.

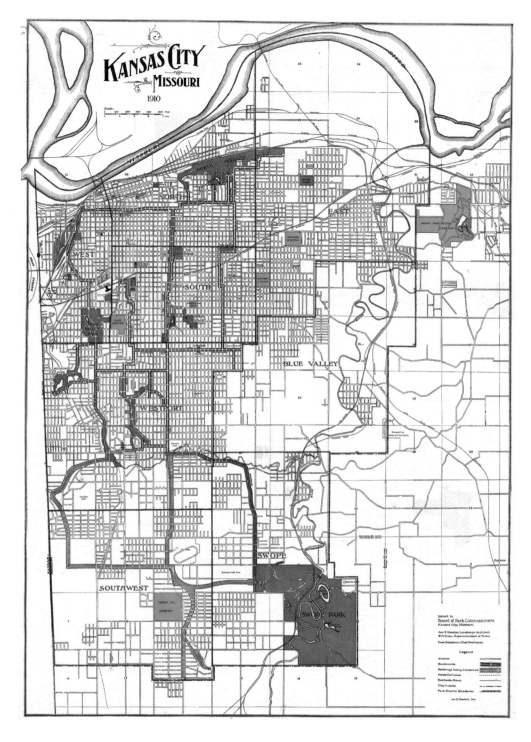

Parks progress as of 1910: Green along streets represented completed boulevards. Among them were Benton, The Paseo and Broadway. Swope Parkway stretched to Swope Park. Brown marked streets being condemned for boulevards, among them The Paseo south of 47th Street and the routes that would become parts of Ward Parkway and Meyer Boulevard.

Club or chamber? The same group, a new name

In late 1916, the Commercial Club changed its name to the Chamber of Commerce of Kansas City. According to reports of the time, the move stemmed from concern on the part of the executive committee that businessmen who differed with the Commercial Club's direction might form a new organization and name it Chamber of Commerce. Business groups in many cities had adopted that name, as had the U. S. Chamber of Commerce.

According to the complaining parties, the executive committee was dominated by a few industries and had accumulated too much power over the club. Many members bridled when, for instance, the committee opposed attempts to promote daylight saving time.

Sustaining memberships, detractors said, gave too much power to certain large businesses.

Defenders and detractors agreed on only one matter — the club needed more "pep," which translated to better attendance and more members.

Resignations were sought, and threats made to form a new civic group. In the end, the organization, eventually the Greater Kansas City Chamber of Commerce, survived the hubbub.

A New Age Dawning

In the space of less than two years, one event transformed American life. Although fought on the soil of Europe, the World War altered Americans' view of the world, expanded their part in it, and gave them new ways to think, get around and communicate. It also saw labor square off against management.

Kansas City sat safely in the middle of a vast continent an ocean away from the front, yet the city and region around it felt the shock of world conflict. Kansas City and its environs sent thousands of its youth off to military training and then off across the sea. Once the United States entered the World War, events at the front in France directly affected families on the home front in middle America.

Compared with wars before and since, America's participation was brief. The United States declared war in April 1917, yet few troops in any numbers arrived in Europe until much later. On November 11, 1918, an armistice was declared. The role played by American soldiers proved decisive nonetheless. Bringing

The Northland remained heavily rural in 1920. Steam-powered harvesting machinery was at work with industry and the Downtown skyline looming in the background.

troops by the thousands and new energy to the Allied side, the Yanks helped break the bloody and tiresome stalemate with the Central Powers.

Kansas City and its region provided more than soldiers. The war brought unprecedented demand for food, which the Plains produced in abundance. Wheat was in demand for the front, so back home the government encouraged Americans to find other things to eat. Potatoes were recommended.

Agricultural processors, implement makers and shippers prospered during the conflict. As a hub for agriculture and railroads, Kansas City got a good chunk of that business. The railroads, however, were taken over by the government with the aim of creating central, efficient direction during the war.

Many companies fared well and job numbers increased but so did inflation; workers noticed and began to demand better pay. The decade of the 1910s culminated in a series of labor actions even while America was still at war. In March 1918, Kansas City laundry workers walked off the job, setting fire to bundles of laundry and throwing rocks at streetcars. Union workers in restaurants, breweries, movie houses and elsewhere joined the walkout, which continued six days. The National Guard was called to try to keep peace and the American Federation of Labor sent a representative to help cool things. Eventually, laundry owners agreed to raise wages and the city's Employers' Association agreed not to make reprisals against striking employees. Streetcar workers joined that walkout and also staged their own strikes, in 1917 for recognition and another in 1918, after the war ended, over pay. The streetcar company hired replacements and eventually restored service to normal. The strikers were out of work and without a union.

Cutting out the middleman

Other, subtler things were happening in businesses in the late 1910s. Across the country, manufacturers began to send their own representatives to sell goods directly to merchants, thus cutting out "the middleman." That middleman was the wholesaler — for so long a mainstay of Kansas City's commerce. The trend was delayed briefly in wartime by the nationwide tie-up of railroads, which meant wholesalers had to maintain

Somehow much traffic made it through this busy and confusing intersection in the late 1920s. Multiple streets entered Main Street at Pershing Road, along with streetcars and pedestrians heading for Union Station, at left. Low-priced autos contributed to the jam.

large stocks near their customers. Once the war ended, and railroads returned from government control to private hands, the switch to manufacturers' direct sales continued. Fewer stocks for distribution from Kansas City wholesale warehouses meant fewer jobs and lower revenues for area wholesalers.

The wholesale component of Kansas City's economy began to be outstripped by other sectors. It would continue to grow through the 1920s, but never as fast as before.

In spring 1919 the boys finally came home — thousands of troops detraining at Union Station to march downtown, then reboarding for mustering out at Fort Riley. The nerve-wracking strains of combat,

and the sights, sounds and customs of a continent most of the doughboys had never visited soon forced those thousands of young Kansans and Missourians into full adulthood.

City kids who had only ventured outside their neighborhoods and country kids to whom the most exotic sight had been the county seat now were veterans not only of war but also of sightseeing in Paris and northern France. These veterans had new ways of looking at the world, which in turn was changing around them. Technology, manners, fashions all morphed rapidly in the wake of the war.

Within only a few years Kansas City

would experience the advent of commercial radio, the arrival of affordable motor cars, a proliferation of huge motion picture theaters, and rampant product advertising in newspapers and magazines and billboards. The dawning of the Jazz Age saw products ranging from ready-to-wear fashions to Victrolas, from breakfast cereal to cigarettes — all driven by advertising and easy credit.

Filled with confidence in themselves, two of the thousands of returning veterans decided to start a men's furnishings store Downtown. With high hopes, in November 1919, Eddie Jacobson and Harry S. Truman opened their doors at 104 W. 12th Street. The name, "Truman & Jacobson" was set in tile at the street entrance. Inside, the shelves and display counters boasted a large stock of shirts, ties, detachable collars, cuff links, gloves and underwear – the standard inventory of a haberdashery, which equipped the well-dressed man of the day.

By 1921, however, falling farm prices and a nationwide economic cooling tested the partners' skill at keeping the business afloat. Silk shirts were no longer selling, and Truman and Jacobson were borrowing. By 1922 the store was $35,000 in the red and the partners called it quits. Instead of bankruptcy, they tried to pay off debts as best they could. A few years later, Jacobson did declare bankruptcy. Truman stayed in debt for nearly two decades.

Meanwhile, the economy righted itself.

But Truman and Jacobson were lucky in a different way. They were alive and healthy. To remember those who had died, and to honor all those who served, Kansas City's civic leaders determined to create a monument.

Lumber magnate R.A. Long headed a committee that would erect not just a monument, but the biggest

A scolding author comes to town

Sinclair Lewis, nationally famous for his novels disparaging boosterism and other mentalities of the age, came to Kansas City in the 1920s to look for material on a forthcoming book. The topic was to be evangelical preachers.

The author had made friends with a Detroit preacher who promised to help Lewis with his research. When the preacher moved to Kansas City, Lewis came here.

Lewis and the preacher soon fell apart, and the author found a new minister to help him. Meanwhile, he took the occasion to offend other ministers and much of the rest of Kansas City.

Speaking to the Rotary Club and Chamber of Commerce, he criticized his audience as complacent boosters. As for the city, Lewis complained that it displayed not only materialistic values but an ersatz culture. Few missed him when he left.

World War I monument in the country. Long's campaign gathered contributions – some from his wealthy friends and fellow businessmen, some from the general public, even pennies from schoolchildren. With the phrase, "Lest We Forget," as a rallying point, the committee raised $2.5 million and a young ally of Long's formed a subcommittee to begin acquiring land for the monument grounds. That colleague was J.C. Nichols, who had parlayed his own skills at fundraising and negotiating into developing the Country Club District of homes.

Quietly, using the techniques he had learned in his own business, Nichols and his committee assembled the land just south of Union Station, land dotted by poor peoples' housing.

By autumn 1921, the grounds were ready to dedicate and the memorial was ready to be built. To mark the occasion, on November 1 of that year hundreds of thousands of Kansas Citians and participants in the American Legion's national convention gathered at the hill just south of Union Station to see the site dedicated by General John J. Pershing and other supreme commanders from France, Great Britain, Belgium and Italy.

As it was for Long, the day for Nichols represented a supreme success. Five years later, the monument would be completed and it, too, dedicated. By then Nichols had become quite used to success.

Birth of the suburbs

His real-estate career started out in 1903, when Nichols was in his early 20s and just out of college. With help from some well-set fraternity brothers from the University of Kansas, Nichols bought land in Kansas City, Kansas. He erected small houses on some of the lots and sold them to working-class families. A prime attribute: his houses sat on high ground, above the bottoms that had been covered by floods earlier that same year.

Then Nichols moved to the Missouri side of the state line, marking out a subdivision south of Brush Creek and naming it Bismark Place.

Nichols proved adept at building a reputation, and at making friends among people with money. In 1908, still in his 20s, he was named a director of the Commerce Trust Company, which would cement a business connection that would remain important for years to come. That same year Nichols had gained control of 1,000 acres to the south of his Bismark Place for further residential development. For that parcel, he had a grand plan.

Some streets would conform to the lay of the land instead of following the strict grid common in most developments. All the lots would have restrictions on the kind of housing and the characteristics of the people who could live on them. Like so many other developers of his day, Nichols barred black people from ownership of his homes.

He called his 1,000 acres the Country Club District, after the nearby Kansas City Country Club.

In 1911, Kansas City, Missouri, completed annexation of the land covered by Nichols' Missouri-side ventures. Meanwhile, just across the state line Nichols bought from the Armour family acreage that would become Mission Hills, an exclusive development. These new and restricted residential districts became home to many of the city's wealthiest and most powerful families.

Nichols' method, which he employed again and again, exceeded what most developers did anywhere in America. He planned not a row of houses here or a block there, but whole neighborhoods with winding streets, trees and occasionally a small park or entrance statuary. His residential streets had to be wide enough for two vehicles to pass, but no wider. The houses he sold were different in style yet similar in value to surrounding homes. He instituted homeowner associations with regular meetings and regular assessments to pay for maintenance of the neighborhood. Within his developments he built small shopping districts, controlled by his company.

Throughout Kansas City's history, neighborhoods had been built and over the years allowed to deteriorate. Quality Hill, which went downhill when the prominent

J.C. Nichols in caricature, above, and in one of his real-life advertisements, below. His favorite way to describe the Country Club district: "1,000 Acres Restricted."

J.C. Nichols turned his shopping district into a Christmas wonderland each year, wrapping streetlights with greenery and placing strings of lights on buildings. Below: The Plaza in the late 1920s, now bounded by apartment towers across Brush Creek.

families who first occupied it moved out, was an example Nichols did not want to repeat. The same was true for Hyde Park and the area along Gladstone Boulevard in the Northeast. Nichols' idea was to do all he could to make property values in his neighborhoods endure.

Although a streetcar line ran down Ward Parkway, these neighborhoods were built for the automobile. Indeed, they were made possible by it, and the symbiotic relationship between suburbia and the motor car helped drive the 1920s boom.

As William S. Worley says in his book, *J.C. Nichols and the Shaping of Kansas City*, Nichols invented few of his tactics, but he skillfully blended the ideas of others into a grand strategy. His success made him a figure in national real-estate circles.

His timing helped. Nichols' early years aligned with the recovery of the Kansas City real-estate market, which had been listless from the bust of the late 1880s until at least the middle of the first decade of the 20th century. The era from 1905 to 1915 proved stable and prosperous for Kansas City and the region around it, and it was in that time that Nichols was getting his business off the ground.

The Country Club Plaza

Then, as the 1920s began to roar, Nichols announced plans to build a large shopping district near his development. It would have a consistent motif, building heights would be limited and the shops would be surrounded by apartments. For the newly abundant motor car, there would be garages and parking lots, all tucked away mostly out of view. This district would draw shoppers not only from Nichols' neighborhoods and the rest of Kansas City, but also from the region. He named it after his big neighborhood, calling it the Country Club Plaza. It would become something of a second Downtown, only tonier. Retailers found the Plaza to their liking, as did retailers in other Nichols-owned neighborhood shopping areas such as Brookside and Romanelli.

Meanwhile, another mini-downtown grew at the bustling 31st and Troost intersection, and workers and shoppers stilled thronged the old downtowns of Kansas City and Kansas City, Kansas.

In retail, one trend was to chain stores, particularly in groceries and drugs. On the new Country Club Plaza, Piggly-Wiggly opened a grocery. Throughout the city,

brothers Isaac and Michael Katz opened new drugstores under their own name beginning in the 1910s. Crown Drugs came along in the early 1920s. Katz and Crown sold not only drugs but also a variety of other goods, and they flooded newspapers with advertisements boasting of their low prices. Chains altered the world of individual merchants, who could not buy in similarly large quantities and thus pay lower prices. They also changed the world of wholesalers, who found that chains were another way retailers could buy directly from manufacturers and cut out middlemen.

For wholesalers, the outlook for the future had continued to dampen since the heady days of the late 19th century. Besides the impact of chains and other stores purchasing directly from manufacturers, wholesalers also had to deal with those in competing cities in the west and southwest. Also, the opening of the Panama Canal had made it unnecessary to deliver all goods to the West Coast by rail through Kansas City.

Kansas City's central location, however, remained important. Exploiting it, in 1925 Sears built a 1.1-million square foot catalogue warehouse at 15th Street and Cleveland on the east side of Kansas City, Missouri. That brought Sears closer to its mail-order competitor, Montgomery Ward, which had outgrown its 19th Street distribution center only a few years after opening it. In 1915 Ward had taken up a much larger residence at 6200 St. John.

Boilers to biscuits

Manufacturing came along, too. Early in the 1920s, a Union Pacific railroad subsidiary organized the Fairfax Industrial District in a crook of the Missouri River next to Kansas City, Kansas. Sealright made containers there, the Darby Company fashioned boilers and other products from steel and Sunshine Biscuits — successor to Jacob Loose's Loose-Wiles biscuits — opened a giant factory.

From 1921 through 1928, factory employment rose 88 percent. In 1925, the area's manufacturing production reached $590 million, moving Kansas City past Milwaukee and close to Pittsburg.

In the Blue River Valley, Sheffield Steel, renamed in 1925 from Kansas City Bolt and Nut, was doing a big business processing scrap metal. In North Kansas City and elsewhere, paint and varnish plants numbered 19 by 1927, putting Kansas City sixth in the country in that category. A leader was Cook Paint, which opened in 1916.

Christmas parades signaled the start of the shopping season Downtown. In 1929, the parade ended with Santa Claus waving to the crowds and chuckling through an onboard microphone and loudspeaker as throngs of children looked on.

Also in North Kansas City, the Corn Products Refining Company opened in 1919, producing syrup and other products made from corn. Corn Products was a large employer and dominated the manufacturing scene. And the women's ready-to-wear industry took off, led by the growing Donnelly Garment Company. In 1928 General Motors opened Chevrolet and Fisher Body plants, adding its production to Ford's.

Small business boom

In the 1920s, things simply sped up. Across America, businesses had rarely had it so good.

Small business shared amply in the rewards. Although dwarfed in size, scope and public acclaim by the giant manufacturers, real-estate companies and banks of the day, thousands of smaller businesses rode smoothly through the era. For example, in the three years from 1923 to 1926, beauty shops increased from 26 to 223.

Other small businesses did well, too, and the Raymond-Green Furniture Company was instructive of what happened in the era. The outfit was formed by two

natives of rural Kansas who met in 1910. Scott Raymond was in his early 30s, having spent the five previous years working for furniture stores and learning the business in Coffeyville, St. Louis and Kansas City. E. G. Green, who had spent his life on the farm and who recently had accumulated a little money from his efforts, was introduced through Raymond's father, briefly the pastor at Green's church.

The two trusted one another and, with only an oral partnership agreement, they both put money into a joint venture in Kansas City. Because of Raymond's experience in selling furniture, they entered that field. In early 1911, the two acquired an existing furniture store on East 12th Street, bought the inventory and went into business as the Raymond-Green Furniture Company.

Within weeks, they moved to a new site a few blocks west near the streetcar intersection at 12th Street and Troost Avenue. Streetcar traffic meant lots of potential customers, particularly among the working-class population of the area. That became their market — inexpensive furniture, much of it used, sold on credit.

The two made a go of it, and their business would survive for more than two decades. In short order, they divided responsibilities. Raymond would buy the stock and arrange for advertising while Green kept the books. Both handled sales. Because of Kansas City's role as a distributing center, their wholesale furniture sources were right in town. Boosted by easy credit and the stimulus of the World War, their business grew. They judged the creditworthiness of their customers by job stability, existence of a family and the amount of other debts.

By the mid-1920s, they moved from 12th and Troost, an area that was fine for streetcar traffic but too narrow for sufficient parking for the city's expanding automobile traffic. Now at 13th Street and Grand Avenue, their business once again rocked along.

Like J.C. Nichols, Raymond and Green had been helped by the good business climate of the 1910s and 1920s. When they began, neither man had vast experience or much capital. The increase in Kansas City's population in that era and gradually rising prices — along with easy credit and perhaps even a communitywide sense of optimism — overcame many problems, such as rather substantial expenses.

The Kansas City area and its businesses overcame much in the 1920s. Combined, the two Kansas Citys grew by 25 percent in population from 1920 to 1930. A wave of school-age children created a boom in school building through the decade.

Indeed, the entire United States hummed along with only occasional hitches through the 1920s. By various measures, economic activity grew by more than 40 percent through the decade and by 1929 the United States was producing half the world's industrial output. Credit, the kind Raymond-Green extended to its customers, made it possible for people of average means to buy some of that burgeoning output

of cars, radios and refrigerators.

Farm prices drop

However, one sector of the U.S. economy lagged badly in the 1920s. That was out on the farm — the thousands of square miles covering several states that had long formed Kansas City's commercial domain. In May 1920, the federal government removed the wartime subsidies for wheat and prices dropped to $1.44 a bushel from $2.15 at the end of 1919. Corn prices dropped too.

Farms mortgaged before the war, when land and crop prices were high, now were worth considerably less. Nevertheless, farmers' mortgage payments remained unchanged. In Washington, the farm block in Congress pushed through new laws giving the secretary of agriculture power to prevent price-rigging by meatpackers, to limit stockyard fees and to regulate grain exchanges. But efforts to prop up commodity prices failed, despite strong support from not only farmers but also implement manufacturers. Without money, farmers couldn't buy the tools they needed.

Despite the farm woes, Kansas City stayed on a binge of moneymaking. The local milling industry, probably helped by the drop in prices for farm goods, enlarged rapidly. By 1924 twelve mills were operating in the Kansas City area.

In 1928, the Republican Party, which had enjoyed a decade of success, held its nominating convention in Kansas City. It chose Herbert Hoover, to head its ticket for president and a Kansan, Senator Charles Curtis, as vice president.

Was the future to be as happy for business and the economy as the last decade?

One who failed in Kansas City

Local resident Walt Disney formed an animated-film studio in Kansas City in the early 1920s, but couldn't make a go of it. His company, Laugh-O-gram, "is worse than broke," he wrote in 1922. So he moved to California, where the climate for his work was much better.

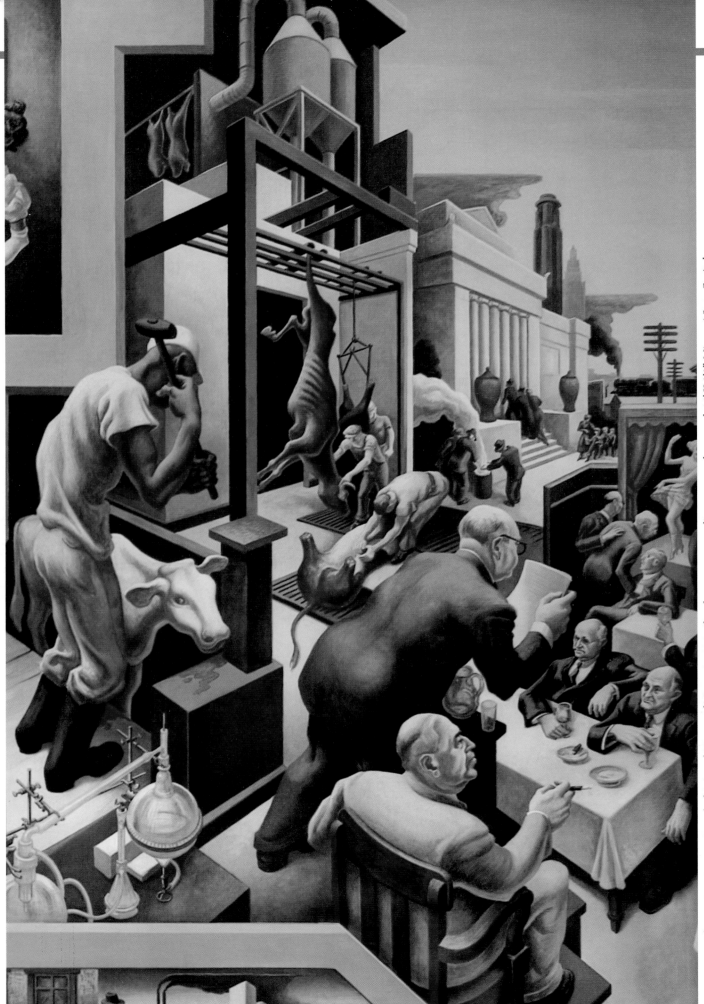

Hard Times

In 1929 events conspired to start the United States economy going downhill, and Kansas City's economy with it.

Families that had taken on debt to purchase all the consumer goods of the freewheeling Twenties began to reduce their spending, particularly on credit. Industrial production began to drop, taking employment down with it. The stock markets crashed, diminishing personal wealth and creating worry and uncertainty about the state of things.

In 1930, industrial production nationwide dropped 21 percent, consumer prices fell and the year ended with a bank panic. In 1931, production dropped 15 percent more and prices fell almost 10 percent. By December 1932, yet another bank panic caused the U.S. economy to crater. National unemployment, only 3 percent in August 1929, reached 25 percent in March 1933.

Some of Kansas City's basic industries had already felt the pressure. Livestock passing through Kansas City's stockyards had been in decline since the middle 1920s, and that would continue in the early 1930s.

Meatpacking had diminished precipitously. In 1918, Kansas City packers received 3.3 million hogs, but by 1939 that number dropped to 519,000, a six-to-one decrease. Nearly 3 million head of cattle entered the slaughterhouses in 1918, but only 1.4 million in 1939. The drought of the 1930s contributed to the decline. Decreased production of corn and other animal feed

Left: Thomas Hart Benton's depiction of Kansas City in the 1930s showed J.C. Nichols and William T. Kemper listening to a henchman of Boss Tom Pendergast, seated with cigarette.

The hungry, most of them men, lined up at the headquarters of Democratic politico Casimir Welch, one of the underbosses in the machine era.

reduced the numbers of cattle and hogs. Packinghouse employment dropped, too, from 16,000 in 1919 to 5,300 in 1939.

Retail prices told a similar, melancholy story. At John Taylor Dry Goods Company at 11th and Main streets, men's ties advertised for $1 in early December 1929. A year later, they were priced at 55 cents. Dancettes, a style of women's underwear, listed for $3.95 at the same point in 1929 but only $1.95 in 1930. Cloche hats, a popular women's style in the 1920s, listed at $1.69 to $3.69 in 1929. All were advertised at $1.29 in 1930.

The market simply couldn't bear 1920s prices any more. In 1931, the Merchants Association, hoping to stimulate sales, urged employers to give workers a half-day off for shopping before Christmas.

Every decade since the Civil War, Kansas City's population had risen by at least 23 percent. In the 1930s, the population of both Kansas Citys actually declined.

As business slowed and hopes for the future began to falter, the city and county governments pushed through a massive building program. At the very least, it would provide work.

The Ten-Year Plan

The public works project would be called the Ten-Year Plan. Its seeds were planted before the Depression, when civic leaders recognized that Kansas City's infrastructure had not kept up with the skyrocketing population.

In 1921, the Chamber of Commerce had formed a "Get-It-Done" committee to push for improvements in streets, hospitals and fire protection, along with schools. The idea gained momentum and through the decade the city widened existing streets, built new thoroughfares and installed new streetlights. A second General Hospital, this one for African-Americans, opened. The school district undertook a campaign of building in which many of the brick schools that stand today were constructed. Lou Holland, president of the Chamber from 1925 to 1927, persuaded the city to lease land just across the Missouri River from Downtown for a new airport. Charles A. Lindbergh, only a few months removed from his historic solo flight across the

Transcontinental and Western Air, headquartered in Kansas City as of 1931, boasted of itself as The Lindbergh Line. The famed aviator was a member of the TWA board.

Boss of the Ten-Year Plan campaign was Conrad Mann, center, head of the Chamber of Commerce. With him stood City Manager H.F. McElroy and Jackson County Presiding Judge Harry S. Truman.

Atlantic, flew in to the site to dedicate the new airport. Later, Holland succeeded in convincing Lindbergh to encourage Transcontinental and Western Air to put its corporate headquarters in Kansas City. In 1931, TWA agreed to do so.

All those projects came and went separately, some of them paid by assessing the real estate in the areas that

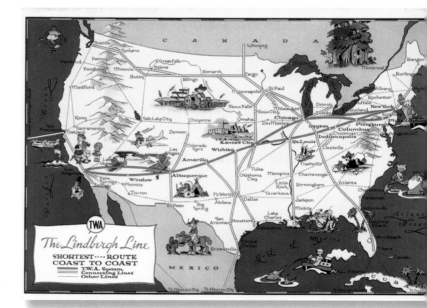

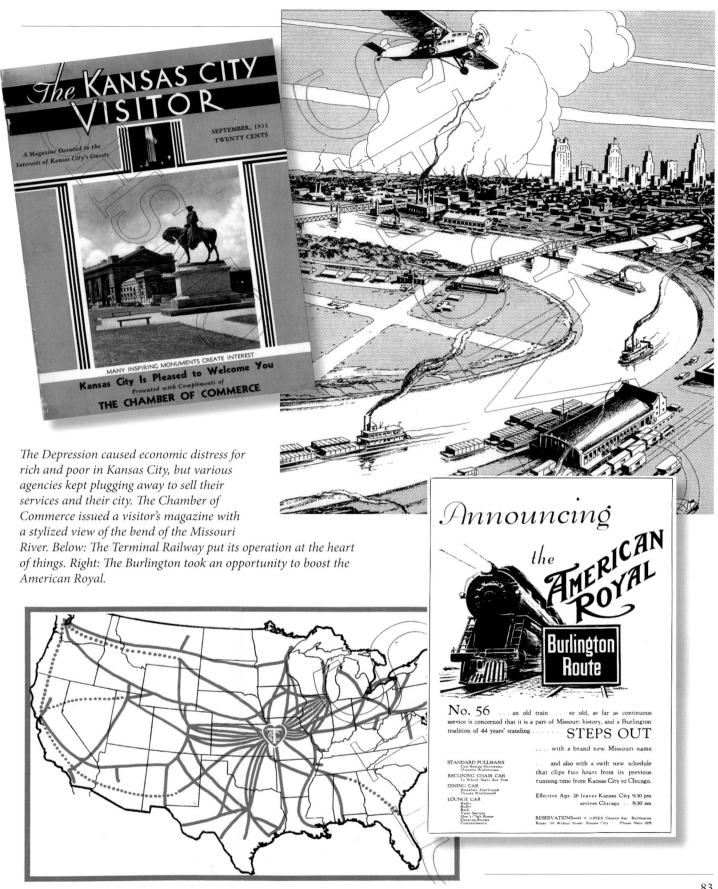

The Depression caused economic distress for rich and poor in Kansas City, but various agencies kept plugging away to sell their services and their city. The Chamber of Commerce issued a visitor's magazine with a stylized view of the bend of the Missouri River. Below: The Terminal Railway put its operation at the heart of things. Right: The Burlington took an opportunity to boost the American Royal.

benefited.

Late in the Twenties the Chamber renewed its push. It called for a comprehensive program of improvements, to be scheduled over a set period and to be supported by bond issues. By the end of the decade, the Chamber, along with a reformist organization called the Civic Research Institute and city officials, agreed that there needed to be a drive to gather information and formulate an overall plan. In 1929 a committee of 100 was named, and in 1930 Chamber President Conrad Mann was chosen to lead the effort. Mann, an extroverted and sometimes brusque German-born brewer, expanded the committee of 100 to a committee of 1,000 and led the push.

The effort was called the Ten-Year Plan of civic improvements, to be continued through the decade. Issuance of bonds would be decided by the voters of Kansas City and Jackson County.

Mann and the Chamber stumped vigorously for the measure. Crucial, however, was support of the dominant political organization, the Pendergast machine. Its

public faces were City Manager H. F. McElroy and Jackson County administrative judge Harry S. Truman, who both campaigned on behalf of the plan, but the real boost came from the powerful election machinery overseen by the big boss, Thomas J. Pendergast. It was small wonder that Pendergast favored the plan; his Ready-Mixed concrete company prospered from contracts it would win for the projects. Also, his most loyal voters were some who would benefit from jobs in construction.

The concrete business

The Chamber and the machine succeeded. In 1931 voters decided 4-to-1 to issue the $39.5 million in bonds and begin construction.

Major Depression-era construction projects included new and skyscraping City Hall and County Courthouse, above, a new Municipal Auditorium, below, and the Kansas City Power & Light Building.

At the Municipal Air Terminal, City Manager McElroy's Son, Henry, and aviation promoter Lou Holland looked on as the mayor's daughter, Eleanor Beach, christened with grape juice a TWA Ford Trimotor named "The Kansas City."

Through the decade, up went a new and massive Municipal Auditorium on 13th Street, right across from Convention Hall, which it replaced. Up went a 32-story City Hall, replacing the 1890s building in the City Market area. A new Jackson County courthouse was in the mix, too. A large section of Brush Creek was paved along the Country Club Plaza — to the dismay of J.C. Nichols, who opposed the new concrete. At the airport, runways were paved, using liberal amounts of the same material. Pendergast's Ready Mixed was ready to serve and did.

Unrelated to the work of government, a new, art-deco headquarters for Kansas City Power & Light Company at 14th Street and Baltimore Avenue joined the skyline in 1931 and Fidelity Bank's 35-story, twin-towered high-rise at Ninth and Walnut streets opened in 1932. Both projects, which gave the appearance of business activity, were under way before the Depression reached its depth.

The federal government chipped in with big new structures, too — a post office at Pershing Road and Broadway in 1933 and a federal courts building at Eighth Street and Grand Avenue.

In total, government spending by city, county, state and federal governments surely provided employment as the Depression began. Indeed, governments frequently tried to maximize the workforce on projects, first as a way to boost payrolls and contribute to consumer spending, and second as a means of popularizing itself with voters.

However, much as the Ten-Year Plan contributed to the skyline, and softened some of the effects of unemployment, it did not immunize Kansas City from the Depression. The agricultural economy, already in poor shape through the 1920s, grew worse. Farms now faced drought, high heat, wind and subsequent erosion in the early and middle 1930s. With the decline in income and population in the hinterland as folks moved off the farm, Kansas City's agriculture-related business suffered, too.

According to figures for the two Kansas Citys gathered by the Chamber of Commerce, net sales by the area's wholesalers and retailers dropped by almost a billion dollars from 1929 to 1935. Employment in those sectors dropped more than 11,000 or nearly 19 percent in the six years, meaning one in five jobs that existed in 1929 had disappeared six years later. Perhaps most telling, payrolls among wholesalers and retailers dropped more than 40 percent.

Building permits plummeted. According to Chamber figures, Kansas City, Missouri, issued 2,415 permits in 1929 but only 1,514 in 1933, a decline of 44 percent. Their value dropped by far more, from $15.3 million in 1929 to $1.7 million in 1933 — a stunning 90 percent decrease over four years.

Housing starts had peaked at more than 3,600 in 1925. In 1930, however, they fell to just under 500 and in 1934 to barely more than 100. The apartment market, too, diminished. In 1932, not a single new unit was built in Kansas City, Missouri.

Big names in town had to work to overcome the effects of the Depression. For J.C. Nichols, grand developments became less grand. The developer, like others in Kansas City, built smaller houses and sold fewer of them. He created a rental department, and when homeowners could no longer make payments on their Nichols homes, he foreclosed and rented them out. The new department also found renters for Nichols homes that went unsold.

The Country Club Plaza saved the Nichols operation. It brought income from shop rents, helping the company weather the precipitous decline in homebuilding and home purchases.

At the small end of the business scale, Scott Raymond's and E.G. Green's Furniture Company began seeing signs of decline in 1930. In 1931 sales slowed markedly, and the company lost $10,000 that year. In 1932, sales dropped to half the pre-Depression number and the partners put employees on schedules working every other day. Among the working class, Raymond and Green's usual customers, people spent what little money they had on food and shelter and not furniture. For a year and a half, Raymond and Green stopped paying rent, yet their landlord was himself desperate enough to let them

Boss Thomas J. Pendergast in action, telling Lloyd Stark that he would not support him for governor. Left: Pendergast's plain and simple headquarters, 1908 Main Street.

continue to occupy the building, in hopes they would begin paying again someday.

Amid worries about their diminishing equity in the business, about a drop in nearby businesses and thus in customer traffic, the partners agreed in 1934 to split up. Both landed in the furniture business, Raymond operating a store with his sons, and Green eventually working for another store.

Their story was typical for smaller businesses across Kansas City and the region.

Kansas City's Depression woes weren't limited to business and the economy. The Pendergast machine reached the zenith of its control in the 1930s and the city it ran lived beyond its means.

Pendergast's machine

The machine was popular with many Kansas Citians, particularly those down on their luck. Acting as a welfare organization, Pendergast lieutenants could help people pay or stave off utility bills and they could help family members in trouble with the law. The hungry could get free dinners staged by the machine. Besides jobs in Ten-Year Plan projects, there were jobs available at City Hall, too. In return for the largesse, the machine expected votes, and got them. If the Pendergast troops were worried about an upcoming election, they registered people from addresses that had no residents, or in several precincts for the same election.

The machine tolerated crime — if the criminals were friendly to the machine. Gambling and prostitution carried on as police, properly compensated, looked the other way. County prosecutors helped criminals avoid time in prison.

The phrase applied to Kansas City in the late 1920s and 1930s was "wide-open town," which meant that you could get away with most anything if you offered the right people something in return.

The city was also wide open for criminals, among them the kidnappers, thieves and gunmen who wandered across Depression-era America. The Barrow gang, led by Clyde Barrow who was accompanied by his girlfriend, Bonnie Parker, spent a couple of nights in Platte County in summer 1933 before authorities routed them out. That same summer, gunmen attempted to free escaped convict Frank Nash in front of Union Station in broad daylight, but wound

After the Union Station massacre, the public crowded around to see the bodies and the blood. The auto on the right was to have carried convict Frank Nash back to prison in Leavenworth.

up killing Nash and four law enforcement men in what became known as the Union Station Massacre.

Also in 1933, gunmen from the city's dominant criminal faction ambushed and killed Ferris Anthon, who was thought to be edging in on the liquor business at the expense of the faction. The man thought to have been Anthon's assailant was caught nearly red-handed, trying to shoot the Jackson County sheriff. With the help of the county prosecutor, his trial was delayed for years. Eventually sent to prison, the gunman was soon pardoned by the governor of Missouri.

On election day in March 1934, four people were killed at polling places. That summer, the mob's best-known figure and front man, John Lazia, was machine-gunned in front of his apartment building.

The city's reputation, already tawdry in the early years of the Pendergast era, took a turn to the violent. None of this was good for business — unless your business was, perhaps, illegal.

In 1939, a series of efforts by local reformers and state and federal prosecutors turned the tide. The boss, Tom Pendergast, was charged with failing to pay income taxes on a slice of a state insurance settlement that had come his way. He pleaded guilty and was sent to Leavenworth. Abruptly, his machine foundered. H. F. McElroy resigned as city manager. McElroy's successors discovered that the books had been cooked, and that

The Nelson Gallery of Art neared completion on the site of Nelson's estate, Oak Hall, in 1933. The same year, the University of Kansas City, left, opened on the other side of Brush Creek. Soon up and running would be the Kansas City Philharmonic, below.

Kansas City was deeply in the red. Reformers organized a "Clean Sweep" campaign and in 1940 threw out most of the Pendergast council members.

Culture in the midlands

Dreary as the 1930s seemed in retrospect under the combined weight of the Depression and machine rule, the area still made advances and found things to celebrate.

One came in December 1933, when a big new art gallery opened. The art was paid for by the estate of William Rockhill Nelson, who had died in 1915. His will had called for his *Kansas City Star* to be sold after the death of his heirs and the proceeds used to buy paintings and sculpture. His wife, his only child, daughter Laura, and her husband, Irwin Kirkwood, were dead by 1927

and the newspaper was sold to a group of employees. As promised, the money bought art. Laura and Irwin's estates, along with the estate of Mary McAfee Atkins, were used to build the new structure named the Nelson Gallery of Art and Atkins Museum.

Another happy moment came with the opening that same year of Kansas City University, a small liberal-arts institution that benefited from land and money donated by William Volker. Volker, an energetic but private philanthropist, had made his money in the wholesale furniture business, concentrating in common household items such as window shades and picture frames.

Fitting with the theme of arts and education, 1933 also saw the founding of the Kansas City Philharmonic, the city's first orchestra since the 1910s.

Meanwhile, the arrival of a new administration in Washington and a new Congress brought

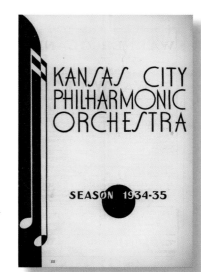

A miniature downtown with its own business association thrived at 31st Street and Troost Avenue in the 1930s.

emergency measures to stem the decline. First off was a four-day bank holiday, called by the new president, Franklin Roosevelt, immediately after his inauguration in March 1933. Congress enacted an Emergency Banking Act, calming what had been a third banking panic.

The United States left the gold standard, the dollar fell on international exchanges, domestic wholesale prices rose and the result was an abrupt turnaround of the Depression deflation. Price inflation took its place.

The WPA

In 1935, the federal Works Progress Administration aimed to put the unemployed to work in building highways, streets, airports, schools, hospitals and other public buildings. As with Kansas City's Ten-Year Plan, the WPA and other government work programs did create jobs and the newly restored earners spent money,

but could not by themselves lift the country out of Depression.

Labor unions were strengthened by new federal laws and by new, vigorous leadership. Some companies began to accept unions' growing clout, but others resisted.

In late 1936, a thousand union workers went on a new kind of strike. Instead of walking out and refusing to return to work, they simply stopped work and stayed in the building. The form was called a sitdown strike. The first came at the Fisher Body Plan in the Leeds District of Kansas City. The immediate causes: the firing of a worker and General Motors' failure to recognize their union, the United Auto Workers. Without car bodies produced by the Fisher plant, the nearby Chevrolet assembly plant ground to a halt as well. The strike ended two days before Christmas, once strikers found that friends and family wouldn't be allowed to deliver food to them.

Steam locomotives underwent a makeover in the Santa Fe shops in the Argentine District of Kansas City, Kansas. The drive wheels were about as tall as the workers.

Katz Drug opened this modern outlet in the 1930s at Main Street and Westport Road. The cat logo was always present for Katz, which billed itself as "World's Largest Cut Rate Drug Stores."

In October 1937, workers at Ford's Kansas City assembly plant, which employed almost 3,200 people, went on their own sit-down strike over the assembly line's speed. The company brought in replacement workers and the union took its charge of unfair labor practices to the federal National Labor Relations Board. In May 1941, the board ordered Ford to rehire the employees and award them back pay of $2.5 million. That year, Ford recognized their union, the United Auto Workers.

Labor organizing led to a split between Thomas Pendergast and one of Kansas City's most powerful business people, J.C. Nichols. The two had gotten along for much of the decade, Nichols cooperating with the boss when it served his interest and vice versa. Until the machine fell, it controlled City Hall and all its permitting, billing, maintenance and law-enforcement powers. But when union construction workers tried to organize Nichols' employees in 1937, Nichols could no longer find common ground with the Boss.

By the end of the 1930s, some businesses were looking up. Butler Manufacturing — which by now had operations in Minneapolis as well as Kansas City, and which had branched out from water tanks and garages to oil-field equipment, cleaning equipment and steel buildings — bid for and won a federal contract to produce thousands of grain bins. The bins were needed to store corn and other grain as part of the government's crop-loan program, which removed crops from the market to bolster prices. Two straight bumper years for the corn crop created the sudden need.

Because the Kansas City plant was operating near capacity, and the Minneapolis plant was, too, Butler bought an abandoned factory near Galesburg, Illinois. It won the bid and delivered more than 20,000 bins in fewer than 75 days. The grain-bin business with the government lasted another decade and a half. Meanwhile, the company expanded its work in Kansas City, where its focus remained.

In the Depression, another city's loss could be Kansas City's gain. Russell and Clara Stover had started a candy manufacturing business in Denver in 1922, and in 1925 opened a plant in Kansas City. The

Butler Manufacturing struck a bonanza when it won the government contract to make grain bins to store crops for federal agriculture price-support programs.

1920s were good for the candy business, as they were for so many businesses, and the Stovers opened a chain of retail stores. After the Depression hit, they were forced to close about half their stores and lost their Denver home. In 1931, they moved headquarters to Kansas City and, with the right marketing touch, kept the company afloat. Eventually, they climbed out of debt. For the rest of the 1930s the Stovers kept their company name, "Mrs. Stover's Bungalow Candies," until 1943, when it would change to Russell Stover candies.

Slowly, the country and Kansas City crept out of the worst of the Depression. The end of the melancholy decade brought the end of the Pendergast machine and a dampening of all the fun in the "wide-open town." But it did not put the economy the full boost it needed to recover. That would come only with the spending required of another great war.

Following pages: Kansas City alight in the night, as photographed from the Liberty Memorial.

REINFORCING
S T E E L

Sheffield—maker of more than thirty steel products —buyer of raw materials and fuel from the territory —an organization meeting important territorial steel needs.

SHEFFIELD
STEEL CORPORATION
KANSAS CITY, MO.

War and its Aftermath

In September 1939, Europe went back to war. German troops and tanks invaded Poland, drawing Great Britain and France and other allies into the conflict. Japan, meanwhile, extended its military grip on Asia.

For a while, the United States remained neutral, but as months passed the country edged closer to the conflict. In September 1940 President Franklin D. Roosevelt signed into law a military draft. Also, he reached a deal to give Britain old U.S. destroyers. By December of that year, the United States was lending goods to Britain and in March 1941, with enactment of the Lend-Lease plan, America began actively producing equipment for the Allies.

American cities vied for the chance at military contracts, and Kansas City — then the 19th-largest city in the country — went to work. The Chamber of Commerce sent brochures to military contractors, but its most effective effort was carried out by a coterie of influential businessmen. Developer J.C. Nichols, furniture

Aircraft workers and others assembled in the thousands on the day North American Aviation's Fairfax bomber plant won its "E" for excellence in war production.

dealer Robert Mehornay, engraver and aviation enthusiast Lou Holland and others traveled to Washington, ostensibly to advise the government on production. They were called "dollar-a-day men," well-to-do businessmen who received a token $1 for each day of their service.

Lou Holland

Kansas City goes to work

Their overriding motive was to grab for Kansas City and the surrounding area some of the new manufacturing capacity envisioned by military planners. They succeeded.

In autumn 1940 Remington Arms announced that it would build an ammunition plant in northeast Jackson County. The operation, named the Lake City Ordnance Plant, would cover 3,200 acres and eventually turn out 200 million rounds of ammunition a month.

In December 1940 the U.S. Army chose the Fairfax Industrial District next to Kansas City, Kansas, as the site of a plant to make bombers for the Air Corps. The factory would be managed by North American Aviation, and at its peak employ 26,000 people. By late December 1941 the first B-25 Mitchell bomber was ready to go, and its first test flight — from Fairfax airport next door to the plant — took place just more than a week later.

By the time of that flight, the United States had come under attack. Earlier in December, Japanese bombers attempted to wipe out the U.S. Pacific fleet at Pearl Harbor in Hawaii. In short order the United States went to war with Japan and Germany. The rumble that Kansas Citians soon noticed overhead was that of B-25s, bound for combat zones. By war's end, more than 6,600 of the airplanes were produced in Fairfax.

Not far from Fairfax and next to the Kansas

Landing ships rolled down the ways and into the Kansas River, above, in sight of the Downtown skyline. The scene was Darby Manufacturing. Below: The Sunflower plant brought jobs and high-explosive manufacturing to western Johnson County.

River, the Darby Corporation shifted production from peacetime metal products to wartime landing craft, which Darby launched into the river. The "prairie ships" would carry tanks and other mechanized Army vehicles in the invasion of Europe.

Near DeSoto in Johnson County, the Sunflower arms plant opened in 1943, supplying explosive propellant for artillery shells. At the American Royal building,

Inside the North American Aviation plant, workers carefully placed tail sections on a B-25 medium bomber, above. Below, women trainees learned to rivet, "Rosies" in waiting, after thousands of men went off to war.

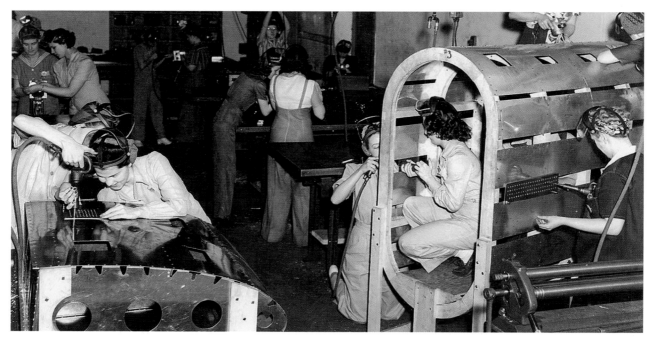

At the Donnelly Garment Company, the company was built on the work of its employees and on the popularity of the inexpensive housedresses it produced. Come wartime, military clothing would take priority.

Commonwealth Glider produced gliders for training and for carrying troops and cargo.

On Bannister Road east of Troost Avenue just south of the Kansas City, Missouri, city limit, the Pratt & Whitney Corporation built a 57-acre complex to produce engines for naval aircraft. At its peak the plant would employ nearly 24,000 people in three shifts. The 2,000-horsepower engines each contained 9,000 parts. At the

beginning, only a few of the workers had operated the high-precision machinery required to make the engines. Yet despite the worries of some wartime planners about that inexperience — and of the difficulty finding suitable skills in the Midwest — the plant met the challenge.

Early on, Pratt & Whitney tried to hire mainly high school graduates with knowledge of special subjects, such as trigonometry. Men were preferred, preferably white. When production lagged later in the war, the company began hiring more women and more black employees, who showed they could do the job. The plan wound up with a commendation from the military for industrial excellence.

Existing industries pitched in, too.

In North Kansas City, Cook Paint made paint for equipment and lining for the cans that held food for GI ration kits. The Phillips refinery turned out high-octane gasoline, Puritan produced compressed air for welding, and local companies turned out gunstocks for American and Allied troops. Aireon made radio and electronic equipment. The Vendo Corporation, makers of soft-drink vending machines, boosted production for military training camps and war plants — the War Department deemed soft drinks "essential for soldier morale" — in addition to producing antennas for radar-detection systems.

For Kansas City's garment industry, military orders took precedence over civilian clothes, and led to a rush of business. Orders flowed in for Army and Navy shirts, trousers and jackets, and for flying suits and for nurses' uniforms.

Besides producing airplanes, engines, boats and uniforms, Kansas City businesses also provided technical training for military personnel. The area's many radio and electronic schools were filled with uniformed students, reaching an estimated 10,000 by late 1943. At the University of Kansas City, aviation cadets took classes and drilled.

At Union Station, as many as 200 passenger trains a day arrived and departed, carrying military personnel.

Before the war was over, 77,000 hires would be made for war-production jobs in the Kansas City area. Adding those already on payrolls, 114,000 would be employed in work directly related to the war effort by 1944. Besides putting Kansas Citians back to work, the new war-related jobs drew thousands of applicants from rural areas. Despite having 40,000 local residents off to war, the Board

Wartime or not, the Chamber of Commerce kept at it, showing residents and non-resident alike how their town contributed to the war effort. Below, Sheffield Steel after the war in the late 1940s.

of Realtors reported that 99.8 percent of housing units were full. Now, the Great Depression had truly ended in Kansas City.

The war ends

In May 1945, Allied troops received Germany's surrender. On August 14, after two atomic bomb attacks on its main island, Japan surrendered. The war for which there had been months of buildup ended abruptly and when it did, so did the war economy.

One day after the Japanese surrender in 1945, North American Aviation's B-25 contract was terminated. In barely a week, more than 4,600 workers were laid off from the Fairfax plant. Operations at Pratt & Whitney ceased, too. It laid off 17,000 workers at once. Sunflower was placed on partial standby.

Nevertheless, a new and buoyant peacetime economy absorbed the loss of war business and jobs. Indeed, Kansas City and the country worked quickly to put the war behind. Despite brief economic travails — inflation flamed up after the government ended wartime price controls, housing was in short supply early on and the local unemployment rate rose briefly — the serious

> *The war for which there had been months of buildup ended quite abruptly. When the war ended, so did the war economy.*

postwar recession feared in some quarters did not happen.

Within a year, General Motors had leased part of the Fairfax complex to make Buicks, Oldsmobiles and Pontiacs. TWA acquired another part to use for its overhaul base. Ford resumed automobile production at its Winchester Avenue plant.

During the war, Americans' spending had been limited by rationing — they could buy only limited quantities of gasoline, sugar and tires — and by apprehension about the future. Auto manufacturers stopped making cars during the war and retooled to build military machinery.

With the end of the war, and of rationing, and of military production, and with U.S. factories once again making consumer products, Americans began to buy. Big catalog-sales outlets such as Sears and Montgomery Ward accounted for one-quarter of retail sales in the Kansas City area. Still shoppers thronged big Downtown department stores and hundreds of smaller shops. Kansas City's big drugstore chains — Katz, Crown Drug and Parkview — stayed busy selling a wide variety of items.

Veterans realized substantial benefits from the Serviceman's Readjustment Act, known as the GI Bill of Rights. The act offered aid with college tuition and advantages in getting home loans. College classes quickly filled with returning GIs, and what most Americans could not afford before the war — a college education — came within reach. With the GI Bill, hundreds of thousands of Americans could afford a house for the first time. New subdivisions went up in city after city.

New growth in suburbs

Kansas City's developers quickly laid out subdivisions to the south in Jackson County and to the southwest in still mostly rural Johnson County. Merriam, Prairie Village, Fairway and other suburbs incorporated in the half-decade after the war. Improved highways paved the way for commuters to work Downtown and live in the suburbs — U.S. 71 from Downtown to the South and the Turkey Creek Expressway from Downtown to the southwest.

Some of the same business leaders who worked

Minnesota Avenue in downtown Kansas City, Kansas, hummed with business and patrons in 1951 as a healthy postwar economy took hold.

Laboratories for the new Midwest Research Institute occupied in their early years the old Westport City Hall. Researchers tested a multitude of ideas for industries.

to bring war contracts to Kansas City, J.C. Nichols and Kenneth Spencer of Spencer Chemical among them, set out even before the German and Japanese surrenders to find a way to keep up the momentum. They envisioned a research center that could keep some contractors and facilities in town and also attract others. In addition, they hoped, the presence of such an institution would stanch the migration of researchers and scientists to the coasts. In 1943 the Midwest Research Institute was formed, modeled after earlier centers such as the Mellon Institute in Pittsburgh and the Battelle Memorial Institute in Columbus, Ohio. After experiments with devising its own projects, MRI found its calling, taking on contracts from businesses that wanted ways to do things better.

At its laboratory in Westport, the Institute and its scientists developed a new means for Spencer Chemical to keep its ammonium nitrate fertilizer from clumping.

For the Folger coffee company, MRI created a palatable instant coffee, and contributed to the development of automatic drip coffeemakers. It devised a coating for M&M candies to make sure the candies didn't melt in the customer's hand — or in shipment or storage. For power companies, MRI studied population trends. It also measured the roughness of airplane runways and explored the causes and treatment of cancer.

On the side, the Institute spawned new-technology companies. To some of them MRI made its labs available and outsourced projects.

Yet even as the postwar era unfolded with new possibilities, some of Kansas City's older business pursuits faltered.

Most notable were the city's meatpackers. Since the 1920s, their combined production and their employee numbers had diminished. After World War II, the

Shoppers flocked in December 1949 to Petticoat Lane, the two blocks of 11th Street between Grand Avenue and Main. At the end of the street stood the new Macy's, which recently had replaced John Taylor Dry Goods.

trend continued; meatpacking was moving away from centralized, urban operations in such places as Kansas City, Chicago and Fort Worth to smaller cities closer to where the cattle were fed and fattened.

Although the Kansas City stockyards saw a record run of cattle in autumn 1943, that proved a temporary spike. Its operations hit a plateau.

Kansas City's milling industry grew, but at a slower pace than in its 1920s boom. Grain from 11 states stretching from the Dakotas to Texas still flowed into Kansas City, and the city ranked second only to Minneapolis-St. Paul in grain-storage capacity. Three big

bakers with local plants did the bulk of the work turning that grain into bread, biscuits, crackers and pretzels — Sunshine Biscuits, National Biscuit and United Biscuit.

In the late 1910s, at the end of the first World War , about one in every two workers in the Kansas City area had a job related to food marketing or processing. By 1947 that ratio had fallen to one in four.

In Kansas City's once-vast agricultural market, the rural population was already in decline, the result of mechanization, which reduced the number of workers. In fact, the rural population of the entire United States had stopped growing in 1910 and by 1930 was clearly on the way down. World War II and the years after only hastened the drop. Mirroring roughly a national trend, from 1940 to 1950 the rural population of Kansas, Missouri, Oklahoma and Nebraska declined by 28 percent. Many of the counties at the edge of the Kansas City market never again matched their peak populations — set in 1900.

Moving off the farm

As rural dwellers left the farm, urban populations rose 26 percent, some of that in cities and some in the towns that took up the task of serving the farm and small-town population that remained.

Agriculture remained an important element in the workings of Kansas City, but now it was only one of several.

At mid-century, wholesaling — 50 years before a massive driver of the local economy — continued to lose steam. Since the 1920s, grocery chains had proliferated, centralizing their own buying and distributing operations. Agricultural cooperatives did the same for farmers. Big department stores, themselves now parts of chains, began buying directly from manufacturers. All this cut into the future of the traditional wholesale business.

Catalog merchandisers still valued Kansas City's transportation connections. Sears and Montgomery Ward shipped tons of items from Kansas City.

Kansas City's manufacturers grew. In 1939, at the tail end of the Depression and eve of World War II, wage earners who made their money in manufacturing numbered 38,500. By 1947 that had risen 67 percent, to 61,800. Food processing remained a sizable chunk of the manufacturing total, but now it was bolstered by growth in the iron and steel industry, apparel-making, automobile manufacturing and printing and publishing.

The apparel-makers employed about 9,600 people in 1949, a bigger workforce than the meatpackers, yet the garment industry did not get much attention. The reason: Most of the people doing the cutting and stitching were spread through 150 small shops occupying upper-floor

Travel, travel everywhere: Reinforcing rods were standing on the path of the Southwest Trafficway that would enter Downtown from the south and southwest, above. Below, Freight locomotives and cars jammed the West Bottoms in 1945.

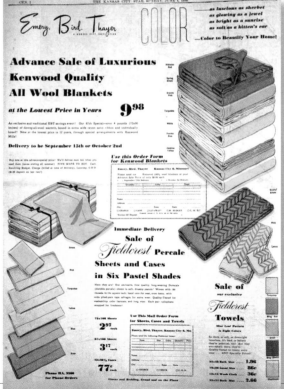

rooms along Broadway in Kansas City's Garment District.

Since the 1890s, Kansas City had been a center for the wholesale dry-goods business, delivering men's and boys' work clothes and other items made in the East to the large rural market served by Kansas City. With the dawn of the 20th century came European immigrants through the port of Galveston, many of them skilled tailors and seamstresses who eventually started their own shops. A few decades later came manufacturers who sought to escape high taxes and high labor costs of the East Coast. With that, clothing was not only distributed from Kansas City, but also manufactured in large quantities here.

The fashions produced in Kansas City were rarely high-end. Instead, local concerns made everyday products such as uniforms, work clothes and housedresses. Because Kansas City did not have a large force of skilled seamsters and seamstresses, apparel producers used the "section system," a sort of assembly-line process in which one worker made collars and another pockets.

In World War II, Kansas City shops made Army and Navy shirts, trousers, jackets, flying suits and nurses' uniforms. After military demand ended, the Kansas City garment industry — like so many other manufacturers — increased direct sales to retailers. One rich market was mail-order houses.

Biggest of the apparel-makers was Nell Donnelly Reed's dressmaking powerhouse, the Donnelly Garment Company. By the late 1940s Donnelly operated in two Kansas City locations, one on Linwood and one on East 17th Street. Another was the Lee Company, which made denim overalls and trousers.

The postwar years were the peak for the Kansas City clothing industry, a heyday that lasted until catalog clothes sales began to decline and small-town clothing shops in the Midwest began going out of business.

The printing industry thrived in Kansas City largely because Joyce Hall's little postcard business of the 1910s had grown into an internationally distributed maker of greeting cards and wrapping paper. Hallmark sponsored a national radio program — soon to make the move to television — "The Hallmark Hall of Fame."

At mid-century, Hall Brothers, which would change its corporate name to Hallmark in 1954, accounted for more than half Kansas City's total jobs in printing through its contracts with 11 printing firms around the

Prairie Village and its miles of curving residential streets formed part of the phenomenal growth of Johnson County and other suburbs after World War II.

metro area. T*he Kansas City Star*, near its all-time peak circulation in 1950, had on the payroll hundreds of printers and pressmen, advertising sales folks, circulation managers and editors and reporters.

About 4,000 people went to work each day in steel works, most of them at Armco's Sheffield facility in the Blue River Valley. Kansas City lay far from any deposits of iron ore, so for its raw material the Sheffield plant used scrap metal. Kansas City was a hub for scrap from the central United States — particularly junked automobiles and discarded farm equipment. Along the Blue River, the scrap was turned into joists, ingots, bars, wire mesh, bolts and nuts.

Next door to the steel plant, Butler Manufacturing was busy fabricating the metal into tanks and buildings for farm storage.

Automobile production soared at Ford's plant on Winchester Avenue, and the General Motors plants in the Leeds district of east Kansas City and at Fairfax in Kansas.

Before long, Ford decided to shift its operation to a new plant in Claycomo, Missouri, north of the Missouri River. About that time, the outbreak of the Korean War intervened and the new facility produced only aircraft wings. After the Korean truce, the entire Ford assembly operation in the mid-1950s would be transferred to Claycomo.

Kansas City companies also made chemicals — soaps, cosmetics, drugs, paints and varnish. Two big

At the Municipal Air Terminal, passengers waited in a sleek lobby.

refineries operated — Standard Oil's plant in Sugar Creek and Phillips' refinery, built in the early 1930s in Fairfax. Other Kansas City companies made mattresses, box springs and office furniture. About 1,200 people were employed making fiberglass for insulation.

Various other businesses still contributed mightily to the Kansas City economy at mid-century — railroads, air transportation, bus services, hotels, restaurants and theaters.

Kansas City's most glamorous employer of the era was TWA, known as Transcontinental & Western Air when it established its headquarters in Kansas City in 1931. Later renamed Trans World Airlines, it gave the town an international cachet.

As many as 7,000 people worked in insurance, finance and real estate.

Studies of the local economy done at mid-century encouraged manufacturing. Food processing, the studies said, had limited growth potential. Instead, more and more diversified manufacturing showed unlimited horizons. Unseen in their potential were service industries, which one day would outstrip manufacturing. The information age was only hinted at by the existence of large, yet crude computers.

For the time being, with Europe and Japan still

recovering from the shock and ruined infrastructure of World War II, manufacturing would be the way of the future.

For Kansas City, that future looked bright. In both population and number of newcomers, the 1950s would prove to be one of Kansas City's busiest decades. The Kansas City area added about a quarter-million people, 90,000 of them immigrants mostly from rural areas. The 1960 census would give the Kansas City metropolitan area its highest population ranking, 19th among U.S. metro areas.

Kansas City's historical commercial advantage — its central location in the continental United States — was responsible. Decades later, the Mid-America Regional Council would look back and declare that in the 1950s the importance of central location probably reached its peak.

Suitably for such an occasion, Kansas City began its decade of progress with an extravaganza. It had been 100 years since the Town of Kansas received a charter from Jackson County, and civic leaders decided to celebrate the centennial in early June 1950. Parades rolled through Downtown and a pageant called "Thrills of a

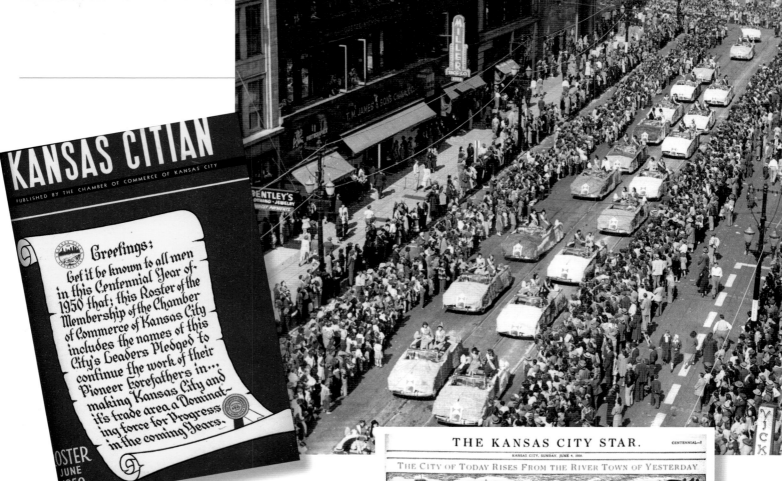

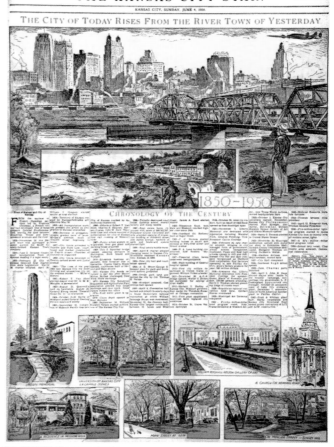

Pulling out all the stops, Kansas City congratulated itself on the century since it was recognized by Jackson County. Pioneer costumes and reference were the order of the day in June 1950, along with parades.

Century," was staged before big crowds at a new outdoor amphitheater in Swope Park.

The thrill was dampened some by the outbreak of conflict in Korea, which broke out only weeks after the Centennial festivities ended. It was dampened even more the next summer, when once again nature intervened in Kansas City's parade.

In summer 1951, after weeks of heavy rainfall across the Great Plains, the Kansas River topped its banks, creating flooding first in central Kansas and then in city after city downstream. On the weekend of July 13, the flooding reached the Kansas City area. Despite emergency workers' efforts to shore up the levees with sandbags, the Kansas River washed into the Argentine district of Kansas City, Kansas, and flooded the Santa Fe rail yards. Within hours, the river topped levies in Armourdale. That area was home not only to working-class residents of Kansas

The new Starlight Theatre opened in June 1951 with a performance of "Flower Drum Song." Patrons on opening night carried raincoats just in case, rain having been the order of the day and night.

City, Kansas, but also to the Procter & Gamble and Colgate Palmolive soap factories and the Wilson, Cudahy and Swift & Co. meatpacking plants. Then the waters rose into the West Bottoms, where 200 acres of stockyards and the massive Armour packing plant operated.

Cattle and pigs floated away as the stockyards went under. By the hundreds, workers were evacuated from inundated meatpacking plants. Some climbed out on aerial cattle chutes, then descended long ladders to patches of land not yet flooded. Warehouse after warehouse filled with water and then with mud. Railroad lines were blocked and trucking came to a halt in the area.

From the air, the West Bottoms, sprawling across both sides of the state line, looked like an inland sea. Water also backed up in the old bed of Turkey Creek and then along Southwest Boulevard in Kansas City, Missouri. Fire broke out there, probably from fuel tanks banging together and igniting fuel spilled on floodwater.

Sightseers gathered at the base of a viaduct to watch the waters rise in the West Bottoms in 1951. The flood would reach much higher in the next few hours.

Runaway barges bashed into the Hannibal bridge, knocking its rotating span open. That was enough to cut off traffic across the Missouri River by both the Burlington Railroad and automobiles, which used a roadway across the top of the bridge.

The flood wasn't done. It poured into the Fairfax District next to Kansas City, Kansas, flooding the General Motors assembly plant, the Owens-Corning Fiberglass plant, Sunshine Biscuits, the Phillips Oil refinery and the TWA overhaul base.

The depth of water from this flood far exceeded that of 1903. Across the Kansas City area, the cost mounted for emergency services. Mosquitos proliferated in low-lying areas, and a stench pervaded the place. Then came a massive effort to clean up the mess, from mud on ground floors to the carcasses of livestock trapped and drowned in the stockyards.

Meatpackers were badly hit. After the flood, Cudahy never reopened its plant. The Bottoms, once the heart of Kansas City's economy, started beating more slowly.

Meatpacking had been migrating to the country, anyway, to place such as Garden City, Kansas, Sioux City, Iowa, and Amarillo, Texas — closer to where the cattle were being raised and fed. Within two decades Kansas City's once-mighty meatpacking plants would all be gone.

The livestock trade itself dispersed. As late as the 1930s Kansas City had a dominant role as a redistribution point for livestock, the point where cattle and hogs arrived from the ranches where they were born and then

were shipped to feeding areas in the corn belt. However, new irrigation techniques made feed-grain production possible in new areas farther from the city and closer to where cattle were raised. Feedlots sprang up across the Plains. Also, farmers began negotiating directly with packers. The livestock trade moved away from giant, centralized stockyards to auction houses in smaller towns across the region.

The relevance of the cowtown name — often beloved but sometimes detested — already was diminishing.

From the western bluffs of Kansas City, Missouri, to the eastern bluffs of Kansas City, Kansas, the great flood of 1951 left its mark in mud and destruction. Afterward, new and higher floodwalls would be installed.

White concrete supports marked the route of the Southwest Trafficway as it was constructed along the west side of Downtown in the early 1950s.

Entering the Modern Era

Jarring as the 1951 flood was for the city's traditional industries, much of the metropolitan Kansas City area sat on high ground and stayed dry. Businesses and homeowners — those above the severely damaged river bottoms — suffered losses in electric power and temporarily a much-diminished water supply. Public transportation from the highlands through low-lying areas was disrupted. Yet most neighborhoods and business districts emerged unscathed, Downtown chief among them.

Downtown had its own problems, less dramatic than the flood but worrisome nonetheless to business leaders of the 1950s. For one, there was traffic congestion caused by the proliferation of automobiles on a street grid laid out in the days of mule-drawn streetcars.

TWA's new headquarters at 18th and Main streets had a space-age look.

Electric streetcars now ran down the center of many a block, reducing maneuvering room for cars. For another, parts of the central business district were deteriorating, particularly along Main Street north of Ninth.

The modern marvel, television, attracted viewers to the windows of the Kansas City Power & Light building, where the electric company installed two sets. Only one station, WDAF, was available and few homes in 1950 had the devices.

City planners proposed a solution for the traffic. They drew up a multi-lane, limited-access expressway loop around the Downtown area. The idea was to create a way for motorists to avoid the grid by motoring part of their way around the circumference. This loop would be connected to outlying parts of the city by multilane streets with few intersections.

One link in the scheme, the Southwest Trafficway, opened to traffic in 1950. The Paseo Bridge across the Missouri River and a wide highway along the path of old Sixth Street were under construction through the north portion of Downtown.

In 1956, the federal Interstate highway program became law, meaning cross-country freeways would connect with the city's expressways. Existing expressways were integrated into the Interstate system. The new Sixth Street was transformed into part of Interstate 70, which would cross the Kansas River valley along the Intercity Viaduct to Kansas City, Kansas. To the southwest in Johnson and Wyandotte counties, construction of Interstate 35 began along Turkey Creek. Eventually, Kansas City, Missouri, would become the center of a spokelike freeway system, attracting trucking companies.

Historically a railway hub, the area became a

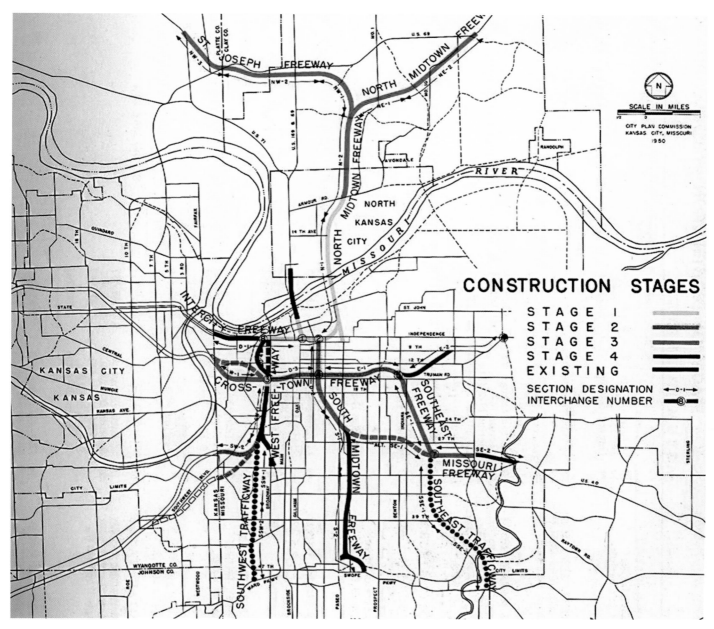

The City Plan Commission's outline of expressways showed a loop around Downtown and routes extending in various directions. Some routes were never built, but several were absorbed into the Interstate highway system.

highway hub, too. With new opportunities for trucking, Sears and Montgomery Ward expanded warehouse space. Also, commuting times for workers improved.

Urban renewal

For Downtown's other difficulty, deterioration, civic leaders came up with a different solution. City Manager L.P. Cookingham, who considered Downtown a "nerve center" of the metropolitan area, warned that it was threatened by blight. The answer of the day was to remove the blight in a process called urban renewal. In that era the idea was common in cities across the country. Beginning in the early 1950s, blocks of stores were declared blighted and scraped clean of buildings.

On either side of Main Street from Sixth to Ninth streets stood decaying buildings decades old. The aging structures were demolished, basements were filled and business owners, residents and transients were moved out. Some blocks were re-made, and from them arose modern concrete, steel and glass office structures. Other

On the north side of Downtown, many of the buildings along Main Street were marked for removal in the urban renewal effort. By 1960, below, several were gone and newer structures standing in their places.

From the top of the Liberty Memorial, a photographer captured this view of Downtown in the early 1950s. Passengers and taxicabs still thronged Union Station.

blocks simply emptied out, replaced by surface parking lots.

In the eyes of 1950s planners, the nerve center of the metropolitan area got relief from clogged streets through expressways and also a partial facelift through urban renewal. By 1957 the streetcars were gone, too, and the tracks paved over.

Those efforts accomplished their goals in the short run, but they failed to revitalize Downtown, which would continue to decline in businesses and residents. The massive removals of the 1950s would be blamed for obliterating parts of the cityscape but doing little to replace them — a facelift that left too many blank spots in the visage of Downtown.

The birth of empires

Areawide, the 1950s marked good times, particularly for the giant distributors, manufacturers and retailers of 1950s Kansas City. Amidst all those giants, two notable small businesses were just beginning, one so tiny it fit into the basement of the owner's home.

Its owner and only employee was Ewing Kauffman, a Cass County, Missouri, native in his mid-30s, and a Navy veteran of World War II. As the one-man sales force, Kauffman spent his days making sales calls on doctors. As the one-man packaging department, he spent his evening hours filling bottles with pills. Kauffman gave his little company the name Marion and the important-sounding word, "Laboratories."

He had spent the immediate postwar years selling pharmaceuticals for an Illinois drug company but when the company tried to limit his sales effort, he quit. Borrowing $5,000 from a bank for seed money, Kauffman bought calcium and high-potency vitamin tablets and each evening bottled them by hand. To the bottles he affixed a label, "Manufactured for Marion Laboratories."

Done with that, he became the shipping department, delivering his packages each night to the post office for mailing.

Kauffman was a good enough salesman to gross $30,000 in his first year. Kauffman found seven investors, ranging from doctors who had done business with him to a high school classmate who had once lent him $20. Each put in $1,000. By 1965, when Kauffman took his company public, each $1,000 investment had grown to about $900,000.

Marion Laboratories would become a multimillion-dollar operation that would make Kauffman a billionaire, enrich the careers and bank accounts of hundreds of employees — whom he called "associates" — and lead not only to his purchase of a major-league baseball team but also to establishment of one of Kansas City's largest charitable foundations. In addition, Marion would become a model for other successful health-related companies for years to come.

Meanwhile, across the country, barely noticeable except from the perspective of later years, the postwar economy began to shift away from the production of products to the production of services. Products cost money to ship, and a central site for moving them had been important to Kansas City since the arrival of railroads. To keep growing, Kansas City would need to keep up with the change.

In early 1955 an accounting service run by brothers Henry and Richard also came upon a way to grow beyond the brothers' dreams. That year, an advertising representative at *The Kansas City Star* suggested to the Blochs that they set a special rate for preparing tax returns. As it happened, the Internal Revenue Service that year ended its own tax-preparation service.

The ad man produced an ad for the Blochs offering tax help for $5. To the brothers' surprise, customers lined up at their door. Within weeks, the two incorporated under the name H&R Block, changing the spelling of their name to avoid mispronunciation. They did so well that the next year they expanded to the East Coast with franchise outlets. H&R Block went public in 1962 and in the mid-1960s the company opened a tax-training school for staff in H&R Block offices. Before long, the company would be known nationwide.

The Blochs formed part of that service sector in Kansas City that would overtaking manufacturing in scale over the next few decades.

New technology and mergers

Manufacturing was changing, too. In Kansas City and across the country, new technology increased the productivity of workers and reduced the need for repetitive labor. By 1959, only 45 percent of non-farm workers were employed in a manual trade, down from nearly two-thirds at the end of World War I in 1918.

Across the landscape of American business, old companies were combining with others. Concentration increased — particularly in manufacturing, communications and banking. At the same time, American business was becoming increasingly international. Oil companies were among the first to look abroad, making big investments in supplies overseas.

Labor organizations concentrated, too. In 1955, the American Federation of Labor and the Congress of Industrial Organizations — which had competed to the point of raiding each other's shops — merged.

On the farm, prices leveled off. Agriculture kept pace with the rest of American business by combining,

Mayor William Kemp got behind the wheel of the 27 millionth Chevrolet produced in the country as it rolled off the assembly line of GM's plant in Leeds. Officials from Detroit flew in for the ceremony.

Baseball fans overflowed the bleachers and sat on the hillside along the left-field line at Municipal Stadium, where the A's could be sure to draw crowds when the New York Yankees came to town.

merging and concentrating. Fewer and bigger farms became a fact of life in rural areas.

From top to bottom in the mid-century economy, life was changing fast. The postwar world brought snazzier, more powerful automobiles; Detroit redesigned its models each year so buyers would be encouraged to purchase more frequently to keep up with the times. Two-car families multiplied. Once out on the wider and smoother freeways, they drove at higher speeds. Early on, the Kansas Turnpike set its speed limit at 80 miles an hour.

At home, Americans spent more for housing and for furnishings. One important piece of furniture, the television, grew from a curiosity of the late 1940s to a dominant feature of domestic life by the middle 1950s. The postwar Baby Boom created millions of viewers. In Kansas City, children's shows filled the after-school hours on local channels with stars such as Frank Wiziarde who, in costume, became Whizzo the Clown.

Major League Baseball arrives

To the delight of many a Kansas City child — and of civic boosters of all ages — Kansas City won a major-league baseball team. In those days baseball, which had only 16 teams and none south or west of St.

Ernie Mehl

Few trees and fewer buildings marked the landscape in 1955 at State Line Road and 75th Street. State Line runs south on the left side of this aerial photograph and 75th extends westward from left to right in the foreground.

Louis, was the most valuable franchise in American professional sports. Kansas City got its team through a bit of luck and a confluence of events. The new owner was Arnold Johnson, a Chicago real-estate man who had acquired an interest in Yankee Stadium in New York and, coincidentally, a piece of the Yankees' AAA team, the Kansas City Blues, and their stadium at 22nd Street and Brooklyn Avenue. The sports editor of *The Kansas City Star*, Ernie Mehl, saw in Johnson an opportunity.

With other Kansas Citians, Mehl persuaded Johnson to put in a bid for the Philadelphia Athletics' franchise, owned by a dying Connie Mack. Quick work made the franchise Johnson's, and he moved the Athletics halfway across the continent to Kansas City. Meanwhile, the city took over and expanded the old Blues stadium, renaming it Municipal. There, on April 12, 1955, Kansas City staged its first top-level baseball game.

The Kansas City A's played their home games in the old core of the city, just east of Downtown. All around it in the 1950s, the city was changing.

For one thing, Kansas City, Missouri, busied itself by annexing vast chunks of the countryside. From 63 square miles in 1947, the city grew to 128 square miles by 1960. The idea behind annexation was to expand the number of taxable properties and also to boost population. The city's annexations — the first since 1909 — began on the south edge with an extension to 85th Street. In 1950, for the first time, the city crossed the Missouri River, adding the Municipal Airport and land surrounding North Kansas City as far north as 56th Street. In 1958, it annexed about 16 square miles on the east and in 1959 fourteen square miles on the south, stretching to 112th Street.

Kansas City was not alone. Independence grew to the east and to the north. Kansas City, Kansas, began planning annexations, too.

Meanwhile, the U.S. Supreme Court changed some of the rules of city life. In 1948 it outlawed restrictive covenants in housing — the kind that kept black people and sometimes other minorities from owning homes in certain neighborhoods and thus created concentrations of black-owned homes in certain parts of town. Now, black families could buy homes in what had been all-white neighborhoods. To do so, they left behind the urban core.

When they arrived in their new neighborhoods, however, they found white families rapidly moving out. A case in point was the area surrounding 37th Street and Brooklyn Avenue on the east side of Kansas City, Missouri. In 1950 census-takers found 4,734 people living in the area, and 99 percent of them were white. That year, the closest predominantly black neighborhood extended no farther south than 27th Street. A decade later, the racial makeup of that same census district had changed radically. Residents in 1960 numbered 4,639, nearly the same as in 1950 but this time forty-four percent were black.

Sometimes the turnover in Kansas City, Missouri, was hastened by "block-busting" real-estate agents, who made it a point to notify white homeowners when black families were moving in, hoping the white families would leave. For the agents, the multiple activity resulted in multiple sales commissions.

In 1954 the Supreme Court outlawed school segregation. The next year, Kansas City's schools began to allow black students. As they began attending formerly all-white schools, some white families withdrew their children. In the 1955-56 school year alone, white enrollment in the Kansas City School District dropped by

Still making steel from scrap metal in the Blue River Valley industrial area, workers at the Sheffield Steel plant poured molten metal into giant molds in June 1955.

1,200.

Driven by the racial change in neighbors and classroom, or by the opportunity to move to a newer home, or by both, white families moved out of the district to surrounding districts. Those destinations included parts of Kansas City, Missouri, that lay outside the Kansas City School District, other school districts in Jackson or Clay counties, and across the state line in Johnson County, Kansas.

Johnson County, which had numbered about 33,300 residents on the eve of World War II, nearly doubled its population to 63,000 in 1950. In the next 10 years, the county more than doubled — to 144,000 in 1960.

The results were stark. Paseo High School in Kansas City, Missouri, was nearly nearly all white in 1955. Eleven years later, Paseo's enrollment was 68.7 percent black. The year 1969 would be the last in which white students formed a majority in the Kansas City School District.

As the people of the city moved here and there and mostly to the suburbs, the look of the city changed, too.

In older, poorer neighborhoods on the fringes of

Downtown, the city used the techniques of urban renewal to declare slums. Residents were displaced and offered new housing in multi-unit projects. Guinotte Manor, T. B. Watkins Homes and Wayne Miner Court were some of them. Once the people left their old neighborhoods, the old buildings came down and often were not replaced.

Like the urban renewal that removed blighted business areas in the northern section of Downtown, these efforts were made possible by enactments and infusions of money from various levels of government — federal, state and local. Typically, clearance was encouraged by private interests, and most enthusiastically by the National Association of Real Estate Brokers. The goal was to make the properties available for private development.

Neighborhoods that flanked the central city were scraped clean. Former residents moved to large housing projects that eventually degenerated into slums themselves, often ridden with crime and poverty. Black-owned business such as groceries, drugstores and cab companies disappeared as the neighborhoods on which they depended evaporated.

Clearly, urban renewal did not halt what by the late 1960s was becoming an increasing flow of businesses and people out of Downtown and out of many older parts of Kansas City, Missouri.

Meanwhile, the expressways intended to clear up traffic and ease the task of traveling through Downtown instead made it easier for workers to live farther and farther away. As housing developments marched outward across the prairie, farther and farther from the urban cores of the two Kansas Citys, retail business followed. By the early 1960s, the depopulation of the central cities was becoming evident and by the 1970s would become obvious. In the Central Business District, total employment would drop 19 percent from 1963 to 1976.

In 1950, the census found 457,000 residents living in 81 square miles of incorporated Kansas City, Missouri. Twenty years later, after annexations almost quadrupled Kansas City's land area, the census-takers counted only about 500,000.

From the middle 1950s into the early 1960s, the civil rights movement was rarely off the front pages of newspapers across America. Increasingly, sit-ins at lunch counters and other acts of mild civil disobedience showed up on network news programs, often accompanied by

Anticipating new business because of Kansas City's recent annexations, the Jones Store in 1954 began an overhaul of its Downtown location.

video from which increasing numbers of Americans got at least some of their news. Some Americans, black and white, were inspired. Others were indignant.

In the late 1950s and early 1960s, the majority of civil-rights marches and demonstrations took place in the American South but Kansas City, falling as it did somewhere in the border lands, was touched, too. By the early 1960s, black people were trying to be served at Kansas City-area cafes, and attempting to enter bowling alleys. Usually, they were barred. Sometimes, police were called to carry them out.

In 1960, the Kansas City Council prohibited racial discrimination by hotels, motels and restaurants, but opponents promptly tied up the measure until 1962, when the Missouri Supreme Court gave it the go-ahead. Until matters were settled, Kansas City hotels could discriminate. And they did. Joe McGuff, then a sports columnist for *The Kansas City Star* and later the newspaper's editor, recalled how New York Yankees catcher Elston Howard, once the only black member of the famous team, had to stay in a hotel in Kansas City, Kansas, when the Yankees came to town to play the Athletics. Meanwhile the rest of the Yankees, the white players, roomed in Downtown Kansas City, Missouri.

The civil rights movement also aimed at segregated

In Clay County, the Antioch Shopping Center assembled dozens of retailers in one, pedestrian-friendly complex surrounded by ample parking. The center, where these visitors strolled in 1956, was one of the first in the area to undertake what became the model.

businesses such as cafes and taverns. Fairyland Park, a big amusement center on Prospect Avenue, refused to change its ban on black attendees despite civil rights demonstrations in 1961 and 1962.

In 1963, the Kansas City Council expanded its public accommodations ordinance, which had overcome court challenges, to include amusement parks, along with swimming pools, commercial golf courses and taverns. Also included were business, technical and vocational schools. After protests were raised by tavern owners and others, the measure went to a referendum. In April 1964, the anti-discrimination measure passed and a month later Fairyland Park admitted its first black patrons. On the other hand, some businesses closed rather than comply.

Retailers who had discouraged black clientele now would have to change their ways. Otherwise, they would face protests and legal action. Employers in all walks of business faced pressure to hire black people in something other than menial jobs.

Some notable employers made the effort. The city's black-owned newspaper, *The Call*, found progress in the 1960s in minority hiring at Hallmark Cards, Tension Envelope and Continental Baking. At the General Motors plant in Leeds, the percentage of black workers had reached 8 percent by 1967, still not at the percentage of black people in the Kansas City population but far higher than the three-tenths of 1 percent recorded at the plant in 1946.

Its parking lots jammed by holiday shoppers in late 1962, the four-year-old Blue Ridge Shopping Center created an unparalleled lineup of retail shops for eastern Jackson County. Interstate 70, then under construction, would make the mall easy to reach, suburban growth easier and Downtown shopping less essential.

Sprawling Growth

By the end of the 1950s, a once-tiny subdivision laid out nearly half a century earlier had grown too big for its governmental britches. The loose organization of Mission Township in Johnson County, Kansas, no longer worked for a community of homes and small businesses now numbering tens of thousands of people. So in 1960 Overland Park, Kansas became a city, joining a growing roster of places orbiting Kansas City, Missouri.

Overland Park's population that first year of incorporation was about 28,000, making it right away the chief city of Johnson County. In the 1960s, it would attract businesses and help create a new and more disparate Kansas City metropolitan area. And Overland Park was not the only place affecting the balance of Greater Kansas City. Blue Springs and Lee's Summit to the east, and Clay and Platte Counties to the north, and other Johnson County cities such as Olathe, Shawnee and Lenexa, and even edge areas newly annexed by Kansas City, Missouri, would only grow bigger and stronger with the years.

At its turn-of-the-century beginning, Overland Park was one of several developments bearing the name "Overland." Overland Heights and Overland Acres adjoined it. The subdivisions were laid out in the early 1900s by developer William Strang on high and hence flood-free ground. Serving all those little neighborhoods was Strang's interurban streetcar line. Nearby, Strang cleared land for a flying field and grandstand where barnstorming pilots performed on Sunday afternoons in the 1910s.

Overland Park of the 1950s, before incorporation as a city, presented a small-town look — except for the buses, which carried people to and from the nearby cities.

Once incorporated, Overland Park wasted little time growing. The boundaries of the new city stretched from Interstate 35 on the north past 103rd Street on the south and as far west as Antioch. Before 1960 was over, the city added land as far west as Switzer Road. By the next year, it reached Quivira Road. In 1968 the Overland Park limits extended west to Pflumm Road and south to 143rd Street.

Led by a generation of confident and vigorous postwar developers, the young city and the county around it rode the charged economy of 1960s America and the spread of interstate highways. Those forces fueled the extension of suburban homes and shops. Eventually the new, safer, younger communities would draw companies in the growing service and information industries.

In 1963 a new shopping center settled in at the northeast corner of 95th Street and Metcalf, then only two-lane streets lined by an occasional housing development. Called the French Market, the twin-towered center was joined in 1967 by the Metcalf South Shopping Center, just south across 95th Street. West across Metcalf, the Glenwood Theater opened in 1966. Next to it stood the Glenwood Manor Motor Hotel. The corner quickly became one of the hottest new retail spots in the metro area.

Construction was wrapping up at Overland Park's big, new French Market shopping center in 1963. Metcalf Avenue, running diagonally from lower left to lower right, and 95th Street formed its boundaries. Both were still two-lane roads.

Where I-35 crossed 87th Street, above, was still largely undeveloped in the late 1960s. Left: Home-selling promotions of the early 1960s.

The Commerce Tower rose from land along Main Street cleared for urban renewal.

United Telephone of Abilene, Kansas, moved its headquarters to the small Johnson County city of Westwood, incorporated in 1949 near the state line. At first, United was little known in the metro area because it served mostly rural telephone customers. It would become better known in years to come as United Telecom and eventually Sprint.

Existing businesses in Kansas City saw an opportunity, too. In 1969, TWA shifted its stewardess-training operations from Downtown Kansas City, Missouri, to a 25-acre campus at Lamar Avenue and 63rd Street in Overland Park, named the Breech Training Academy. Soon the school was training men for the same task, and so renaming the job "flight attendant," and then training attendants for other airlines.

The academy saved an important function of the airline for the Kansas City area. TWA, which still called itself "Kansas City's Hometown Airline," had begun moving administrative functions to New York City and reservation jobs to St. Louis. Kansas City also held on to TWA's overhaul base, which had moved from Fairfax to a site well north of Downtown.

Downtown Kansas City, Missouri, boasted its own additions. Commerce Bank in 1965 erected a skyscraper, the Commerce Tower at Ninth and Main Streets, in the area cleared by urban renewal. The tower boasted a set of ethnic restaurants featuring Irish, Austrian, Italian, Asian and French cuisines — all under the umbrella name, Top of the Tower. Three years later, another modern structure, TenMainCenter, opened at the corner of 10th and Main Streets.

But that same year, 1968, a landmark of long standing went dark. The Emery, Bird, Thayer department

Johnson County was not first with big shopping centers. The Blue Springs Mall opened in 1958 in eastern Jackson County, and the Ward Parkway Shopping Center in 1959 along State Line Road in Kansas City, Missouri. Other, smaller centers and strip developments appeared along the way.

What set Johnson County apart was its phenomenal growing power. From 1960 to 1970, the population of Johnson County would increase by more than 50 percent, reaching 220,000, surpassing Wyandotte County and becoming the second-largest county in the metropolitan area after Jackson in Missouri.

Corporate growth and opportunity

Businesses set out to share in the boom. In 1966,

TWA was Kansas City's proud hometown airline in the 1960s, when it flew out of the Municipal Air Terminal, above. Flight attendants trained at a new academy in northeast Johnson County.

store, a Downtown institution for more than a century, closed its building on 11th Street — or Petticoat Lane — between Walnut Street and Grand Avenue. Even if some new commercial buildings were going up, retailing Downtown was coming down.

Not in danger in the 1960s were public construction projects, of which Kansas City set out to build some prime examples.

In 1966, voters approved by a huge margin a $150 million bond issue to construct a new Mid-Continent International Airport, replacing the convenient but outdated Municipal Air Terminal just across the river from Downtown. The next year, Jackson County voters approved a $43.5 million twin-stadium sports complex.

Both projects easily outdid any previous public construction. Both would prove successful and both would have two things in common. Neither was close to

Following pages: Downtown retained some of its vitality in 1961. On this block of Walnut Street, looking north from 12th, were three jewelers, two women's wear stores, a cafeteria, a bank, a drugstore and other merchants.

MERCANTILE
BANK
AND TRUST COMPANY
1119 WALNUT
KANSAS CITY'S CONVE
CAFETERIA
Grigg's

Downtown but, once you reached them, both were easy to use.

The airport site lay 15 or so miles to the north on Platte County ground only recently annexed by Kansas City. Safety dictated that the airport be placed well away from heavy concentrations of people, yet the far-longer commute from south of the river was startling to Kansas Citians accustomed to simply crossing the Missouri to old Municipal Air Terminal on the other bank. Travel time to the new airport, now named Kansas City International, was supposed to have been minimized by a light-rail line, but that never materialized. The plan for multiple terminals, each with close-in parking, did work for Kansas Citians, who could get from their cars to their gate in a matter of minutes.

New stadiums and new teams

The baseball and football stadiums at what would be named the Harry S. Truman Sports Complex would go up on the eastern edge of Kansas City, Missouri, not far from the city limit of Independence. Ample parking and excellent views of the playing field made the two stadiums the best in America when they opened.

Kansas City baseball fans of the early 1960s endured the eccentric owner of the A's, Charles Finley. Finley continually experimented with the trappings of baseball but, annoyingly, also continually threatened to move the team. In 1968 he did.

Municipal Stadium, here in its football configuration, hosted the Chiefs, the A's and later the Royals.

But who would play in them?

On the football field, there was little question. In 1963, the city acquired its first professional football team when Texas millionaire Lamar Hunt moved his Dallas Texans to Kansas City. The team, renamed the Chiefs, played in the American Football League, an invention of Hunt and other owners of franchises in Denver, Los Angeles, Houston, Oakland, Buffalo, New York and Boston. As the team improved, along with the new football league, it sold more and more tickets to games in Municipal Stadium, which it shared with the baseball Athletics. After the Chiefs won the league championship in 1966, they played in the first championship game against the National Football League, a game that took on a name suggested by Hunt — the

Super Bowl. They would go to the championship game again after the 1969 season. That time, they would win.

Things were different in baseball. In 1967, the year voters approved the stadiums, the Athletics were run by Charles O. Finley, who had bought the franchise in 1962 after the death of original owner Arnold Johnson. Almost from the time he took over, Finley dismayed Kansas City with repeated threats to pull the team out of town. At the end of the 1967 season, with planning for the new, 40,000-seat baseball stadium under way, Finley made good on his threat. He packed up the A's and moved the franchise to Oakland, California.

By the late 1960s, Jackson County's two new stadiums had taken shape, left. A radical concept for the time, the Truman Sports Complex had separate buildings for baseball and football. Other American cities were building single stadiums convertible to either sport. Above: Ewing Kauffman was persuaded to buy a new franchise for the city. His wife, Muriel, and friend Earl Smith celebrated a record season-ticket sale. Until the Sports Complex was done, the new Royals would share Municipal Stadium with the Chiefs.

Kansas City business leaders pulled every string they could to provide their new baseball stadium an occupant. Finally baseball's owners and the league offices agreed to award two new expansion franchises that would begin play in 1969. If someone or some group in Kansas City put up $10 million, the city would get a team.

Who would own it? Earl Smith, an official of the Smith-Grieves printing company, approached a Kansas Citian who had the money — self-made pharmaceutical millionaire Ewing Kauffman. At first reluctant, Kauffman was persuaded when Smith arranged a visit to the offices

of the California Angels, then owned by Gene Autry. Autry, the cowboy singer and a friend of Smith's, opened the Angels' books. Kauffman looked them over and promptly agreed to buy the franchise.

For the first time in modern baseball history, a Kansas City-area resident owned the local major-league baseball team. Kauffman talked about how good Kansas City had been for him and set out to put a winning team on the field, unlike the bedraggled Kansas City A's. In 1976 the Royals would win their first of multiple championships.

Even as public and private money flowed in the late 1960s and suburban development rolled ever outward, social forces strained civic nerves.

Civil unrest

Black Americans were growing frustrated. Despite the end of legal segregation in schools, housing and public places, despite new voting rights laws and promises of adequate housing and better health care, most remained well down the economic ladder. Black people in Kansas City and most other American cities lived largely in concentrated neighborhoods separated by distance and political clout from the benefits enjoyed by white America.

In the Watts section of Los Angeles in 1965 and in Detroit in 1967, black residents rioted. The Watts riot extended over six days, cost tens of millions in damage and left 34 dead and more than a thousand people hurt. The Detroit riot lasted five days, left 43 dead, hundreds hurt and more than 2,000 buildings destroyed. Both events began in confrontations between policemen and black residents.

Kansas City avoided widespread violence until April 1968. Only days after the assassination of civil rights leader Martin Luther King Jr. in Memphis, black residents marched in the streets. In Kansas City, Kansas,

Civil rights demonstrators marched peacefully through downtown Kansas City, Kansas, after the assassination of Dr. Martin Luther King, Jr. School officials let out classes for the day.

Matters turned violent in 1968 in Kansas City, Missouri, where marchers and helmeted police faced off, and the police began tossing tear gas. That evening began a deadly series of riots that lasted five days.

which had a sizable black population, the school district called off classes the day of King's funeral, April 9, and the demonstrations remained peaceful. Schools in Kansas City, Missouri, stayed in session that day. Trouble followed.

High school students on the city's east side began a protest march that attracted followers. From Parade Park at Truman Road and the Paseo, the marchers headed west along Interstate 70 toward Downtown and City Hall. After speeches were made there, someone threw a bottle. Police, who wore riot helmets, tossed tear gas canisters at the crowd. Violence was reported here and there during the rest of the day. That night looting, rioting and burning broke out on the east side. The uproar lasted five days, despite a citywide curfew.

When the destruction was surveyed, the damaged totaled more than $1 million, much of it on the east side but some Downtown, where department-store windows were broken. Six people died and hundreds were arrested.

The riots made it clear to white civic leaders that they needed to pay attention to the inner city. The events raised the consciousness of the city's black residents, and some black leaders would say later that the era empowered black people to launch new businesses and become involved in politics. The city enacted another equal-rights law, a fair-housing ordinance.

For other Kansas Citians, the riots made it seem that the city had become a danger zone. Escape to the suburbs was their solution.

Meanwhile, on campuses in Kansas City and in nearby college towns, protesters marched against the military draft, the war in Southeast Asia, and in some cases the capitalist system. Among the demonstrators were sons and daughters of Kansas City businessmen and businesswomen.

At job sites, construction unions were having their say, too. With the new stadiums and the new airport on the way, strikes caused delay after delay. In 1969, Kansas

Dutton Brookfield

City led the country in days lost to construction strikes. The opening of the new stadiums had to be put off almost two years. Dutton Brookfield, head of the uniform manufacturer Unitog, took on the task of heading the Sports Authority and navigated the issues surrounding construction of the stadiums.

As in so many other places across the country, the 1960s in Kansas City ended with the economy humming and the public conversation dissonant.

Downtown, surrounded. By the late 1960s the ring of interstate highways was nearing completion. The view is to the east.

Riding High

Civic flags were waving as the 1970s got under way. Kansas Citians saw big things on the horizon and nothing, it seemed, would halt the plans of the growing metropolis.

In the farthest northern reaches of incorporated Kansas City, a sprawling, three-terminal airport went into service in 1972, replacing the tight confines of old Municipal Air Terminal. The city confidently renamed the airport Kansas City International, and scheduled a flight or two to another country to back up the "international" part of it. Vice President Spiro Agnew flew in for the opening ceremonies.

The same year, the Kansas City Chiefs began play on the artificial turf of sleek, new, yet incomplete Arrowhead Stadium, where fans flocked despite some uninstalled seats and a few non-functioning restrooms. The next spring, the Royals opened the baseball season across the

Left: Ewing and Muriel Kauffman, happy in their roles as Kansas City's baseball royalty. Above: Arrowhead Stadium, packed for a Chiefs game.

parking lot at their new stadium.

Chiefs owner Lamar Hunt's Worlds of Fun amusement park welcomed thrill-seekers, many of whom now viewed the rides at old Fairyland Park as tame in comparison.

Just south of Downtown, Hallmark's Crown Center welcomed patrons to an amalgam of shops, eateries, apartments and offices.

At the Country Club Plaza, the Alameda Plaza Hotel rose over Brush Creek. The first-class hotel provided a big addition to a Country Club Plaza that was continually moving upscale.

Into the spotlight

To alert the world to Kansas City's massive modern additions, a group of businessmen led by Hallmark's Donald Hall in 1972 launched a promotional campaign.

The effort recognized that the outside world did not necessarily think well or ill of Kansas City — it simply didn't think about Kansas City at all. So began Kansas City Prime Time, an all-out march of publicity and marketing. Prime Time's workers enticed reporters for newspapers around the country and for national magazines into writing articles about the city. The publicity crews prepared television spots boasting that Kansas City had "more fountains than any place but Rome" and "more boulevard miles than Paris."

The campaign bought billboards reciting Prime Time's new label for Kansas City: "One of the few liveable cities left."

In this remaining liveable city, the Baby Boom generation entered the job market in force, making itself felt in offices during business hours and outside in the afterhours. Waves of 20- and 30-somethings flocked to nightspots, and entertainment clusters set out to serve

Welcome To
Kansas City.
One of the few liveable cities left.
1976

KANSAS CITY'S PRIME TIME IS NOW!
1972

THE CHAMBER OF COMMERCE OF GREATER KANSAS CITY

Kansas City's new, three-terminal airport went into service in autumn 1972, left, as the Prime Time campaign boasted about it and other attributes of Kansas City.

Following pages: River Quay in 1974, north on Delaware.

them.

The first one took root in the Old Town area of Kansas City, just north of the freeway loop. It was created by a man who had turned from academe to entrepreneurship.

In 1961, Marion Trozzolo, a former Rockhurst faculty member, combined two existing products — a new chemical coating called Teflon and the age-old frying pan — into a money-making new product called the Happy Pan. Billed as a utensil on which food wouldn't stick while it was cooking, the Happy Pan was all the rage among homemakers. Trozzolo used some of the returns from his invention to buy properties near Kansas City's historic City Market, an area called Old Town because it lay in and near the original Town of Kansas. It also had a few blocks of 19th-century buildings still standing.

Trozzolo began renting his old buildings to certain kinds of businesses — restaurants, taverns, music venues and craft shops.

In 1972, he gave his development a name: River Quay. The word "quay" was a variant of "key," one meaning of which is a landing for watercraft. Trozzolo used "Quay" to refer to the old rock steamboat landing that had given the Town of Kansas its start. His 20th-century River Quay would have

a 19th-century ambience and, if things worked well, a trendy reputation. Summer weekends in the River Quay in the early 1970s brought crowds to Delaware Street and Wyandotte and to the cross streets Third, Fourth and Fifth. Patrons dined, drank, listened to music, ate ice cream and browsed the shops of silversmiths and antique dealers.

For a couple of summers, the River Quay owned the urban spotlight. Then Trozzolo sold out to a New Orleans developer. At the same time, strip clubs, bars and other establishments considered unsavory by the Quay's original merchants began to infiltrate the area. The original, rather lighthearted and hip atmosphere of

the area faded. As quickly as it blossomed, the Quay fell from public favor, and shortly the name would become associated with mob violence.

Another part of town with 19th-century buildings, Westport, picked up the baton. Once its own city, older even than Kansas City, Westport had slumbered with residences and a few small businesses since Kansas City annexed it in 1897. In the 1960s, it attracted counterculture devotees. Now, with River Quay's decline, the young fun-seekers of Kansas City moved their evenings to Westport. Small taverns and restaurants followed.

On a large scale

At the other end of the spectrum, big public and private construction projects kept popping up. In the West Bottoms — now home to a shrunken stockyards, fewer railroad tracks and no meatpacking plants since Armour closed its doors a few years before — Kansas City built Kemper Arena. The entertainment emporium opened in 1974 with two major-league tenants, the Kings of the National Basketball Association and the Scouts of the National Hockey League.

In Johnson County, 1975 saw the advent of Oak Park Mall, a shopping center of unprecedented scale in the metro area. The same year, Corporate Woods office park opened its first five buildings on the south side of Interstate 435. Farther out, in Lenexa and beyond Interstate 435, J.C. Penney established a catalog warehouse with twice the floor space of Oak Park Mall.

The encouraging developments of the early 1970s reached their apex in 1976. First the country's attention focused on Kansas City and Kemper Arena, where the Republican National Convention gathered to decide the battle for the nomination between President Gerald Ford and Ronald Reagan. The delegates chose Ford, and paired him with a Kansan, Bob Dole, as his running mate. It was Kansas City's first national political convention since

Kemper Arena's distinctive exoskeleton kept sight lines unimpeded for spectators inside. The arena became home court for the Kansas City Kings basketball team and briefly housed the Kansas City Scouts hockey team in its two years in town. Also on the bill through the year: concerts, conventions and American Royal events.

A Crown Center guide pointed out features of the retail, office and housing complext to visitors in 1974. The project, which sat on a hillside overlooking Downtown, was a creation of Hallmark.

Corporate Woods, an office park along Interstate 435, gave clear signals from its opening in 1975 that Johnson County was becoming a player in the metropolitan area business scene.

1928. For the occasion the three big television networks brought in cameras, anchors and morning shows, demonstrators walked the streets and occupied Penn Valley Park and costumed delegates took it all in. The Prime Time campaign could not have asked for more.

That autumn the Royals won the American League's western division. Nothing like it had ever happened in Kansas City baseball. After years of disappointment at the performance of the Athletics and their mercurial out-of-town owners, Kansas Citians deemed the Royals' championship a signal achievement. At the seventh-inning stretch of game after game, owner Ewing Kauffman and his wife, Muriel Kauffman, waved to the fans from their suite at the new stadium and the fans waved back. The ultrasuccessful Kansas City businessman and his wife were receiving nearly universal acclaim.

As Kansas City prided itself on its grand decade, the region around it prospered, too. In the 1970s the Soviet Union, a longtime Cold War foe, began buying wheat from American farmers. The new overseas market ended long years in which each American wheat harvest brought overproduction of crops, shortages of rail cars to move them and grain piled, uselessly, outside elevators.

Everything was clicking in the 1970s. Yet, as always, world events and the power of nature had their way.

The ground in Kansas City already was saturated by long rains when a concentrated storm dumped torrents into the Brush Creek basin one September evening in 1977. At the Country Club Plaza, cars bobbed in the high waters.

A string of crises

In 1973, an oil crisis brought on by war in the Middle East drove up the price of gasoline and other petroleum products. Shortages of gasoline caused many gasoline stations to close on Sundays, and the highway speed limit was reduced to 55 miles an hour to save fuel. A federal recommendation to save electricity by turning off Christmas lights led the Country Club Plaza to douse its annual display, but only temporarily. Those first steps of the energy crisis were followed later in the decade by increases in the cost of natural gas, and thus of home heating in the midwest.

Inevitably, the U.S. economy — to which Kansas City was now closely linked — grew messier. The country entered a recession in late 1973 that lasted more than a year. Inflation picked up steam through the decade in a cycle of rising prices and wages.

Unrelated to the economy, except as it created a bad reputation for Kansas City, organized crime in the middle 1970s began a field day of murder and revenge. In the River Quay, disputes among tavern owners, some of them closely tied to the mob, led to shootings and arson fires. In late March 1977, an explosion heard over much of the city leveled two nightclubs in the once-pleasant Quay district. In the old northeast section of Kansas City, and in Midtown and Clay County, mobsters gunned down one another. One mobster's body was found in the trunk of a car parked at the Kansas City International Airport, the still-new and prime symbol of the livable city.

Nature continued to take a hand in events, this time striking right in the city's vitals. In September 1977, a rare, concentrated rainstorm flooded the watershed of Brush Creek. Flood waters rolled down the narrow creek, along the paved section east of State Line Road and into the Country Club Plaza. Basements flooded, first-floor showrooms and restaurants were inundated and automobiles washed from parking places and underground garages. From the Plaza the waters stormed downstream to the Blue River. Along the way, the flood trapped people in buildings and homes and by the time the water receded Kansas City counted 25 dead and $100 million in damages.

Only a few months later, in January 1978, fire broke out at Kersey Coates' proud, 19th-century hotel at Broadway and 10th Street. The south edge of the hotel was destroyed and 20 people died.

In 1979, yet another calamitous rainstorm, this one

Property destruction reached its peak in the mob wars of the 1970s when an explosion leveled two nightclubs in the River Quay. Murders, however, would continue.

with high winds, caused the roof of Kemper Arena to collapse. Fortunately, no one was inside. Unfortunately, events scheduled months in advance — including the Kings' NBA season — had to find new homes. The hockey Scouts didn't need to reschedule; already the team had left town for greener pastures.

For most of the decade, Kansas City followed the country's pace in employment growth. When the whole United States did well, so did the city. When the country sneezed, the city sneezed, too. But in 1979 employment growth locally began to lag the rest of the country, which was already feeling the effects of skyrocketing interest rates. In the 1970s, statisticians determined, more than 40,000 people flocked out of the metropolitan area in search of new work. Many were first-time job-hunters. They were part of the Baby Boom cohort just entering the job market — only they were entering it somewhere besides Kansas City.

Beginning in 1979 and continuing into the early 1980s, the region lost 20,000 manufacturing jobs. Total non-farm employment in the metro area fell for three consecutive years.

In the five counties surrounding Kansas City — Jackson, Johnson, Clay, Platte and Wyandotte —

Luckily, no events were scheduled in Kemper Arena the night in 1979 when high winds and rain conspired to tear the roof from its suspension.

population grew by only 3 percent through the 1970s, reaching 1.25 million, according to the 1980 census. Compared with previous decades since the war — when the five-county total had grown by double digits every 10 years — that record was anemic. Within the city limits of Kansas City, Missouri, population fell 11 percent, to 448,000. In Kansas City, Kansas, it declined 4 percent, to 161,000.

Meanwhile, the Kansas City school district began to unravel, battered by the flight of young families across district and state lines and by unwillingness on the part of those residents who remained to support the schools with taxes. A lawsuit against the district over past segregation tied it up for years in litigation and later in court-ordered tax increases and directives. As the school district went, many said, so went the attractiveness of Kansas City, Missouri, to business.

A harbinger of the age in local business was the sale of one high-profile Kansas City company to an outside organization, signaling a trend that would only grow in years to come. The Kansas City Star Company, saddled by expenses stemming partly from its efforts at diversifying,

Medical personnel arrived early, right, followed by construction workers and investigators when suspended skywalks fell on dancers at the Hyatt Regency hotel in 1981. More than a hundred people died.

put itself on the block. In February 1977, the newspaper founded by William Rockhill Nelson and Samuel Morss in 1880 passed into the ownership of a New York-based broadcasting and newspaper group, Capital Cities Communications.

Inflation, recession and another disaster

Kansas City had begun the 1970s on a wave of possibilities, exciting and headline-making. Now, as the 70s ended and the 80s began, hopes were tempered by the

reality of runaway inflation, high interest rates, a nearly static population and a new nationwide recession.

In 1980, inflation neared 15 percent, the cost of borrowing soared and the Federal Reserve intervened to try to halt it, raising its funds rate as high as 20 percent. The Fed won the battle — annual inflation dropped below 5 percent within a few years — but at the cost of a recession brought on as business and consumers cut spending.

The same year, the Soviet Union invaded

Afghanistan, and the United States responded by embargoing the same grain sales that had made agriculture prosper in the Great Plains through the 1970s. The boom quickly died, causing farmers in Kansas and other states in the nearby wheat belt to default on loans. Across the region, rural banks went out of business.

By 1982, mortgage rates rocketed well into the teens, dampening home buying and construction. That same year, U.S. unemployment hit 10.8 percent. The Kansas City area lost thousands more jobs in manufacturing as companies pared down, left town or simply closed. GM's Leeds and Fairfax plants and Ford's plant in Claycomo cut workers. Montgomery Ward closed its 1.25-million square foot warehouse at 6200 St. John Avenue. In 1985, when the company halted its mail-order business, 1,400 workers were thrown out of work.

Amid the economic gloom, Kansas City came face-to-face with a catastrophic engineering failure that in a matter of seconds cost the lives of 114 people. It happened at the newly opened Hyatt Regency hotel, part of the Crown Center complex. On July 17, 1981, in the midst of the hotel's regular Friday night tea dance, a heavy, suspended walkway crashed to the floor, crushing and maiming the dancers below it.

The city once again rose to the occasion. Within hours, a line of donors formed at the Community Blood Center. Rescue workers, health professionals and heavy equipment operators worked long hours to extricate and care for those who survived. Yet there was also fingerpointing and filing of lawsuits that took years to work through.

A facelift for Downtown

In the middle 1980s, the local economy got some relief from two sectors — retail and real estate.

In 1984, retail sales in the metro area jumped 15 percent and credit card use rose by 30 percent. Employment growth recovered, once again tracking closely the U.S. pattern.

With city tax breaks as motivation, developers put more than 2 million square feet of office space on the drawing boards. Kansas City's skyline — little changed since the early 1930s, took on a new and loftier look.

First came a new hotel, Downtown's first major one in 60 years. It aimed to boost the city's convention trade. The site chosen was on 12th Street just north of Barney Allis Plaza. The Vista International, as the hotel

The Vista, which supporters hoped would answer the need for a Downtown hotel and show, as the sign indicated, that Kansas City was working.

was named, occupied a block once lined by bars and burlesque houses, Kansas City's infamous 12th Street Strip. The Vista was the product of nearly a decade of effort by business leaders, most prominently Irvine O. Hockaday of Kansas City Southern Industries and R. Crosby Kemper Jr. of United Missouri Bank. In the end, funds from Kemper, more than 30 area banks, insurance companies and the federal government built the hotel, which opened in January 1985.

Much more was to come, as a result of a developer

who had made a career and a fortune in the suburbs.

Frank Morgan, the Kansas City-born son of Russian immigrants, began his working life in the garment industry, and then switched to real estate. With his uncle, Sherman Dreiseszun, and others Morgan assembled large properties in Johnson County. In the 1960s, Morgan's group developed the French Market and Metcalf South at 95th Street and Metcalf. Their Oak Park Mall opened in 1975. Then they moved to other parts of the metro area — Metro North Mall in the Northland, Indian Springs Mall in Kansas City, Kansas, and Mission Center in Mission. The group also built malls in other cities — Denver, Cincinnati, Toledo and Tulsa.

In the 1980s Morgan turned his sights Downtown. Through Morgan partnerships — among them Executive Hills Inc. and Copaken White & Blitt — One Kansas City Place and the AT&T Town Pavilion were erected. They became the tallest and second-tallest skyscrapers in Kansas City and, with the massive Vista hotel, they formed the most notable changes in downtown's skyline in years.

By 1987, the Vista, too, had come under Morgan control after the hotel's investors began to despair about its financial prospects. Morgan also gained control of the landmark Muehlebach Hotel cater-cornered from the Vista.

Like Morgan, in the middle 1980s many area developers were riding high. Then suddenly, Congress changed federal tax laws, and obliterated breaks for certain investments that developers had relied on. Locally,

Rich and reclusive, Frank Morgan assembled properties north and south and in the middle, giving parts of Kansas City a new look.

the realization also dawned that the metropolitan area was becoming overbuilt. In 1986 and 1987, longtime developer Kroh Brothers — creator of the city of Leawood and developer of the Ward Parkway Shopping Center — collapsed in a sea of debt. Locally as well as nationally, the real-estate market, having given a boost to the local economy, entered a slump that would last into the early 1990s. Commercial property value dropped, although home prices held their own. From 1986 to 1991, metropolitan-area construction contracts fell and foreclosures rose nearly one-third. Rents paid to developers of shopping centers and strip malls dropped, too.

Morgan branched out into banking, vigorously granting real-estate loans to borrowers who might not

Still under construction in 1987, the new AT&T Town Pavilion and One Kansas City place already had outdone the longtime leaders on the Kansas City skyline — the art-deco Kansas City Power & Light building, the old Southwestern Bell building and City Hall.

have received them from more conservative banks in town. Although Morgan struck many longtime civic leaders as an upstart, some of the city's longtime institutions eventually did business with him — among them Kansas City Southern Industries, the J.C. Nichols Company and Hallmark.

Morgan's progress in re-making chunks of Downtown resulted partly from sizable tax breaks handed out by the city government. Yet the Morgan group was not the only entity to receive them, and the government of Kansas City, Missouri, was not the only one to hand them out.

City vs. city

In the middle 1980s, Kansas City, Kansas, gave General Motors tax advantages in an attempt to keep the carmaker's operations in town. The move succeeded, and the automaker built a new automobile assembly plant on property formerly occupied by Fairfax Airport. To do so, it moved some operations out of the plant originally built for North American Aviation. Before the decade was done, the old bomber plant was gone.

Kansas' gain was Missouri's loss. At the same time GM was planning its new Fairfax site, it closed the Leeds

Urban cowboy: At what was left of the Kansas City stockyards, 1980s cowpunchers didn't look the part of old-timers. They wore hard hats and herded cattle aboard three-wheeled scooters.

plant in the Blue River Valley. That occurred in 1988, and ended some six decades of operation at the location. At its peak, the Leeds operation produced 60 vehicles an hour.

In 1993, however, Kansas City, Kansas, could not beat a $10 million tax abatement granted by the Johnson County town of De Soto to lure away Sealright Company Inc., Fairfax-based makers of packaging for frozen desserts. Suburbs had learned the technique that bigger cities originally developed to retain businesses and turned it to their advantage.

Over the next few decades, cities across the metropolitan area would dangle tax breaks to lure companies away from other cities, some of them neighbors in the Kansas City metropolitan area. Whether a new company came from inside the metropolitan area, or from outside the region, the result was that existing

taxpayers in the company's new home city subsidized it through taxes. Open to question was how much the area gained in the exchange.

As the 1980s ended, tax breaks, living costs, school problems and people simply looking for something new gave new momentum to the growth and transformation of greater Kansas City.

Over the decade, 15,000 people migrated to the area for work, resuming the pattern that had been disrupted by the out-migration of the late 1970s. The big winner was Johnson County, Kansas. It gained 31 percent in population in the 1980s while Jackson County, Missouri, grew only 1 percent. Overland Park grew by 36 percent while the two Kansas Citys lost more than 24,000 residents in the same span.

Inevitably, business would follow the pattern.

Surely the greatest sports moment to happen in Kansas City occurred in October 1985, when the Royals won the World Series over the St. Louis Cardinals. After the final out of the seventh game, third baseman George Brett lifted winning pitcher Brett Saberhagen in a victory hug. The next day, the city toasted the team with a parade Downtown.

Before the crucial 1996 election on the bistate tax, Union Station and its planned science museum put on a rally to boost support. More than 10,000 attended.

Redefining Business

When the 1990s arrived, Kansas City stood at the threshold of a new era of communication. About mid-decade, a worldwide data network would begin to affect everyday life from home to office. Combined with a profusion of cellular towers and satellites and compact personal computers and tiny communications devices, the network would change the nature of doing business.

As the Internet epoch neared, and as if signaling the passing of an age, Kansas City lost the last vestige of the industry that once defined its place in the world.

On September 26, 1991, the Kansas City Stockyards — reduced to 34 acres north of Kemper Arena — held its last regular cattle auction. Through the 20th century, sales had moved to the country, to local auction rings or to any place deals were made among livestock owners, feedlots and packinghouses. With the end of the day's auction, the Kansas City Stockyards let go 50 employees, temporarily leaving only six to handle sales of a few hogs and sheep. Soon, none would remain in an industry that once employed thousands in Kansas City.

The cowboys and clerks who no longer had a job in the stockyards entered a local labor force where unemployment reached 6 per cent that June. The city and the country were in another recession. This time, the economic blow came from the savings and loan industry and the blow fell hard in Kansas City.

The story began in the early 1980s, when longtime federal

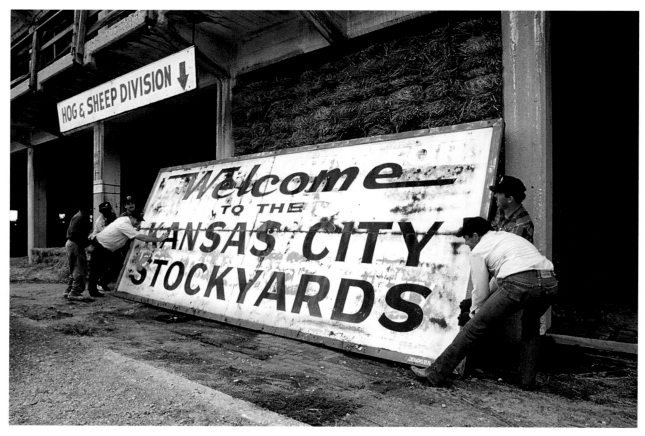

A collectible now: This sign was part of the memorabilia put up for auction as the Kansas City stockyards, a local institution since the 1870s, ended its operations.

restrictions on savings and loans were removed. Unfettered, some of the S&Ls created a bevy of new investment vehicles, offering high interest rates and causing the institutions to scramble for capital. Savings and loans made speculative real estate and commercial loans and some grew exponentially — but some suffered loss after loss and failed, or came to the verge of failure. Regulators estimated that fraud was involved in up to one of every three cases. When federal insurance for S&L losses ran out, the government decided to bail out the S&Ls and sell their assets. In the process, real estate values plummeted and many S&Ls went out of business.

In 1991 the government seized several such institutions in Kansas City, finding their capital had fallen below regulatory requirements. Among them was Home Savings, which had been taken over by Frank Morgan in 1985 as he added to his real estate and financial empire. In 1992, regulators seized two other

Morgan banks and the government charged Morgan and partners with rigging bids for office leases. Two years later the financier, under a cloud of legal problems, died.

Kansas City clawed its way out of this recession in 1993, when real estate — surely the area's longest-lasting business pursuit — came back. Investors put behind them the slump caused by the savings and loan and real-estate bust and began spending money.

Faster than the country

The next year, the growth rate in the Kansas City region outpaced overall expansion in the United States. It kept growing, driven by higher employment and more spending. And real estate wasn't the only hot business.

Hospitals, banks, restaurants and retailers all started hiring. Casinos — approved by Missouri voters in 1992 — first opened in 1994, having created construction jobs beforehand and more jobs afterward for thousands of workers in their restaurants and hotels and gambling floors.

Along 119th Street in Leawood, Town Center Plaza went up. Near Olathe, the Great Mall of the Great Plains created space for scores of stores.

Jobs in the service sector now easily outnumbered those in any single category, and formed one-third of the area workforce. That sea change had happened in three decades. As late as 1969, manufacturing employed the most persons in the Kansas City area. Yet as the 20th century waned, service jobs caught up and sped past. In the 1970s, service employment grew by more than 40 percent locally while manufacturing jobs rose only 7 percent. In the 1980s, service went up 44 percent and manufacturing 10 percent.

Technological change and innovation

The change in the composition of the business world and the workforce did not stop there. By now,

When casinos were introduced in Missouri, law required them to float in rivers, which led to creative solutions such as a cove for the Argosy casino, below, on the Missouri. The Hilton Flamingo floated in its own pond supplied by river water. Above: A day at the slots.

THE GREAT MALL
OF THE GREAT PLAINS

information was driving much of the world's commerce, sped along by a combination of technical innovations. The Internet created the connections, software developers made the tools, telecommunications advances provided the coverage and miniaturization multiplied exponentially the devices for sending and receiving data.

Kansas City-area companies rode the wave, and several helped lead it.

United Telecommunications, the telephone company that had moved to Johnson County in 1966 from Abilene, Kansas, joined its long-distance operation to Connecticut-based GTE's Sprint in 1986. In 1989 and 1990, the local company increased its ownership share and by 1992, it controlled all of Sprint. Along the way, it became the largest employer in the metropolitan area. By 1997 Sprint would have 10,000 people on the payroll locally with offices in 50 or more buildings across the metro area. That year, the company unveiled plans for a 20-building, 200-acre office campus on 119th Street in Overland Park.

In 1979, three computer analysts who worked for the Arthur Anderson & Co. accounting firm had broken away and founded Cerner Corporation, a software company. Cerner set out to develop information technology in the medical industry. After growing rapidly in the late 1980s and slowing down briefly in the early 1990s, Cerner found its niche integrating information systems for health-care companies. In 1992 its stock rocketed up 342 percent and the firm soared on through the rest of the century.

Garmin, founded in Olathe in 1989, sold its first

Left: The Great Mall of the Great Plains in Olathe.

A representative of Garmin showed off the company's fish finders to visitors at the Kansas City Sportshow in 2000. The firm's name was a melding of the first names of its founders, Garry Burrell, left, and Min Kao.

global positioning system device in 1991, and then rose to become the top manufacturer of electronic navigation equipment in the United States. It branched into fitness devices, guidance for airplanes, automobiles and boats.

Using technology developed to keep track of railcars and their revenue, a Kansas City Southern subsidiary ventured into processing records for the mutual funds industry. DST was spun off by the parent railroad in 1995 and not only continued in financial services but also operated a real-estate subsidiary that quietly transformed the western edge of Downtown.

And there would be many more. Unlike Sprint, Cerner, Garmin and DST, a multitude of information companies started in a technology boom something like the real-estate bubble of the 1880s.

The Leawood Town Center Plaza at Nall Avenue and 119th Street. The retail complex was in the final days of preparing for its opening in 1996.

As long as the decade lasted, business remained strong. Kansas City added about a quarter of a million jobs in the 1990s. Services and retail trade accounted for two-thirds of them.

More than ever, Kansas City's market was the rest of the country and the world. By 1997, 44 percent of the region's private, non-farms sales went to customers outside the region. Conversely, the same percent of goods and services bought here came from outside.

Fixing up the city

The good news of the 1990s for business was matched on the civic front.

Bartle Hall, the key to the city's longstanding effort to draw conventions, was expanded in 1994. In 1996 voters on both sides of the state line approved, for the first time, a tax affecting them all. The so-called bistate cultural tax helped restore Union Station and build a science-education center there. The station, having for years suffered the ravages of weather, time and neglect, was made ready and re-opened with its science center by 1999. At 18th and Vine streets, the hub of the black community's business and entertainment before desegregation, a Negro Leagues baseball museum along with a jazz museum came to life in 1997. In 1998 Kansas City voters approved money to repair the Liberty Memorial. Like Union Station, it had suffered from neglect for too many years.

The final decades of the 20th century brought another trend — more Kansas City companies, large and small, losing their local headquarters. A spate of mergers and acquisitions changed several important players on the Kansas City business scene.

Galyan's, a sporting goods store at Town Center, featured a climbing wall where customers could try their skill.

In 1989 Marion Laboratories, a high performer in the pharmaceutical world, merged with Merrell Dow and created Marion Merrell Dow. From the proceeds about 300 of Marion's "associates" became millionaires. Ewing Kauffman, the man who started Marion in his basement, by the late 1980s had net worth of more than $1 billion. Later, the merged company would join German-based Hoechst, and then the resulting Hoechst Marion Rousell would merge with Rhone-Poulenc of France and eventually become part of Sanofi-Aventis, later simply Sanofi. Each change led to job moves and staff cuts in Kansas City.

In the perspective of history, that was too bad. A 2006 study by Heike Mayer, an urban affairs scholar, reported that local biological research, clinical trials and pharmaceutical research had their origins in Marion Labs, in former employees who set out on their own. In Mayer's words, Marion had served as a "surrogate university" for the Kansas City region. No Marion meant no surrogate university for the future. Nevertheless, many of Marion's spinoffs survived nicely.

Business Men's Assurance, founded in 1909 in Kansas City to provide accident insurance for traveling businessmen and later branched out to life insurance and other pursuits, sold to an Italian firm in 1990. In 2003 the Italian company split up what was left of BMA and the name went out of existence. The landmark BMA Tower at 31st Street and Southwest Trafficway was sold in 2002.

And there were more. Stuart Hall, for nearly half a century a maker of paper products in Kansas City, was acquired in 1992 by the Newell Company of Illinois. In 1998, Sealright sold to Huhtamaki, a packaging company based in Finland. Unitog, manufacturers of uniforms for industrial use, was purchased in 1999 by Cintas Corporation, which closed Unitog's corporate headquarters Downtown

DST Systems headquarters at the southeast corner of 11th Street and Broadway Downtown.

and put its building up for sale. The Rival Company, makers of consumer products including the Crock-Pot slow cooker, sold in 1999 to the Holmes Group, based in Massachusetts. In 2004, an Australian Company would buy century-old Butler Manufacturing.

Even the J.C. Nichols Company was taken over in 1998. As founder and operator of the Country Club

From around the world, calls came to Cerner's support staff in North Kansas City in 1997.

If a movie theater with one screen could make money, why couldn't several screens make several times as much? Stan Durwood, foreground, with associates, dreamed up the idea of the multiplex and sold it nationwide through his company, AMC Entertainment. He also came up with the idea of a Power and Light district to revive Downtown, but died in 1999 before it could take shape.

Plaza, and as developer of mile after mile of attractive and stable neighborhoods and cities like Mission Hills, Prairie Village and Fairway, the Nichols Company had had an immense effect on the retail and residential character of Kansas City. A growing burden of debt and a battle between management and disgruntled shareholders, however, led to its sale to Highwoods Properties of North Carolina.

The outcome of selling to outsiders was unpredictable. *The Kansas City Star*, sold in the late 1970s, did better than before the sale. The company shed bad investments, cut expenses, increased profits and began expanding in products and employees. On the other hand, Marion Laboratories gradually disappeared.

Either way, the loss of a company headquarters could mean the loss of a company's best-paying jobs and of contributing members of civic leadership. For companies not headquartered in Kansas City, incentives and social pressures were fewer to make charitable contributions and to pitch in with civic projects. Richard P. Coleman, a longtime student of Kansas City society and author of *The Kansas City Establishment: Leadership through Two Centuries in a Midwestern Metropolis*, found that the loss of headquarters had contributed to a drop in the numbers of the social elite, which he referred to as the Establishment. Nevertheless, he found, the Establishment remained powerful in local matters. The majority of those

Following pages: Very carefully, a helicopter maneuvered four "Sky Station" sculptures atop Bartle Hall pylons in 1994.

The Kansas City headquarters of Unitog in 1999, before the uniform supplier was purchased by an outside company and its building sold.

powerbrokers could trace one or more generations of civic leaders in their families through a hundred years locally.

Going out with a bang and a megabyte

The decade — and the 20th century — would end with about 1 million people employed in metro Kansas City, according to the U.S. Bureau of Economic Analysis. At times in the 1990s, some businesses found it hard to get workers. The Chamber of Commerce sponsored a program that advertised vacancies in customer service and technical support in cities in Illinois, and also sent brochures to career counselors, all in an effort to bring workers to Kansas City.

The landmark BMA tower at the rest of the hill at 31st Street and Southwest Trafficway. The Kansas City company it symbolized was bought by an Italian firm.

Yet, at the end of the century, what was Kansas City? Those million or so workers lived in 11 counties, extending east and south to Ray, Lafayette and Clinton in Missouri and south to Miami in Kansas. That was the latest and most expansive definition the Census Bureau had given the metropolitan area. The 2000 census found 1.7 million people in those 11 counties.

The words "Kansas City" meant something far more expansive than they had even 50 years before. Making it possible was the ubiquity of automobiles and the area's unsurpassed system of freeways. In the mid-1990s a study found that the average resident of the Kansas City metro area traveled 25 miles a day by car. Of the 33 biggest metro areas in the United States, Kansas City stood fourth in that category.

So, too, did the word "Kansas City business" take on new meaning. For some companies and their employees, the Internet made going to work — if you could call it "going" anywhere — even easier than travel by automobile. Now, workers would "telework" from home. By the end of the 90s, more than 90,000 home-based businesses were counted in the metro area. For those hundreds of thousands who still commuted to a place of work, a 20-minute drive got them from Downtown Kansas City to Lenexa. The same 20-minute drive in 1949, before expressways, would have gotten them just past the state line, only to Westwood.

Even more important, the Internet in the 1990s freed many companies to set up shop anywhere they wanted and serve any market they wanted. Such a business might be limited only by access to the World Wide Web or shipping restraints. The new phalanx of information providers, of course, faced none of the latter.

As the 20th century closed, Kansas City's economy percolated, people had jobs and businesses made money.

The metropolitan view: Thirteen miles separate the Corporate Woods office complex along Interstate 435 in the foreground from Downtown Kansas City, Missouri, in the distance. Between them and nearly on a line with them, is commercial development surrounding 95th Street and Metcalf Avenue.

Still a Good Place to Live

Amid fireworks, high hopes and civic to-do lists that challenged Kansas City to accomplish great things, the metropolis embarked on the 21st century. On New Year's Day 2001, archivists, city officials and spectators gathered at Union Station. There they opened the Century Box, the container into which the leaders of a century before had placed artifacts of their time and wishes for the future.

The mayor, Kay Barnes, read aloud a message written by James A. Reed, Kansas City's mayor back when the box was sealed and stored away in 1901. Reed addressed his century-later successor this way:

"Dear Sir...."

Things had changed in 100 years and even as fierce

Above: Mayor Kay Barnes looked on as David Boutros, a Kansas City historian and archivist, lifted artifacts from the Century Box. Left: The Sprint Center, a new Downtown venue for sports and entertainment, neared completion in autumn 2007.

an intelligence as Reed's had not guessed that, one day, one of his successors might be female. Reed's hundred-year-old note went on about events of the century that had just elapsed:

"The ox cart has given place to the locomotive… the telegraph and telephone have taken the place of mounted couriers."

By January 1, 2001, steam locomotives had given

way to diesel and passengers traveled mostly by airplane and automobile. The Internet had sped up everything from personal messages to financial transactions. Soon the role of the telephone would be shared by texting. Many Kansas Citians had never read a telegram.

Bolts from the blue

On that first day of the 21st century, a new world already had arrived, and rather abruptly.

Only months earlier, the city's nascent tech sector had taken a beating. The widely feared switchover of computers to years beginning with "20" — the Y2K problem — had gone smoothly. Computer experts and their companies succeeded in selling new systems and fending off problems. Then the technological success turned sour. Once the worries about Y2K ended, businesses stopped buying new systems. Investors sold off formerly high-flying technology stocks, among them the stocks of internet startups or "dot-com" companies. The blow struck Silicon Valley in California, and it resounded on Kansas City's Silicon Prairie. As their value declined, once-promising area companies shut down, and a once-promising umbrella group, the Silicon Prairie Technology Association, closed.

The dot-com bust contributed to a brief and comparatively mild recession in the United States. Then, only months after the Century Box was opened, terrorists commandeered commercial jetliners and flew them into the Twin Towers in New York and the Pentagon in Washington. As a result of that event on September 11, 2001, the stock market plummeted. Transportation was shut down for a while and only slowly reintroduced with new security measures in place. At airports, long lines formed at gates. Other parts of Kansas City's important transportation industry — trucking and railroads, which carried hazardous materials – saw increased precautions in shipments and training of operators. With that came delays and increased expenses.

A new world

Those events transpired in a Kansas City whose shape and size would have jarred all but the wildest

Left: DST's output production facility produced electronic statements in the Westside Business Park along Southwest Boulevard. Facing page: Ironworker Richard Green of Kansas City at work on the new IRS Service Center on Pershing Road.

Preceding pages: Sprint's campus at 119th Street and Roe in Overland Park registered its own ZIP code.

dreamers in the year that the 19th century ended.

Census-takers in 1900 found more than 163,000 people living in Kansas City, Missouri. Adding Kansas City, Kansas, the number rose to about 215,000. Together, the two Kansas Citys contained two-thirds of all the people in the five surrounding counties — Jackson, Wyandotte, Johnson, Clay and Platte.

By the middle of the 20th century, the dominance of the two Kansas Citys increased as new residents swelled their populations. In 1950, the two Kansas Citys accounted for an even greater 71 percent of the five-county population. Kansas City, Missouri, alone claimed more than half. That same year Kansas City, Missouri, for the first time pushed its boundary north of the Missouri River, to 56th Street. To the south the city extended to 85th Street.

In the next half-century, the two cities' dominance dwindled. By 2000 Kansas City, Missouri, had nearly quadrupled its land area, reaching to the north well into Clay and Platte counties, and all the way south to Cass County. Yet its population had fallen below the 1950 number. Now, the two Kansas Citys contained only 39 percent of the population of the five closest counties, which now counted 1.5 million people. And record-keepers had expanded the metropolitan area to 11 counties. Of that wider definition, the two cities accounted for 33 percent.

Indeed, Kansas City, Kansas, no longer was the second-largest city. That place had gone to Overland Park, the Johnson County suburb that had not existed as an incorporated city in 1950.

The second half of the century saw Overland Park and its neighbors in Johnson County attract hundreds of new businesses and hundreds of thousands of new residents. The evidence showed in Corporate Woods and along Metcalf Avenue and College Boulevard, and in streets that only a decade or two before had been country roads. By 2000 Johnson County boasted six times as many people as in 1950, and ranked as the second-largest

Carol Marinovich

county in the area after Jackson. Johnson accounted for 30 percent of metro area jobs, Jackson County 39 percent.

Johnson County was not alone. To the east and southeast of Kansas City, homes and businesses popped up in Blue Springs and Lee's Summit in Jackson County. The same pattern held in the Northland — Clay and Platte counties — whose businesses and residents had long complained of being ignored by their counterparts south of the Missouri River.

In 1950, Platte County had been so small — fewer than 15,000 people — and so rural that statisticians did not include it in their definition of the Kansas City metro area. By 2000 the county had quintupled in size. Platte and Clay counties contained a quarter of a million people that year, and by 2010 the two counties would swell past 300,000.

Northland residential real-estate activity had grown strongly for at least a decade and now commercial activity was catching up. Many of that area's new residents were high earners who chose their homes in places such as Riss Lake in Parkville and near the National and Tiffany Greens golf courses.

In 2002 developers broke ground for the Zona Rosa shopping and residential development on 93 acres at Interstate 29 and Barry Road. The center opened in 2004. Big-box retailers moved in along Barry Road and new subdivisions went up in Kearney, Excelsior Springs, Liberty and other cities.

Renewals and revivals

By the middle of the new century's first decade, even two long-neglected parts of the metro area saw things looking up.

The first was Wyandotte County, which ranked historically as a mostly blue-collar area. It was home to some of the city's basic industries such as meatpacking, railroads and soap factories, and to their workers. The county and Kansas City, Kansas, had trudged along for years, every census since 1970 finding fewer people in each. Property values fell so low that residents paid some of the highest property-tax rates in the metro area to make up the difference.

Under the leadership of the city's first woman mayor, Carol Marinovich, the city

The Kansas Speedway brought not only NASCAR racers and fans to western Wyandotte County, but also mammoth furniture and outdoor stores, a soccer stadium, a casino and a multitude of restaurants, stores and entertainments.

and county were joined in 1997 under the title Unified Government. That same year, a partnership of the city-county and the state of Kansas lured the International Speedway Corporation to choose western Wyandotte County — rolling hills dotted by a few homes and farms — as the site for a new NASCAR track. Racing began in 2001, but that was only the start of things.

The track drew attention throughout the Midwest, and before the first season of racing was done, Omaha-based Nebraska Furniture Mart announced it would open a store in the same development, called Village West. That announcement was followed by a Cabela's outdoor-equipment store. Then a shopping district called The Legends opened in 2005. Restaurants and retailers flocked to the area, as did customers. Four years later, a

project that would bring a new soccer stadium in 2011 and a new development for the Cerner Corporation were announced. In 2012, Hollywood Casino would be added to the list of Village West attractions.

As if by magic, farmland was turned into a buzzing new city-within-a-city.

Then there was that other long-neglected part of the metropolitan area, Downtown Kansas City, Missouri, and in particular the south portion of the freeway loop. A part of the once-undisputed business and entertainment hub, the south loop had become a checkerboard of parking lots and vacant buildings. Mayor Barnes helped assemble a deal to build a new arena and an entertainment district there, hoping to draw businesses and people to one of the deadest parts of the old Downtown.

First came a new headquarters for H&R Block, which opened Downtown in 2006. That same year, guests once again could check in at a refurbished President Hotel. In 2007 the Sprint Center, a circular glass-walled arena, held its inaugural season of sports and concerts. New restaurants and taverns opened in the adjoining Power & Light District, named for the distinctive skyscraper at 14th Street and Baltimore Avenue.

Beyond the loop to the south, Kansas Citians and tourists alike took in the new National World War I Museum at the Liberty Memorial. Near Brush Creek, the Bloch Building was added to the Nelson-Atkins Museum of Art, a contemporary appearance joined to the formal 1930s original structure.

Figures dressed as World War I soldiers slog through the mud of a recreated western front at the National World War I Museum at Liberty Memorial.

A skyline addition

In 2011, the Downtown skyline received an unmistakable addition: the Kauffman Center for the Performing Arts. The soaring, scalloped structure for multiple modes of music and performance was the dream of Julia Irene Kauffman, daughter of Ewing and Muriel Kauffman and one more in the string of additions to local life by the Kauffman family. The center did not arrive easily. A proposed bistate tax to support it and other projects — modeled after the tax that revived Union Station — failed at the polls. Instead, private support came through.

The new landmarks and redone old ones made the first decade of the new century one of the most spirited eras for public building in the history of the metropolitan area.

For several years, business matched the pace. In 2003, for instance, Garmin reported record sales and laid plans to increase the size of its plant in Olathe. Kansas City engineering firms fed the nationwide and worldwide demand for new sports stadiums and new water systems,

Above: Head man Neal Patterson spoke to employees and guests at the opening of a Cerner building in North Kansas City.
Right: A festival of Italian music, food and dancing drew a crowd to the Northland's new Zona Rosa complex in 2008.

roads and bridges. Animal health companies kept Kansas City ahead of its peers in life sciences.

Yet challenges still came from outside and also from within.

TWA — which Kansas City once called its hometown airline but which had which moved its headquarters to New York and its hub to St. Louis — was taken over by rival American Airlines in 2001. For a few years, American maintained the overhaul base, which for

Preceding pages: The Bloch Addition at the Nelson-Atkins Museum of Art.

decades before had been a fixture in the Northland and employer of thousands of Kansas Citians. In 2010, the airline moved out.

The agribusiness sector was buffeted in mid-2002 when Farmland Industries filed for bankruptcy. Farmland, once America's largest farmer-owned cooperative and a Fortune 500 company, was hurt by slumping sales of fertilizer and by unsustainable debt. The cooperative had taken on that debt in the 1990s as it tried to grow and compete with other agribusiness giants.

Another of the city's onetime members of the Fortune 500, Interstate Bakeries, filed for Chapter 11 bankruptcy in September 2004. Interstate was the largest wholesale baker in the United States. Emerging in 2009, Interstate moved its headquarters to Dallas

In 2005, Colgate-Palmolive Co. said it would close its plant in the Armourdale section of Kansas City, Kansas, eliminating 250 manufacturing jobs. The plant had been a fixture since the early 1900s.

Easily the biggest reversal of the new century — the Great Recession — began, according to economists, at the end of 2007. Kansas City felt the severe shock within a year. Offspring of a mixture of an overheated real-estate market nationwide, questionable mortgages and questionable investment vehicles based on them, the Great Recession cut heavily into businesses and employment. Many Kansas City small businesses would not survive and many big businesses would muddle through only by cutting costs, products, services and employees.

In early 2009, Sprint Nextel laid off thousands of local workers, and Hallmark laid off hundreds. YRC Worldwide, the former Yellow Freight trucking giant, eliminated hundreds more, as did Harley Davidson at its motorcycle plant. Sanofi-Aventis said it would close its Kansas City manufacturing plant.

Late that year, nearly 90,000 people reportedly were looking for work in the Kansas City area. In August 2010 the local unemployment rate hit a peak, 9.1 percent. Kansas City area shared in the pain of the entire country, but at times it fared even worse, the local unemployment

Frank Ellis, chairman and CEO of Swope Community Enterprises, talked about a new urban neighborhood initiative in 2012. The Greater Kansas City Chamber of Commerce, of which Ellis was chairman, and United Way jointly undertook the effort to rehabilitate areas between 23rd and 55th streets and Troost Avenue and U.S. 71 in Kansas City, Missouri. With Ellis was Dianne Cleaver, left, vice chair of United Way of Greater Kansas City's board of trustees.

rate exceeding the U.S. rate for a while.

Gross metropolitan product, the local production of goods and services, slumped 1.4 percent from 2008 to 2010. Not until 2011 did it begin to grow again. Meanwhile, studies showed that 85 percent of the metro area's $93 million product came from providing services and 15 percent from producing goods.

In Greater Kansas City in the new century, Dun & Bradstreet counted more than 84,000 businesses. By its definition of small business — 249 or fewer employees — a little more than 83,000 of those fell in the small-business category. Those companies employed about two-thirds of the workers in the metro area. Eighty percent of members of the Greater Kansas City Chamber of Commerce were small businesses.

Right: Before it opened in 2011, the Kauffman Center for the Performing Arts offered a preview of its theaters and glass-enclosed lobby to advance ticket buyers.

That made 83,000 or so businesses that were unlikely to make much news — or much of a splash when they opened or when they went out of business. They might be auto repair shops, home remodelers, appliance stores, travel agencies, liquor stores, cobblers, tailors, restaurants, taverns, financial advisers.

Employing as they did the greatest portion of the local job force, small businesses were for the most part doing well in 2008, when employment in the metropolitan area neared 1,027,000. Two years later, when employment bottomed out at less than 945,000, those businesses for the most part were struggling to keep going. By summer 2012, area employment had regained some health, nearing 990,000.

Through it all, there were the small businesses that enjoyed fierce support from customers. Gates Bar-B-Q was one, a mainstay of the competitive local barbecue scene since the 1940s. Boulevard Brewing, founded only in 1989, delivered its multitude of products all over the city — and to 26 states.

As much as some sectors felt the pain of the recession, others kept a vigorous pulse.

Health-related pursuits stayed mostly healthy. A decade into the new century, more than 130,000 people worked in hospitals, nursing care facilities, diagnostic laboratories and in doctors' and dentists' offices across the metro area. Medical testing played a substantial role as did development and commercialization of drugs.

Fifty-three thousand people in the area worked in transportation in 2012, more than 15,500 in trucking, 8,500 in warehousing and storage and nearly 5,000 in railroading.

In a world linked by the internet, central location still counted for something in the 21st century, and Kansas City remained an important hub for railroads and highways. BNSF, the successor to the Burlington railroad, whose investors built the Kansas City bridge, and the Santa Fe, which helped open the southwest, planned a 1,000-acre rail yard and warehouse complex called an

For the Gates family, barbecue restaurants are a tradition. Gates Bar-B-Q owner and civic leader Ollie Gates sat inside one of his chain of eateries. His was one of Kansas City's oldest small businesses.

intermodal facility in south Johnson County. Another intermodal facility was expanding next to Kansas City International Airport. At the old Richards Gebaur Air Force Base, CenterPoint was developing a 970-acre facility.

Realities, and overcoming the odds

No city has achieved perfection, and surely Kansas City has a ways to go to reach it. Some parts of the area have too much crime and too little education and other parts need streets and sidewalks fixed and vacant houses torn down. The Greater Kansas City Chamber of Commerce has set goals for the city to achieve, an acknowledgment of Kansas City's needs as well as its possibilities.

It has long been said that the Kansas City area survives most economic distress because of the diversity of its businesses, which insulates it against problems that devastate a single sector. The other side of the coin: Kansas City seldom shares in the big growth bubbles that help for a while, and then turn and afflict other places.

As long as this part of the world has been settled, business has survived. Many have come and gone. There

Expanding its brewing capacity along with its national reach, Boulevard Brewing Company opened this addition in 2006.

were all those saddlers and hardware salesmen and warehouse operators and blacksmiths who started little businesses in a town out west, the Town of Kansas. Hardly any survived that great recession called the Civil War.

Yet through the years an admirable number of Kansas Citians started small, survived and made it big.

Ewing Kauffman gave his new company the name Marion Laboratories so his customers wouldn't get the impression that he was its only employee — which in the beginning he was. Kauffman made it so big he left a fortune that is helping Kansas City almost 20 years after his death and will for years to come. His company eventually was bought and bought again, downsized to the point that it planned to disappear completely by the middle 2010s. But the Kauffman name lives on in buildings, charities and life of the city.

Sprint began as a tiny telephone system serving Abilene, Kansas, when Abilene resident Dwight

Eisenhower was still a teenager. In the 21st century, Sprint Nextel ranked as the Kansas City area's biggest private employer, a player on the giant stage of telecommunications whose headquarters has moved to Virginia and then back to Kansas City. In the vicissitudes of modern life and modern business, and the world of instant communications, that kind of thing happens.

Cerner Corporation, just a little company started a little more than three decades ago by three computer guys, found a recession-resistant niche. It rode medical record-keeping to dominance in its field. In 2012, Cerner employed 6,500 in Kansas City area and 10,500 worldwide.

There's Kansas City Life, owned from its beginning by Kansas Citians and still owned by them today.

Or Commerce Bank and UMB, both operated by branches of the same clan, Kemper, and both having survived in that rare American business type — the

The Power & Light District packed its central square in 2008 when "American Idol" finalist and Blue Springs native David Cook made an appearance. Cook eventually won the singing competition on the television contest.

locally owned and thriving bank.

In 2010 Joyce Hall's little postcard sales operation, which first operated out of the YMCA, marked its 100th anniversary at its headquarters in Crown Center.

For some decades now, Kansas City has been proud to say it cannot be pigeonholed as one kind of business town or another.

Because Kansas City has no mountains or oceans, it has little world tourism business. However, as it has throughout its existence, the city draws people from miles around for entertainment, shopping and business. These days, they attend football games and the theater, gamble legally in casinos, eat at fine restaurants, and

Kansas City Life's stone lioness on Broadway.

spend nights on the town.

Kansas City is not a capital of finance. It has little in the way of extraction industry — no coal or iron ore or oil with which the town's fortunes entirely rest. If Kansas City has been identified in the popular imagination, it has been associated with cattle and cuts of steak. Today, the cattle are long gone.

A branch-office town: That remains one characterization of the metro area, a description that recent events only confirm. AMC Entertainment, locally based and pioneer of the multi-screen theater complex, now is part of a Chinese company. Applebee's restaurant chain was bought by out-of-towners. Butler Manufacturing now operates under an Australian firm.

What Kansas City does have is an economy with its finger in so many pies that it can't be categorized, unless "diverse" is a category. At the Mid-America Regional Council, the local agency charged with analyzing metropolitan-wide information, Frank Lenk has this description:

"We're like a lot of other cities, only slightly different. We're a different flavor of … chocolate."

The difference lies at least partly in Kansas City's quality of life. The area's low cost of living, inexpensive housing and many good school systems have for years attracted companies and people and then held them. Another has been the productivity of Kansas Citians. According to the Mid-America Regional Council, the area's manufacturing work force is measurably more productive than the national average.

In 2011, the Kansas City area ranked 26th in the country in production of goods and services, although its population ranked 33rd.

Kansas City has dependable, hard-working people who live in a metropolitan area without huge traffic jams or high day-to-day tension.

The good place

In 2010, the Greater Kansas City Chamber of Commerce moved its offices into Union Station. The immediate effect was to help the nearly century-old monument make ends meet by paying rent, but the symbolism was remarkable.

The Chamber now operated out of the building universally accepted as the city's centerpiece, and the move harked to the long-ago era when Kersey Coates and his fellow town-builders strove mightily to get a railroad — any railroad — to build track to this tiny community at the bend of the Missouri.

And it was Union Station that now sheltered the new Century Box, the one filled with contemporary artifacts and messages on January 1, 2001, after the ceremonies opening the old 1901 container.

The last time that one century passed into another, civic leaders were in the midst of their push for an expansive system of parks and boulevards to make the city — as Commercial Club President Frank Faxon had wished in 1890 — "a good place to live in."

Kansas Citians built those parks and boulevards,

The 100-year-old offices and boardroom of lumber magnate R. A. Long were restored by UMB, which occupies the R. A. Long building, one of Kansas City's first skyscrapers.

and went on to build homes and neighborhoods that would become national models for attractiveness and comfort. The work was done on a solid, diverse economic foundation that has weathered business cycles and breathtaking events.

The area has had its share of risk-takers who created great wealth from entrepreneurial inspiration. But it has ceased to be the hog-wild kind of town of the 1880s. The boisterous, smoky, smelly and risky city of those days has cleaned up its act.

For hundreds of thousands of residents, the passage of the decades has meant steady improvement in the quality of their lives. The metropolis still attracts thousands of people and businesses because of that very thing — the chance to live, work and operate in surroundings that would have astounded Frank Faxon.

A good place to live, to work, and to do business? By almost any reckoning, Kansas City has exceeded the hopes of its early dreamers.

Certainly, it is one of America's enduring success stories.

THE CHAMBER

Greater Kansas City Chamber of Commerce

125 YEARS

Greater Kansas City Chamber of Commerce

Making History, Celebrating Kansas City

Kansas City's bright future is steeped in its rich tradition. It's a place that has been and continues to be many things: trail head, river stop, rail hub, cow town, cultural melting pot, entertainment Mecca, tourist destination, technology leader.

In 125 years, this city has grown in many ways, but business has always been the cornerstone of the community; taking risks, meeting challenges, evolving, fostering collaboration, creating ties.

Just as a bridge over the river offered a connection to success, our rich history links us to a future of opportunity.

In the following pages, Greater Kansas City Chamber member businesses will share the basis of their foundation; each one individually an integral part of the past 125 years, and collectively creating a greater region than any of us could achieve alone.

Member Profiles

Greater Kansas City Chamber of Commerce
The Chamber Then & Now

What is now the Greater Kansas City Chamber of Commerce started out in 1887 as the "Commercial Club." It was a time when Kansas City was still shaking off the dust from its rough-and-tumble start as a frontier town perched on the edge of the "Great American Desert."

By 1887, that so-called desert was filled with cattle ranchers from Canada to Mexico. It was a time of great technological change — the city got its first telephones 1879; electricity came to town in 1881; refrigerated rail cars prompted the growth of Kansas City's meatpacking industry; new corrugated rollers cracked the wheat from Great Plains farmers and turned the city into a flour-milling center; typewriters came into use, along with sewing machines and vacuum cleaners.

Between 1880 and 1890, Kansas City's population more than doubled, swelling from 55,000 to 132,000. Cable cars criss-crossed the city, carrying 20,000 people a day. Union Depot, with its 125-foot clock tower, presided over the busy rail yards in the West Bottoms. New construction was everywhere: the decade of the 1880s saw new board-of-trade and federal buildings, as well as the "towering" New York Life and New England buildings.

Not that everything was rosy. The nation's first "Great Depression," which began with the Panic of 1873, had seemed to be easing as the decade of the 1880s began. But when banks and manufacturing collapsed in 1884, recession followed. (Corn prices fell so far that Kansas farmers

KC Museum-Union Station archives

For 125 years and counting, the leaders of the Commercial Club, later known as the Chamber of Commerce, have been a who's who of community-minded businesspeople, one after another focused on the growth and prosperity of Kansas City.

burned their crop for fuel. Corn had become cheaper than wood or coal.)

In Kansas City, meanwhile, the infrastructure demands of a growing city were readily apparent, including basics like paved streets, water and sewer systems. Trade with Mexico beckoned. Economic competition with other Western towns was fierce even as cities and states forged new trade relationships with their neighbors.

"An unending career of prosperity and usefulness…"

The city's business leaders organized the first chamber of commerce in 1856 with a goal of bringing the railroads to Kansas City. Their "great railroad campaign" culminated 13 years later with the opening of the Hannibal Bridge across the Missouri River. The group eventually went dormant in 1873. (The handwritten minutes from the meetings of that first chamber are still in The Chamber's archives.)

By the mid-1880s, business in Kansas City was starting to organize itself. Real estate dealers got together to form an exchange. The city's bankers formed a new clearing house association for more flexibility in financing. And a new Mercantile Exchange had been created (but wasn't particularly effective).

Business leaders wanted something more. As *The Kansas City Star* explained in 1913:

"At that time, Kansas City was like a great vine. It spread over the ground with no trellis to direct its tentacles which were branching out in all the departments of commerce. Two or three business men were sitting at a lunch counter one day when it was proposed that a commercial club be organized to take charge of the city's growth along civic as well as commercial lines."

That casual lunch counter conversation led to a small meeting of business leaders. The men gathered at the Brunswick Hotel one hot July night in 1887 — Frank Faxon, George Fuller, Charles Campbell, J.M. Patterson, J.C. James, T.B. Bullene, and L.E. Irwin. As the 1913 *Star* article described it:

"To reach the meeting place they stumbled along dark, uneven streets, leaping the mudholes and taking desperate chances with the sidewalks of native lumber, which the rain and sun had warped and twisted into rainbow shapes. Those who came from afar carried

William Bradford Grimes, the first Chamber President

lanterns."

They decided the new Commercial Club of Kansas City would be devoted to the welfare of the city's businesses and the city itself. As one of the founders, Frank Faxon, explained in a speech a few months later, their goal was to "Make Kansas City a good place to live in."

That goal became the motto of the new Commercial Club.

The first general meeting was held on July 29, 1887. That same day, *The Star* editorialized:

"The Commercial Club of Kansas City has organized. May it have an unending career of prosperity and usefulness. If it will keep alive and active there is a career of honor and usefulness before it…"

Bruce Mathews

The leadership team of the Greater Kansas City Chamber of Commerce includes Rick Perry, Senior Vice President and Chief Administrative Officer; Kristi Smith Wyatt, Senior Vice President of Public Policy & Programming; Melea McRae, Senior Vice President and Chief Marketing Officer; and Chamber President and Chief Executive Officer Jim Heeter.

"A good place to live in…"

The Commercial Club formally opened the doors of its new, "spacious" room in the Essex Block on Nov. 18, 1887. The Club marked the occasion with its first banquet, attended, *The Star* reported the next day, "by a large number of representative business men."

"The Coates house orchestra was stationed behind a bank of foliage at the entrance to the dining room, and at 8 o'clock the guests marched to the dining room to the strains of a lively march."

The Commercial Club of Kansas City was open for business. In the next month, delegations of club members traveled to Fort Scott to investigate the potential of a new sugar mill. Another group visited the "City of Mexico" to invite officials and business owners there to visit Kansas City and, eventually, establish trade relationships.

Kansas City was growing both in population and commerce. The newly-formed business organization began advocating for the paving and lighting of the city's streets, for better city government through changes in the city charter; for railroad development and fair shipping and insurance rates; for a new, modern General Hospital; and for the "great enterprise of our parks and boulevards."

In early 1900, Kansas City was getting ready to host the Democratic National Convention. City leaders had tried to get the 1892 and 1896 conventions and failed. Here was the chance to show off the city and its modern new convention hall.

Disaster struck on April 4 when fire completely consumed the hall. That same day, members of the Commercial Club organized the effort to rebuild in time to host the Democrats. It was a huge — and successful — community effort:

"Businessmen arranged with suppliers of construction material for priority shipments and with railroads for special transportation service. The day after the fire architect Frederick E. Hill, who had designed the hall, was retained to design a new one…A hundred and fifty men worked with shovels, chisels, and hacksaws to clear the site." (*K.C.- A History of Kansas City, Missouri*, by A. Theodore Brown and Lyle W. Dorset.)

Ninety days later, the Democrats held their convention in Kansas City, nominating William Jennings Bryan for president. (There were still a few parts of the hall unfinished, but those were well-hidden thanks to the convenient draping of flags and banners.)

When Kansas City needed a new train station, the Commercial Club Board of Directors went en masse to a meeting of the K.C. Terminal Railway Company and demanded it. That same day, the railway company appointed an executive committee to oversee the effort that led to the 1914 opening of Union Station.

As the Commercial Club closed out its 25th year, *The Kansas City Star* summarized, "The dash and the daring of the Commercial Club came to be accepted as the Kansas City spirit."

In the years that followed, the Commercial Club became the Kansas City Chamber of Commerce and then, recognizing the regional nature of the businesses and community it served, the Greater Kansas City Chamber of Commerce.

During its first 125 years, the Greater Kansas City Chamber led campaigns to construct the American Royal, Liberty Memorial, new schools, KCI, and Starlight Theatre. Kansas City's Depression-era Ten Year Plan was the joint creation of political boss Tom Pendergast, City Manager H.F. McElroy, and Chamber President

> *The Big 5 goals are designed to create jobs and raise the quality of life in the Kansas City area, focusing on entrepreneurship, the arts, urban revitalization, life sciences and animal health.*

Conrad Mann. The plan created jobs and built City Hall, police headquarters, the Jackson County Courthouse, and Municipal Auditorium. Streets were improved, as were sewers, city parks, public safety, and water works.

They also paved Brush Creek — to prevent flooding. (Pendergast, it should be pointed out, owned a concrete company.)

The more things change…

"I find it fascinating that so many of our issues and challenges are similar to those facing that small group of business leaders back in 1887," says Jim Heeter, President and Chief Executive Officer of The Chamber. "Street improvements, sewer construction, health care, trade and business development — but now we're operating at regional and global levels."

The Chamber's Big 5 goals for "Big KC" are the most recent example of The Chamber's leadership, Heeter says. The Big 5 are designed to create jobs and raise the quality of life in the Kansas City area, focusing on entrepreneurship, the arts, urban revitalization, life sciences and animal health.

"As an organization, we've been focused on civic betterment and helping our members for 125 years," Heeter says. "That's the 'Kansas City Spirit' behind The Chamber's leadership on the earnings tax campaign, our efforts in Jefferson City, Topeka, and Washington, the Big 5, and our decision to move our offices to Union Station.

"There's an interesting symmetry to working inside Union Station," Heeter adds. "The Chamber sparked its construction, saved it from the wrecking ball by leading the bi-state tax campaign, and stepped up to help the station's bottom line by becoming a tenant. Its history, in many ways, is a reflection of our history…"

On Nov. 20, 2012, the Greater Kansas City Chamber holds its 125th Annual Dinner. The crowd will be larger than that first party back in 1887; guests won't enter marching to the tune of a John Philip Sousa; and the celebration won't last until 12:30 a.m. But the motto – or goal, if you will — is the same: make Kansas City a good place in which to live.

Bayer CropScience

One of the world's leading innovative crop science companies in the areas of seeds, crop protection and non-agricultural pest control.

The Bayer CropScience Kansas City operations have been a part of the Kansas City community for over 50 years. The site provides products critical to farmers not only in the United States but around the world, safeguarding crops against damaging pests, weeds and plant diseases.

How would it feel to know you were responsible for setting the dinner table for more than 7 billion people worldwide? **Bayer CropScience** in Kansas City is part of a team that is finding ways to feed a hungry planet just as farming acreage decreases and climate change causes increased crop stress.

The Kansas City facility of Bayer CropScience is meeting the challenge by providing farmers around the world with innovative crop protection products and the means to safeguard their crops against damaging pests, weeds and plant diseases. It all helps to assure maximum food production from each acre.

The company's global headquarters is in Monheim, Germany. With 21,000 employees worldwide and annual sales of roughly €7.3 billion, it is one of the world's leading innovative crop science companies in the areas of seeds, crop protection and non-agricultural pest control.

A member of the Kansas City community for over 50 years, Bayer CropScience has been known by different names over that time: ChemAgro, Mobay, Miles. But the company has always been a part of Bayer.

Groundbreaking for the Kansas City facility occurred in the fall of 1956 in what had previously been a field of corn. In fact, the groundbreaking ceremony had to be delayed for some days waiting for the farmer to harvest his crop. The original land purchase was 25 acres,

Bruce Mathews

with options on 75 more acres.

Situated today on 240 acres in the northeast industrial section of the city, the Bayer site provides products critical to farmers not only in the United States but around the world, with a significant portion of its production slated for export.

Growers have come to rely on the products manufactured at the Kansas City plant to protect crops ranging from citrus to cereals, from vegetables to cotton, and more.

One such product embraced by farmers across the Midwest and beyond is the pre-emergence corn herbicide Corvus®. This innovative product controls more than 50 types of harvest-limiting weeds for a full growing season, with applications measured in just ounces versus the pints or quarts per acre required by other herbicides; and it works whether conditions are wet or hot and dry.

While the Bayer CropScience site can reflect on a half-century of success in Kansas City, its perspective is decidedly on the future. Capital investment at the site during its five decades of growth brings its assets to a figure exceeding $1 billion. Additional investment in the production of the advanced chemistries required by modern sustainable agriculture continues today.

While the site's primary purpose is to provide the technologies farmers in countries across the globe need to help feed a hungry planet, its foremost priority is

the safety of its employees and neighbors. The facility's excellent safety record attests to the success of meeting the safety expectations of both the company and the community.

As with safety, the Bayer site's diligent attention to climate concerns is reflected in its application of advanced technologies to safeguard the quality of air, water and land, thereby minimizing environmental effect.

This sense of broader obligation by Bayer extends to its role in the Kansas City community, as well, with a demonstrated commitment to helping address educational, cultural and social service needs. To provide means for working together with neighbors and the community in various ways, Bayer established a Community Advisory Panel (CAP) in cooperation with others in our community.

The CAP members represent nearby neighborhood associations, environmental organizations and public safety forces, among others. These community-oriented individuals meet regularly with Bayer site management to address issues of mutual interest. Bayer considers the CAP to be among its most important initiatives.

In Kansas City, Bayer CropScience moves forward confidently to its next half-century as a globally competitive, sustainable operation critical to helping feed a growing world population, while earnestly attentive to its safety, environmental and social responsibilities.

Bayer HealthCare, Animal Health Division

One of the top international manufacturers and suppliers for animal health focusing its research and development activities in the livestock and companion animal segments aligned with the Bayer mission of "science for a better life."

Bruce Mathews

Bayer's current main entrance and administration building.

From the cattle stockyards of yesteryear to the suburban family's loyal companion of today, Kansas Citians have an enduring relationship with animals.

It comes as no surprise that the United States headquarters for one of the top international manufacturers and suppliers for animal health products is based right here in the Kansas City metro community. With its simple-but-telling mantra — "Protecting, Curing, Caring…Together" — the **Bayer HealthCare, Animal Health Division** is a natural fit with the past, as well as the future of business in Kansas City.

The company has been a leader in researching and developing new products, and new forms of administering these products, for the animal health industry since the early 1900s. The origins of today's company began with Cutter Laboratories, based in Fresno, Calif., (founded 1897) as well as Haver-Glover Laboratories, based in Shawnee, Kan., (founded 1921). Bayer bought Cutter in 1974, merging its Chemagro animal health product group with the Cutter operations to form Bayvet.

Today, Bayer HealthCare Animal Health Division focuses its research and development activities in the livestock and companion animal segments. The company employs about 500 people in the Kansas City area, and nearly 3,000 worldwide.

As part of a collective industry effort, the Bayer HealthCare Animal Health division helped spearhead the development of the Kansas City Animal Health Corridor Intiative. This is where the single largest concentration

Bayer Animal Health archives

Bayer's original building and main entrance.

of animal health and nutrition interests in the world can be found. Kansas City-area animal health companies represent nearly a third of total sales in the $19 billion global animal health market.

Bayer HealthCare Animal Health Division is a part of Bayer HealthCare. Bayer HealthCare is a subgroup of Bayer AG, based in Leverkusen, Germany. Conducting business in more than 120 countries, the Bayer HealthCare Animal Health Division manufactures and markets approximately 100 different veterinary drugs and care products for livestock and companion animals worldwide. With sales of approximately EUR 1.2 billion in 2011, the BayerHealthCare Animal Health Division is one of the world's leading manufacturers of veterinary drugs.

To create these world class products, Bayer scientists first research and develop products at the company's flagship facility and Global Animal Health Headquarters in Monheim, Germany. Then the products are manufactured in various countries throughout the world. Bayer HealthCare's Animal Health Division is proud to call Shawnee, Kan., home to its North America Headquarters. Key types of products the Animal Health division manufactures include:

> *Kansas City-area animal health companies represent nearly a third of total sales in the $19 billion global animal health market.*

- Fast, effective solutions to pest problems such as Tempo® for darkling beetles, house flies and spiders and cattle ear tags that control face flies, horn flies and gulf coast ticks.
- Infectious disease treatments for livestock and companion animals such as Baytril® 100 and Baytril® respectively
- Parasiticides such as Advantage® and K9 Advantix® to keep companion animals protected from fleas and ticks.
- Drontal®, Drontal® Plus, Profender and Advantage® Multi — products that control endoparasites such as heartworm, tapeworms and other types of internal parasites in pets

The company's Shawnee site is Bayer's North America Animal Health Headquarters. At this site, animal health drugs are manufactured and the headquarters boast excellent safety records.

The company is dedicated to operating sustainably and in harmony with the environment. It commits all employees to the Responsible Care Policy, which encourages employees to conserve resources and minimize the environmental impact of the company's activities. In fact, the company installed new wastewater treatment systems at headquarters and its manufacturing plant in fall of 2011, allowing the business to recycle 20,000 gallons of water per day, or more than 1 million gallons in a time span of nine months.

Today, The Bayer HealthCare Animal Health Division is proud to be part of the Animal Health Corridor. The company is enthusiastic about the future of Kansas City and the prospective future of animal health in this global marketplace.

Belger Cartage Service, Inc.

Belger, a family-founded business now in its third generation, offers crane services, machinery installation and de-installation, specialized heavy hauling and warehousing.

A 20-ton conventional truck crane loads safe deposit boxes in this 1940s photo. Larry Belger (in the white shirt) stands in front of the crane's rear outrigger box. In the 21st century, Belger's turnkey services continue to include lifting and heavy hauling.

In 1919, while other printers were using horse-drawn wagons to move paper stock and printed matter in and out of Kansas City printing plants, visionary Richard Belger purchased a 1919 Dodge truck to better serve his printing customers. His foresight, knowledge of the industry and commitment to service led the fledgling **Belger Cartage Service, Inc.** to grow steadily and eventually include six locations in four states.

Those services now include crane services, machinery installation and de-installation, specialized heavy hauling and warehousing. With headquarters in Kansas City, Mo., grandson C. Richard (Dick) Belger continues the Belger family tradition to the third generation.

From the transportation and erection of windmill rotors to plant turnarounds and industrial storage,

Belger has been involved in historic and iconic projects throughout the Midwest. Belger's fleet has expanded beyond that first truck to include hundreds of cranes and heavy lifters. Industries served have also grown to include power generation, utilities, aircraft, oil and construction.

"Better Call Belger " has become a well-recognized term when the job demands the highest quality service coupled with uncompromising customer satisfaction at a competitive price. This philosophy has allowed Belger Cartage Service to establish a record of continuing growth.

The company was founded as a family endeavor. Today, employees are still considered a family of highly trained individuals committed to their customers and to the communities in which they live and work. By working hard to provide a stable atmosphere for its employees, Belger has reaped the benefit of outstanding loyalty and participation. Their dedication and experience enhances the quality of Belger's safety and customer satisfaction programs.

Founder Richard Belger established the principle that service to the customer and community was the most important guide to the company's actions. He believed that the most successful companies are active participants in working to improve the quality of life in their communities.

The Belger Arts Center is an example of the company's active dedication to creating meaningful change through educational programs that show lasting impact and long-term commitment to community.

> *Founder Richard Belger established the principle that service to the customer and community was the most important guide to the company's actions.*

The Belger Arts Center, singly and in partnership with other educational, community and arts organizations, hosts rotating exhibitions of contemporary art, docent led tours and hands-on activities for children and visitors of all ages. Since partnering with Red Star Studios in 2009, programming has expanded to include contemporary ceramics exhibitions, hands-on ceramics classes and an artist-in-residence program.

In her article, "Truckloads of Art," (April 28, 2010), in Review: Mid-America's Visual Arts Publication, Adelia Ganson wrote, "The center provides a valuable resource for art and art history students and educators as well as fun-seekers mingling in the Crossroads on First Fridays. …"The center shares a building with Belger Cartage Service, where the company corporate offices are full of artwork themselves and sandwiched between the open spaces on the ground and third floors, which are used for exhibitions. The collection of the John and Maxine Belger Family Foundation causes the building to seemingly burst with art, each piece more beautiful, complicated and

Belger's 550-ton crawler crane hoists windmill blades 270 feet into position during maintenance operations.

larger than the last."

Richard Belger was a problem-solver. His commitment to finding creative solutions continues today as the cornerstone of Belger's ongoing success.

Today, Dick Belger proudly carries on the tradition of quality service established by his grandfather almost a century ago. He credits company growth to the ability to listen to customers and adapt to their changing needs. Dick Belger's support of positive transformation of communities through the development of creative capacity is a tribute to his grandfather's creative problem-solving and commitment to community.

Blue KC

Blue KC has been serving customers for 75 years, and its commitment to the Kansas City community remains just as strong as the day it was founded by community physicians and individuals.

Mark McDonald

Blue KC headquarters in beautiful downtown Kansas City. Below, Betty "Grace" Jackson, Blue KC's first customer.

As Kansas City's first health insurance company, **Blue Cross and Blue Shield of Kansas City (Blue KC).** has been serving customers' health insurance needs since 1938, when a worker from Wolfermann's Bakery convinced her boss he should provide health insurance to their workers.

That worker, Betty "Grace" Jackson, and Wolfermann's Bakery became the first customers of Blue KC. Originally called "Blue Cross of Kansas City," the company was started by local physicians, hospitals and individuals, and provided hospital services with seven network hospitals. The company grew quickly, and by the end of 1938 served 14,000 members and had ten network hospitals.

In 1943, Kansas City Blue Shield was formed to provide members with a prepayment plan for physician services. Blue Shield grew quickly, as well, and in 1950 it was the first Blue plan to introduce extended benefits to individuals not covered by an employer. That practice continues today, and is one of the fastest growing markets Blue KC serves.

In the 1960s, Blue Shield introduced a Medicare program to serve the health insurance needs of a growing senior citizen market.

Finally, in 1982, Blue Cross of Kansas City and Kansas City Blue Shield united to become Blue Cross and Blue Shield of Kansas City. Since that time, the company has continued to grow and currently serves more than one million customers here in Kansas City, as well as across the country, providing a variety of innovative employer and individual health plans and comprehensive wellness programs.

In 2012, Blue KC was honored to receive J.D. Power and Associates' ranking for "Highest Member Satisfaction among Commercial Health Plans in the Heartland Region."

As the Greater Kansas City Chamber of Commerce celebrates its 125th anniversary here in Kansas City, Blue KC is getting ready to celebrate its own significant milestone. In 2013, Blue KC will have been serving customers for 75 years, and its commitment to the Kansas City community remains just as strong as on the day it was founded.

As the only local, not-for-profit commercial health insurance company in Kansas City, Blue KC's commitment to the community runs deep.

Its mission statement is "We will use our role as the area's leading health insurer to provide affordable access to healthcare and to improve the health and wellness of our members." That mission statement drives the nearly 1,000 employees at Blue KC to continually work to provide excellent service and a variety of affordable plans and programs to fit the community's changing health insurance needs.

Mark McDonald

Blue KC employees participate in the launch of B-cycle.

As a long-time member of the community, Blue KC believes strongly in the idea of giving back, and investing time and dollars to keep area neighborhoods and school districts strong and children healthy.

Annually, Blue KC provides significant support to a variety of community initiatives serving this objective. Programs around this effort include assisting area safety net health organizations to be able to serve more people;

providing financial assistance to member school districts and allied healthcare institutions so they may enhance the learning experiences of their students; and providing programs in the community that educate and encourage residents to live healthier lifestyles.

In addition, employees collectively volunteer thousands of hours of their time to help a variety of community organizations, and Blue KC's executives hold leadership positions on the boards of many local organizations. At Blue KC, the giving comes from all levels, and makes a difference for Kansas City's residents.

Wayne Powell, Vice President Executive Services and Chief of Staff, remarked, "Last year, we helped more than 300 community organizations with our financial and volunteer assistance. It's heartwarming to see our employees and our management team come together when the need is so great and be able to help our friends and neighbors right here in Kansas City."

Blue KC continues to serve the ever-changing landscape that is the Kansas City market. To address changes to the industry as a result of health care reform, Blue KC has set into play a strategic plan targeted at maintaining its leadership position in the market.

David Gentile, President and Chief Executive Officer of Blue KC, states, "The next generation of health care must be built around wellness and a greater sense of accountability on all of our parts. Providers must ensure quality outcomes; employers need to encourage employees to take advantage of wellness programs offered; and individuals must understand that good health begins with them. As Kansas City's wellness leader, Blue KC is doing its part by providing benefits, programs and education to help people make the right decisions regarding their health."

Under the careful guidance of David Gentile, Blue

BCBS

Blue KC employees compete in walks and runs across the metro area.

KC's strategy is built upon this wellness framework. The company has ramped up its already significant provider collaboration activities, and is currently working with Kansas City's hospitals and medical community on a shared approach to align care incentives and deliver effective care.

Blue KC helped bring the first patient-centered medical home program to Kansas City, a concept of care in which the patient and physician collaborate in the care approach for that patient to bring the best possible outcome.

In addition, providing value-based benefit designs are an essential part of the plan, as they bring cost-effective care while enhancing the quality of care customers expect.

Last, but certainly not least, Blue KC is putting a laser focus on its retail market and consumerism. Estimated to grow the fastest once health care reform really comes into play in 2014, the retail market promises big opportunities, as well as big challenges for Blue KC.

Gentile said, "Health care is generational. We are now focused on finding the right mix of products and programs to appeal to the different generations we continue to serve."

As part of this overarching strategy, Blue KC recently introduced community initiatives that address childhood

> *As the only local, not-for-profit commercial health insurance company in Kansas City, Blue KC's commitment to the community runs deep.*

obesity. With partners like the Chiefs Sports Lab powered by Blue KC, Girls on the Run, and B-cycle, Blue KC is powering up wellness initiatives across the community.

Blue KC has taken a leadership role in this arena because it believes that healthy children mean a healthy future for Kansas City. Reversing the childhood obesity trend is not a quick fix, and Blue KC has a long-term commitment to healthier living by the whole community.

Dawnavan Davis, Ph.D., Director of Health Promotions at Blue KC, said, "The future of Kansas City rests on the health of our children. At Blue KC, we're committed to making a healthy difference in the lives of children and families. From the community programs we help bring to life, to the tools and resources we offer through BeWellKC.BlueKC.com, Blue KC is doing its part to improve the health of our community."

Blue KC has been a part of the fabric of Kansas City for 75 years, and looks forward to continuing to serve the community for many more years.

Boyle Meat Company

Over the past 80 years, Boyle's is proud to remain a nationwide company making great products and keeping up with technology by allowing customers to order via the web.

Every time you bite into a thick, juicy Kansas City strip steak, take a moment to remember the men from Kansas City who made it famous. Robert "Bob" Warren Boyle started Boyle Meat Company in 1932 at 1301 Vine Street in Kansas City, Mo. It was just a little meat market in its early days, also known as Seibers & Boyle. Most of the customers were walk-in and carry-out.

World War II called and Boyle left his hometown and was stationed in Italy. As the Quartermaster in the Army, he provided food to soldiers in the European Theatre.

Boyle came back from the war with $10,000, half in the form of a G.I. Loan. He started calling on restaurants, country clubs, hotels, hospitals and other institutions, steadily building his wholesale meat business. He would take orders in the afternoon, prepare the orders that evening and the next morning he was out bright and early making the deliveries. In 1946, Arin Brumbaugh joined Boyle as a partner in the meat company and remained so until Brumbaugh's death many years later.

> *Not long after establishing its meats as premier cuts and his steaks as "famous," Boyle Meat Company introduced the Kansas City strip steak...*

Not long after establishing its meats as premier cuts and its steaks as "famous," Boyle Meat Company and other meat purveyors introduced the Kansas City strip steak in the mid-40s. The New York strip steak had nothing on this delicious, boneless strip steak.

In 1955, Boyle Meat Company introduced Boyle's Famous Corned Beef Company. Traditionally, butchers made corned beef by throwing waste scraps into brine, but Boyle decided to produce corned beef out of his best cuts of meat and started using brisket. Back in the '50s, '60s and '70s, the corned beef revenue was growing at 25 percent per year. At that time, Boyle's Famous Corned Beef was selling about 12 million pounds of meat and Boyle Meat, which sold about 5 million pounds, combined had annual revenue of $10 million to $15 million.

For Boyle, his Irish heritage was important enough to create his famous leprechaun logo, which has been an icon of Boyle Meat Company and Boyle's Famous Corned Beef Company from the beginning. Boyle was branding

in more ways than one before branding was a trendy term used in today's market.

At this time in 1975, Boyle Meat owned 75 percent and Bob Boyle owned 25 percent of Kansas City Cold Storage. All three companies were located at 416-500 E. 3rd Street, in the Kansas City Cold Storage building next to the ASB Bridge. Boyle's stayed in the Kansas City Cold Storage facility until 1997 before moving to the West Bottoms at 1638 St. Louis Ave. Boyle's has been very active in the revitalization of the West Bottoms.

Boyle passed away in 1993, and his widow, Viola Pearl (known as Olie), sold the company in 1997 to Don Wendl from Des Moines, Iowa. Wendl was one of the Boyle's loyal customers and did not want to lose a good product. He is currently the sole owner of Boyle's and has carried on the Boyle tradition of quality, selling millions of pounds of meat per year and creating a and multi-million dollar corporation.

Over the past 80 years, Boyle's is proud to remain a nationwide company making great products and keeping up with technology by allowing customers to order via the web at www.boylesteaks.com and www.boylescornedbeef.com.

More importantly, Boyle's has had the opportunity and enjoyment of working with many fine individuals, groups and charities such as the Ban Johnson Amateur Baseball League, Avila College, American Royal, Stop Violence, Kansas City Day, Red Friday, KCPT Auction, Boys & Girls Club, Scout Troops, Rotary Youth Camp, the Greater Kansas City Chamber of Commerce, and the Convention and Visitors Association of Kansas City.

Boyle has been and always will be all about supporting Kansas City and its children.

The Builders' Association

In 2012, The Builders' Association represented about 900 general contractor, subcontractor and supplier member companies employing about 20,000 people.

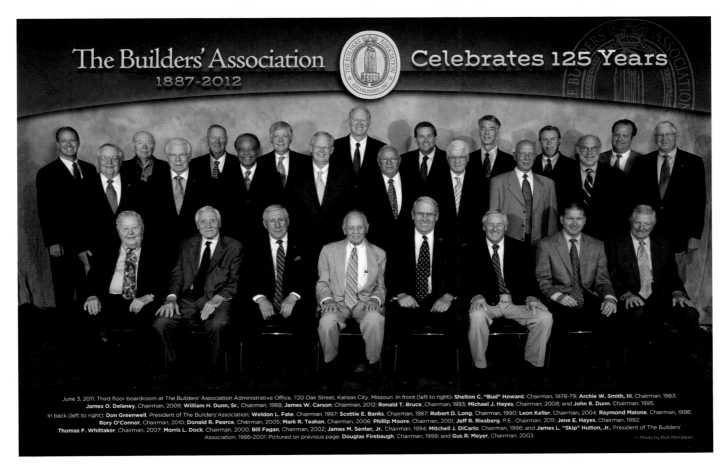

June 3, 2011: Third floor boardroom at The Builders' Association Administrative Office, 720 Oak Street, Kansas City, Missouri. In front (left to right): **Shelton C. "Bud" Howard**, Chairman, 1978-79; **Archie W. Smith, III**, Chairman, 1983; **James O. Delaney**, Chairman, 2009; **William H. Dunn, Sr.**, Chairman, 1988; **James W. Carson**, Chairman, 2012; **Ronald T. Bruce**, Chairman, 1993; **Michael J. Hayes**, Chairman, 2008; and **John B. Dunn**, Chairman, 1995. In back (left to right): **Don Greenwell**, President of The Builders' Association; **Weldon L. Fate**, Chairman, 1997; **Scottie E. Banks**, Chairman, 1987; **Robert D. Long**, Chairman, 1990; **Leon Keller**, Chairman, 2004; **Raymond Malone**, Chairman, 1998; **Rory O'Connor**, Chairman, 2010; **Donald R. Pearce**, Chairman, 2005; **Mark R. Teahan**, Chairman, 2006; **Phillip Moore**, Chairman, 2001; **Jeff R. Riesberg**, P.E., Chairman, 2011; **Jene E. Hayes**, Chairman, 1992; **Thomas F. Whittaker**, Chairman, 2007; **Morris L. Dock**, Chairman, 2000; **Bill Fagan**, Chairman, 2002; **James M. Senter, Jr.**, Chairman, 1994; **Mitchell J. DiCarlo**, Chairman, 1996; and **James L. "Skip" Hutton, Jr.**, President of The Builders' Association, 1986-2001. Pictured on previous page: **Douglas Firebaugh**, Chairman, 1999; and **Gus R. Meyer**, Chairman, 2003.   — Photo by Rick McKibben

The Builders' Association and the Greater Kansas City Chamber of Commerce have an important anniversary in common: Both organizations were founded in 1887. The association takes pride in this shared longevity as well as its chamber membership and participation.

On August 9, 1887, The Builders' Association opened its first office in Kansas City's historic River Market area. On August 9, 2012, the association celebrated Founders' Day at 720 Oak, its current home.

At Founders' Day ceremonies Kansas City Mayor Sly James stated, "For 125 years you have helped to shape this city. You've built monuments that are both big and consequential. Your logo carries a singular building in the middle of it and it's a building that I care about quite a bit because it's City Hall, and you built that. Now you're going to continue to help build the things that we need in order to maintain and grow our status as a world-class city."

The Builders' Association is positioned to do just that, with a broad range of services both traditional and high-tech.

The Builders' Association has embraced the fast-evolving digital landscape with innovative services designed to give its member companies a competitive edge.

Members use the Builders' EPR (electronic plan room) to find projects, bid work and increase their revenue. A new software product called ProjectConX supports not only the bid process but the entire project management process throughout construction. The association has become a leader in the development and delivery of web-based education and training among construction trade associations and continues to expand its services in this area. It now offers multimedia services to member companies so they can reach their customers (and prospects) with powerful, affordable video messages.

"Our unique strength is our ability to develop services more efficiently than our members could on their own, so they can focus their time and resources on growing their businesses," said Don Greenwell, president.

The Builders' Association offers a wide variety of risk-management services. Specializing in nearly 50 safety training programs, its Safety, Health and Environmental Services staff provides the resources companies need to manage jobsite risks.

The association's insurance affiliate, Midwest Builders' Casualty, is a leading provider of workers' compensation and is rated A- (Excellent) by A.M. Best. The association also demonstrates its commitment to enterprise risk management through CISAP, the Construction Industry Substance Abuse Program.

Construction trade apprenticeship programs are available at the Association's Education and Training Center in North Kansas City as well as at its offices in Jefferson City and Springfield. The association collaborates with industry partners to promote development of the construction industry's future workforce. The continued flow of talented young people into the industry is also facilitated by The Builders'

The Builders' Association Anniversary Banquets, an annual tradition, feature distinguished speakers and guests and are attended by hundreds of its members.

Association Scholarship Foundation.

The Builders' Association Government Relations staff advances the industry through management of legislative and regulatory issues, while its Labor Relations staff facilitates productive work practices and helps ensure that projects can proceed without interruption.

Along with its sister organization, the Kansas City Chapter, AGC, The Builders' Association hosts events that provide its members a myriad of business development opportunities. The association also informs and celebrates its membership through the quarterly Modern Builder magazine.

In 2012, The Builders' Association represented about 900 general contractor, subcontractor and supplier member companies employing about 20,000 people. It has offices and plan rooms in Kansas City, Jefferson City, Columbia, and Springfield, as well as its more than 100,000 square foot Education and Training Center in North Kansas City.

While its efforts to refine and develop its services are ongoing, its mission remains the same: "The Builders' Association shall provide high quality and valued services that contribute to the betterment of each individual member and the construction industry."

The Builders' Association invites you to visit www.buildersassociation.com or call (816) 531-4741.

Burns & McDonnell

Burns & McDonnell has come a long way since its early days. From design and construction in 1900 of a combined water and light plant for Iola, Kan., above — aptly described by Clinton Burns as "our first good job" — to design and construction of the massive Iatan 2 energy center for KCP&L and partners in Weston, Mo., at right, Burns & McDonnell always has focused on a single mission: Make our clients successful.

Burns & McDonnell Builds on Client Success

At employee-owned Burns & McDonnell, each person on every job works under a single, simple and shared mission: Make our clients successful.

"We know that the only way we will continue to be successful is to continue to do whatever it takes to satisfy our clients," says Greg Graves, the firm's chairman, president and CEO. "We are all focused on client success and we have a personal, tangible stake in doing whatever it takes to achieve that outcome."

Such culture of commitment is reaffirmed every day at Burns & McDonnell, as more than a quarter century of employee ownership continues to strengthen a tradition of service and excellence born in 1898 inside a small office in downtown Kansas City, Mo.

Back then, two young engineering graduates of Stanford University set up shop inside the old New England Life Mutual Insurance Co. building at the northeast corner of Ninth and Wyandotte streets. Clinton S. Burns and Robert E. McDonnell had "scientifically located" Kansas City as the metropolitan area with the most communities in need of municipal water, sewer and power service — that is, potential customers — within 200 miles, the farthest the two could travel overnight by train.

Today, what began as Burns & McDonnell Consulting Engineers remains very much at home in Kansas City, but with an expanded reach. The firm now provides engineering, architecture, construction, environmental and consulting solutions worldwide, based out of its headquarters on Ward Parkway and working through more than 30 regional and international offices.

Employees own 100 percent of the firm, under a stock plan launched in 1986. Empowered by the broad responsibilities, entrepreneurial spirit and financial rewards that result, the 3,700 employee-owners of Burns & McDonnell regularly respond with unsurpassed

Missouri Gov. Jay Nixon, left, and Kansas City Mayor Sly James congratulated Greg Graves, chairman, president and CEO of Burns & McDonnell, as the firm announced plans for a new auditorium and additional employees at its world headquarters. The 450-seat auditorium accommodates professionals visiting Kansas City for conferences on sustainability and other topics.

customer service to deliver projects ahead of schedule and under budget.

Such commitment carries over into community services, organizations and efforts.

Through the Burns & McDonnell Foundation, employee-owners provide monetary and service-oriented assistance. Financial contributions range from matching gifts of up to $250 to area nonprofits designated by individual employee-owners, to donating $1 million to the University of Kansas Cancer Center.

The corporate gift, in 2010, established a clinical high risk prostate cancer prevention program at the center, which earned designation as a National Cancer Institute two years later.

"For more than a century, Burns & McDonnell has helped build infrastructure to improve the quality of life in this country," Graves says. "With this gift, we build hope for prostate cancer patients throughout the Midwest."

Fellow employee-owners also help build hope for others through a variety of community initiatives, lending their expertise and generosity to numerous activities and endeavors.

"At Burns & McDonnell, our focus is to do work that matters, every day," says Melissa Lavin-Hickey, director of the Burns & McDonnell Foundation. "That objective extends to our community efforts."

The company's giving, volunteering and grant programs are focused in four strategic areas:

• Educational outreach, including support for STEM — science, technology, engineering and math — initiatives that awaken curiosity, expand imaginations and broaden opportunities for young people. Burns & McDonnell established the Engineerium at Union Station and sponsored the Battle of the Brains to encourage and motivate area students to create an exhibit for Science City.

• Environmental responsibility, building off a major component of business efforts to provide community support. In the Center School District — through a 10-year educational partnership known as "Learn Green. Live Green" — young people realize

When Clinton Burns and Robert McDonnell chose Kansas City, the two Stanford University graduates first settled in the old New England Life Mutual Insurance Co. building (inset) at the northeast corner of Ninth and Wyandotte streets. Today the company remains a fixture in Kansas City, with nearly 2,400 employee-owners in town and an expansive world headquarters at 9400 Ward Parkway.

sustainability benefits through an outdoor rain garden classroom that cleanses rainwater, and fruits and vegetables grown in community gardens irrigated with the clean water.

• Human services, backed through identification of a major charity each year and assistance provided for many more. Among them is Christmas in October, during which dozens of employee-owners roll up their sleeves to repair homes of residents who lack the necessary skills or resources.

• Arts and culture, areas that promote creativity, inspiration and imagination — resources that Burns & McDonnell professionals draw upon each day. Employee-owners support the Kansas City Ballet, the Nelson-Atkins Museum of Art and other programs and organizations that fuel the community's individuality and character through word, image, music, body and building.

"We share our passion with specific, targeted efforts," Lavin-Hickey says. "We provide financial support, but we also teach. We swim, walk and run to raise funds. We paint and plant. We create and support exciting educational programs, and we nurture young people into thinking big."

Big thinking translates into plenty of work at Burns & McDonnell. The company handles some of the largest and most complex engineering and construction jobs in the world — from running high-powered electric transmission lines through a national forest into Southern

A 2011 celebration in the Grand Ballroom at Bartle Hall marked the 25th anniversary of the company's conversion to employee ownership, through an employee stock ownership plan (ESOP). Since then the ESOP Association honored Burns & McDonnell as its 2012 ESOP Company of the Year, and Fortune magazine ranked the firm No. 26 among the country's "100 Best Companies to Work For."

California, to creating marshes that are restoring the Florida Everglades, to overseeing construction of a new international airport in the booming Persian Gulf hub of Doha, Qatar, and beyond.

The ability to handle complex situations is nothing new, even when it comes to the company's own structure. After its formation as a partnership in 1898, the engineering firm eventually was sold to then steel giant Armco Steel.

However, in 1985, Armco decided to put Burns & McDonnell up for sale. Talk swirled of a German company's interest in snapping up one of Kansas City's major professional companies.

Enter Newton Campbell and Dave Ruf Jr., two Burns & McDonnell executives who offered a different plan: The firm's 1,300 employees would buy the firm through an employee stock ownership plan (ESOP), a plan financed by corporate officers and a loan secured through R. Crosby Kemper Jr. and United Missouri Bank. As of Jan. 1, 1986, all Burns & McDonnell employees had gained an additional job title: owner.

Eight years later, Kemper looked on as Campbell and Ruf burned the mortgage, much to the delight of fellow employee-owners whose long-term financial success would be tied to the superior client services they provide.

The ownership culture continues to thrive. The ESOP Association recognized Burns & McDonnell as its 2012 ESOP Company of the Year, and Fortune magazine ranked the firm No. 26 on its annual list of "100 Best Companies to Work For."

"We work on important stuff," Graves says. "We appreciate how hard our people work. And we know, because we're 100 percent employee-owned, that we will be rewarded for how hard we work."

CBIZ, Inc. /EFL Associates

CBIZ's innovative business model, which combines expertise across financial services, employee benefits consulting, executive recruiting and other disciplines, provides clients with a level of insight and coordination that is unique in the marketplace.

Kansas City has a reputation for producing great entrepreneurs, and the story of how a group of insurance brokers, accountants and executive search experts came together to form the Kansas City office of **CBIZ, Inc.** highlights the power of a shared vision.

The three main players forming this powerhouse group are O'Byrne & Associates, Mayer Hoffman McCann and EFL Associates.

In 1962, Robert D. O'Byrne started an insurance agency focused on the principles of knowledge, outstanding service, integrity and "always doing the right thing for employees, business partners and clients." Ultimately expanding beyond traditional life insurance sales, the firm's employee benefits brokerage business soon became the focus of the company.

By the late 1980s O'Byrne & Associates employed nearly 100 people, and in 1988 Robert A. (Rob) O'Byrne became president of the firm. In1995, the company was recognized as the small business of the year by the Greater Kansas City Chamber and the company and its affiliate expanded to multiple markets across the United States.

Mayer Hoffman McCann's origins can be traced back to 1954. After working for an established accounting firm, Ernie Mayer started his own Kansas City CPA practice in an effort to "take control of his own destiny." By 1960, Ernie had teamed up with like-

Bruce Mathews

CBIZ/EFL executives, left to right: Rick Mills, Carolyn Watley, Jay Meschke, Angie Salmon, and Rob O'Byrne

minded partners, Martin White and Bill Hoffman, and over the next 18 years the firm's audit, accounting and tax services continued to thrive. Renamed Mayer Hoffman McCann (MHM) in 1978, the firm expanded through

Entrepreneurs, left to right: Bob O'Byrne, Pete Lemke and Ernie Mayer.

acquisitions and organic growth while serving clients throughout the United States and abroad. In 2002, Rick Mills became the president of MHM Kansas City.

With roots dating back to 1976, executive search firm EFL Associates was established in 1982 by Dick Eyler, Bill Franquemont and Pete Lemke. Headquartered in Kansas City, the firm opened a Denver office in 1986 and began conducting searches for clients across the country and internationally. EFL's reputation for effectively recruiting passive senior candidates fueled its growth to become one of the top 40 retained executive search firms in the country. President Jay Meschke joined the firm in 1992, and Pete Lemke remained as CEO until his retirement in 2010.

These start-up stories, while impressive, may have ultimately been unremarkable had they continued as stand-alone organizations. Instead, O'Byrne & Associates (1997), Mayer Hoffman McCann (1998), and EFL Associates (2008) joined CBIZ, Inc., along with several other local entities, creating a blended firm of experts with the ability to serve clients in a unique and innovative way.

"The manner in which CBIZ Kansas City came together has created a very powerful business model," remarked Carolyn Watley, president of CBIZ Benefits & Insurance Services in Kansas City. "The combination of

> *CBIZ, Inc. is now the seventh largest accounting firm in the nation, the second largest benefits specialist and in the top 2% of retained executive search firms*

specialty firms allows us to assemble a team of experts to address a multitude of business issues on behalf of our clients — from tax, accounting and M&A activities to employee benefit design and executive recruiting."

"This blend of subject matter expertise provides our clients with a level of insight and coordination that isn't possible with separate vendors," said Angie Salmon, senior vice president of EFL Associates. "In a recent discussion about executive search, for example, we recognized that one of our clients had an opportunity for significant tax credits and cash incentives based on company growth projections. By collaborating with one of CBIZ's incentives experts, our client now expects to receive over $500,000 that would have otherwise gone unrealized."

CBIZ, Inc. is now the seventh largest accounting firm in the nation, the second largest benefits specialist and in the top 2% of retained executive search firms. Although the CBIZ Kansas City office employs over 500 professionals, the client-centric culture and entrepreneurial spirit upon which O'Byrne & Associates, Mayer Hoffman McCann and EFL Associates were founded continues to flourish.

DuraComm Corp.

International manufacturer of AC-to-DC switch mode power supplies, wind and solar energy, and commercial and industrial LED and induction lighting solutions

Bruce Mathews

CEO Benny Lee stands in the reception area of the DuraComm building which he recently renovated and expanded to accommodate growth and to provide a more energy efficient workplace.

What are the driving forces behind a successful serial entrepreneur?

Kansas City businessman Benny Lee says he continues to be inspired by both the satisfaction and the enjoyment of building a company. Lee, a Taiwan native, leads several diverse enterprises, including Eliton, a folding cello business; Nimbus, a retailer of accessories for tablet computers. His larger venture, **DuraComm Corp.,** is an international manufacturer of AC-to-DC switch mode power supplies, wind energy and commercial and industrial LED and induction lighting solutions.

Lee is also one of the area's most energized advocates of building stronger American and Asian relationships. He is a board member and past president of the Asian American Chamber of Commerce of Kansas City and first vice-president of the International Relations Council of Kansas City.

"I like to emphasize the importance of continued business and cultural exchange in our city so we can better participate in the growing global economy," says Lee.

Realizing the growth potential at DuraComm, Lee became majority shareholder in 2007, and then the sole owner in 2010. His vision for the company includes achieving expanded marketplace diversification for DuraComm and replicating success strategies from his prior endeavor, Top Innovations. Top Innovations is an award-wining multi-product international business Lee founded in 1987 and sold in 2008.

Lee credits DuraComm's reputation for innovation to his technicians, engineers, and technical salespeople, who excel in developing new ideas for products and turning them into reality.

"My team and I are focusing on developing product lines for three distinct divisions," says Lee. "They are DuraComm Power Supplies, DuraComm Lighting, and DuraComm Solar. Proudly, all are experiencing exponential growth."

To provide a better workplace environment and to accommodate the continuing business expansion, Lee relocated DuraComm in 2011 to a more optimum 47,000-sq.-ft. location at 6655 Troost in Kansas City. He then renovated the 45-year-old building to be more energy efficient.

One major project of this renovation involved the design and installation of a 24.80 KW Solar PV system. The structure was also retrofitted with DuraComm LED lighting equipment and energy usage is now monitored by a wireless smart metering system distributed by DuraComm.

DuraComm has received recent acclaim for its growth, leadership, business culture and ingenuity. Lee accepted the Missouri Governor's Minority and Small Business Award and the Kansas City Manufacturer of the Year award in 2011. DuraComm was honored by "Kansas City Business Magazine" as 2012 Top Company honoree, and Lee was selected as a Ernst & Young Entrepreneur of the Year—Central Midwest Regional Finalist. The U.S. Small Business Administration recognized Lee with

Bruce Mathews

In DuraComm Lighting's modern LED testing lab, CEO Benny Lee verifies critical elements of lighting specifications, such as lumen output and color rendering in LED products for commercial and industrial use. Through continual testing, DuraComm makes quality control a paramount value at their business.

> *Lee credits DuraComm's reputation for innovation to his technicians, engineers, and technical salespeople, who excel in developing new ideas for products and turning them into reality.*

its Region VII 2011 Minority Business Champion designation for his support of minority and small business.

Believing in the importance of organizations that aids in fueling business growth, Lee has accepted leadership responsibilities on committees and in groups that assist, educate and promote minority-owned businesses, small business and entrepreneurship.

He serves on the board of directors of the Greater Kansas City Chamber of Commerce and is an "Entrepreneur in Residence" and mentor at the Institute for Entrepreneurship and Innovation at the University of Missouri–Kansas City.

Lee and his companies are highly involved in community support, charitable giving and philanthropy. Lee served on the executive board of the Tocqueville Society of the United Way.

He formed a club to bring music of the world to Kansas City and sponsors music scholarships at Park University, where he formerly served as trustee. Lee is a patron of the Kauffman Center for the Performing Arts and the Kansas City Symphony. He assisted in establishing the Chinese sculpture exhibit at the International Sculpture Garden in Overland Park, Kansas.

"I enjoy contributing to Kansas City, which I believe is a wonderful place to live, raise a family and own all kinds of businesses."

Hallmark Cards, Inc.

Hallmark products — ranging from greeting cards and gift wrap to Recordable Storybooks and Interactive Story Buddy™ characters — can be found at more than 38,000 retail outlets domestically and online at Hallmark.com. The company publishes in 30 languages.

Hallmark's world headquarters in Kansas City, Mo., is home to the creative teams of artists, writers, photographers and designers who dream up new ways to meet people's emotional needs. Below, J.C. Hall, circa 1911, soon after he moved to Kansas City to start his greeting card business. (Courtesy of the Hallmark Archives, Hallmark Cards, Inc.)

Telling the story of Hallmark Cards, Inc., is like flipping the pages of an American scrapbook. It includes three generations of family leaders, new product innovations, famous characters, retailing breakthroughs and a set of timeless values — service, quality, caring and creativity.

Hallmark's story begins in 1910, when 18-year-old Joyce Clyde (J.C.) Hall stepped off a train in Kansas City, Mo., with nothing but two shoeboxes of postcards under his arm. He had little money — not even enough to take a horse-drawn cab to his lodgings at the YMCA — but he had an entrepreneurial spirit and the determination of a pioneer. Hall quickly made a name for himself with the picture postcards he sold.

Rollie Hall soon joined his brother in business in Kansas City, and they named the company Hall Brothers. On Jan. 11, 1915, a fire destroyed their office and inventory. They took the only salvageable item — their safe — and set up shop again. With $17,000 in debt, they pressed onward.

When they recognized the public's desire for more privacy in their communication, the company started offering high-quality valentines and Christmas cards mailed in envelopes. The fateful fire resulted in the Halls' decision to buy printing presses and produce their own greeting cards in 1915.

Hallmark developed its patented "Eye-Vision" cards display in the 1930s, giving shoppers an easier way to browse greeting cards. Before this innovation, greeting cards were kept in boxes. (Courtesy of the Hallmark Archives, Hallmark Cards, Inc.)

Early Innovation. Armed with the success of the early Hall Brothers greeting cards, J.C. and his brother continued to innovate. Their first foray into other product lines came in 1917 when the Hall brothers "invented" modern gift wrap.

During the peak Christmas season, they ran out of solid-colored gift dressing and improvised by selling fancy decorated French envelope linings. Those sold out so quickly that the brothers decided to begin printing their own gift wrap.

J.C. Hall also was an innovator in marketing his cards. He was intrigued by the word "hallmark," used by goldsmiths as a mark of quality. J.C. liked that it not only said quality, but also included his family name. So, in 1928, the company began marketing its brand by using the Hallmark name on the back of every card. That same year, Hallmark was the first in the greeting card industry to advertise nationally with an ad, written by J.C. Hall, in *Ladies' Home Journal*.

In 1932, Hallmark signed its first licensing agreement with one of the 20th century's most recognizable names — Walt Disney. Another 1930s

innovation was the company's patented "Eye-Vision" greeting card displays, which took cards out of shop drawers and put them on display racks where people could easily see and read them.

Building a Brand. The burgeoning Hallmark brand solidified its position in American history in 1944 with nine simple words. One of the most recognized slogans in advertising, "When You Care Enough to Send the Very Best," was born from notes jotted down by Ed Goodman, a sales and marketing executive at Hallmark, on a 3 x 5 index card.

In 1951, Hallmark sponsored the first original opera created especially for television, "Amahl and the Night Visitors." J.C. Hall decided to sponsor the Christmas Eve program to thank all the people who bought Hallmark cards. This would be the first in a series of specials that would become the Hallmark Hall of Fame.

In the more than 60 years since, Hallmark Hall of

Don Hall and J.C. Hall look over the master-plan model of Crown Center in the late 1960s. (Courtesy of the Hallmark Archives, Hallmark Cards, Inc.)

Crown Center surrounds Hallmark's headquarters in downtown Kansas City and offers office space, hotel and meeting facilities, and condominium living. This vibrant district provides options for shopping, dining, live theatre, family attractions, and a year-round schedule of events.

Fame productions have won 80 Emmy Awards, making it the most-honored dramatic program in the history of television.

By the time the company name was officially changed from Hall Brothers to Hallmark Cards, Inc., in 1954, the tradition of entrepreneurship and innovation started by J.C. Hall was deeply ingrained.

Growing and Expanding. Under the leadership of Donald J. Hall, son of J.C., who became president and CEO in 1966, Hallmark expanded its presence in Kansas City and took its business around the globe with the start of Hallmark International operations.

In the early 1960s, J.C. and Don Hall looked out over the area surrounding their company's Kansas City headquarters and did not like what they saw: rutted parking lots, abandoned warehouses, and a limestone hill cluttered with signs and tarpaper shacks. They believed their company deserved a better setting for its home — and that the city which had given much to them deserved better than the blighted landscape.

They had two choices — follow the stream of businesses fleeing downtown Kansas City for the suburbs; or stay and make the city environment better. They chose to stay.

Crown Center Redevelopment Corporation, a Hallmark subsidiary, was formed to make the Halls' vision a reality. The Hall family sought the counsel of nationally known designers and urban planners. They invested millions of dollars, and then patiently waited for that investment to pay off, understanding that the returns on a project such as Crown Center would be realized only over the long term.

With its first phases opening in the early 1970s, Crown Center stood as a prime example of urban revitalization, turning a blighted 85-acre section of Kansas City into a thriving retail, residential, office and entertainment complex. Today, Crown Center is a key tourism destination for families, with new attractions like Sea Life Aquarium and Legoland Discovery Center, entertaining 5 million visitors each year.

Under Don Hall's leadership, Hallmark and the Hall family also strengthened its commitment to numerous Kansas City civic and charitable initiatives. With a legacy of generosity that continues today, Hallmark maintains a philanthropic strategy of supporting projects in Kansas City and in the other communities where it operates facilities. The corporate foundation commits to projects that enable the company to provide not just funds, but also employee volunteers and product donations.

Branching Out. During the 1980s, the company formalized the Hallmark Gold Crown® store program, bringing together a network of independently owned and operated retailers to build on the strength of the Hallmark brand and products.

Around the same time, Hallmark began acquiring complementary companies to reach new markets and expand into new areas of business. Today those subsidiaries include Crayola, maker of Crayola® brand crayons and art products; DaySpring, producer of greeting cards for Christian consumers; and Crown Media, the publicly-traded parent company of cable's Hallmark Channel.

Into the Second Century. As the greeting card industry's leading brand, Hallmark leaves its mark on more than just cards. The Hall family's third generation — Donald J. Hall, Jr. and David E. Hall, both grandsons of the founder — continue the legacy of strong leadership and innovation. Don steers the worldwide company as

Hallmark Gold Crown® stores showcase Hallmark's products in neighborhoods across the country.

president and CEO, while Dave leads the North American businesses, including wholesale and retail operations.

Today, Hallmark products — ranging from greeting cards and gift wrap to Recordable Storybooks and Interactive Story Buddy™ characters — can be found at more than 38,000 retail outlets domestically and online at Hallmark.com. The company publishes in 30 languages, and its products are available in more than 100 countries around the globe. Hallmark Gold Crown® stores bring the most extensive selection of Hallmark products to neighborhoods across the U.S. and Canada.

Quality family entertainment, started with the Hallmark Hall of Fame in 1951, has expanded with the Hallmark Channel and Hallmark Movie Channel cable television networks reaching millions of households with family-oriented programming.

This Kansas City company has come a long way from that teenage entrepreneur with two shoeboxes of postcards and a big dream. But even as the company and the world have changed, Hallmark continues to stay close to people's emotional needs, understanding what is universal in the human heart and meeting those needs with products and experiences that bring people together.

Helzberg Diamonds

Once a family-owned Kansas City business giant, Helzberg Diamonds is now a member of the American Gem Society®, has more than 230 stores nationwide, and a thriving e-commerce business.

1948: Helzberg's House of Treasures

Bruce Mathews

2010: Helzberg Collections

Helzberg Diamonds' history reads like a romance novel featuring a love affair with a quality product, generations of ingenious family members with a flair for marketing and business, and eventually, a marriage with a multi-billionaire.

Morris Helzberg opened the original Helzberg store in a 12-foot building at 529 Minnesota Ave. When Morris passed away suddenly in 1922, responsibility for the small jewelry store fell to his youngest son, 14-year-old Barnett.

Barnett became an exuberant business man and just six years later at age 20, he made his biggest move, opening another store at Eleventh and Walnut, sealing his reputation as a prominent jeweler in the Midwest.

Barnett beat the odds of the Great Depression and doubled the size of his store at Eleventh and Walnut in 1932. It was the only expansion of the year in Kansas City and made Helzberg a symbol of courage to the community.

One of Barnett's most significant achievements of the decade was development of the Certified Perfect Diamonds Program — diamonds that the jewelry industry labeled as perfect under 10-power magnification.

Helzberg's claim to be "Middle West's Largest Jewelers" became a self-fulfilling prophecy as the company grew and expanded over the next decade. As the country was drawn into World War II, advertising took on a patriotic tone. At the end of the war, Helzberg boldly expanded beyond downtown Kansas City into the growing suburbs.

It was during the mid-1940s that Barnett made his greatest contribution to the jewelry industry through his effort to establish the Diamond Council of America, an institution for teaching jewelers and sales personnel the science of diamonds and gemology.

In 1948, Barnett opened the store of his dreams, Helzberg's House of Treasures on the Country Club Plaza in Kansas City. The store was designed in Fifth Avenue style, on three levels and sold fine china and silver in addition to jewelry.

Helzberg Diamonds came of age in the 1950s, operating 15 stores in six markets, along with a mail order division. Fulfillment of mail orders was handled mostly in house from the Helzberg General Office at 1013A McGee. As always, Barnett's promotions succeeded, and in 1950, a spectacular showing of the Harry Winston Court of jewels drew thousands to the Country Club Plaza.

Soon, Barnett Jr. and Charles joined their father in the family business. The third generation of Helzberg boys kept the company on top. In 1963, Barnett Sr. stepped up to chairman of the board giving 29-year-old Barnett Jr. responsibility for leading the company. Then, in 1967, Shirley Bush accepted young Barnett's proposal of marriage and the I Am Loved® button was born — a modestly conceived promotion that made history.

During the 1970s, Helzberg Diamonds matured as a

In 1948, Barnett opened the store of his dreams, Helzberg's House of Treasures on the Country Club Plaza in Kansas City. The store was designed in Fifth Avenue style, on three levels and sold fine china and silver in addition to jewelry.

national retail chain. Pursuing an aggressive expansion plan, the company opened, on average, three new stores per year. By the end of the decade Helzberg Diamonds operated 42 stores in 16 states.

Helzberg Diamonds entered the '80s an industry leader. During this period, modern marketing and merchandising were integrated with the company's long-standing traditions of quality and service — the Helzberg name became synonymous with both.

The next decade saw the company expand to 101 stores in 22 states. Barnett Helzberg Jr. retired in 1995, leaving the company an exceptional opportunity for growth by selling to Warren Buffett's Berkshire Hathaway.

In 1996, the company ventured into the world of online sales by launching its e-commerce site – helzberg. com — and by the end of the decade grew to 200 stores.

The latest heroine to enter the pages of the Helzberg novel is Beryl Raff, a 26-year veteran of the jewelry industry. Under her leadership, Helzberg became the first nationwide jeweler to qualify for membership in the American Gem Society®. AGS is an association dedicated to consumer protection, education, ethics and integrity in the jewelry industry. Beryl oversees 230 stores nationwide, and the thriving e-commerce business. For this once family-owned, Kansas City business giant, the story continues to unfold.

H&R Block, Inc.

H&R Block operates in 11,000 company-owned and franchise retail locations in the United States and worldwide. It is the only tax services company to offer retail and digital tax preparation solutions.

On the 13th block of Main Street in downtown Kansas City sits a 17-story office building. This glass structure, in customary green, welcomes visitors and associates to **H&R Block**'s international headquarters.

It is here, perhaps, where co-founder Henry W. Bloch can best appreciate what he and his brother Richard built nearly 60 years ago. Today, the company is the world's largest tax services company, preparing more than 500 million tax returns worldwide since it first opened its doors in 1955.

The company now operates in 11,000 company-owned and franchise retail locations in the United States, and has international operations in Canada, Australia, India and Brazil. In addition, the company is the only tax services company to offer retail and digital tax preparation solutions.

When Henry studied at Harvard Business School following his stint in World War II, a chance visit to the library played a pivotal role in the birth of the business. He read a copy of a speech by a Harvard professor who said there were three kinds of business: big, small and labor. "Big business and labor were both very powerful, but small business really had no one to turn to," he said, "and small business was really the backbone of this country. The future," he declared, "would be in helping small businesses."

Henry's vision was to provide services to small businesses like temporary workers, plus accounting, collection and management services, and, yes, even income tax preparation. Henry's vision became United Business Company.

In 1954, United Business Company's 12 employees

H&R Block headquarters building on 13th and Main in Kansas City, Mo.

were keeping books for various clients, and Henry and his brother, Richard, were working seven days a week, long into each night. Both brothers realized something had to give so they looked to remove time-consuming tax preparation from their services. This was also the year the basic tax code the IRS uses was introduced.

One of the brothers' clients, John White, who worked in display advertising for *The Kansas City Star* and was concerned that he would have no one to prepare his taxes, suggested, "Why don't you really try making a business out of taxes before you get out entirely?" A small ad was made showing a man behind an eight ball, with a simple headline: Taxes, $5. White convinced the Blochs to run the ad twice. The first day the ad ran, the office was full of people.

On Jan. 25, 1955, Henry and Richard replaced United Business Company with a new firm specializing exclusively in income tax return preparation: H&R Block, Inc.

In 1956 H&R Block expanded to open seven offices in New York City. A year later, H&R Block began opening offices under a new business model that would later be called franchising, and H&R Block doors swung open on Main Streets across the country. The company went public Feb. 13, 1962, with a $300,000 offering — 75,000 shares at $4 per share. H&R Block became listed on the New York Stock Exchange in 1969.

Today H&R Block has a retail office within five miles of every American and helps taxpayers file their taxes anyway, anywhere and anyhow they want. What started as a pen and paper business has evolved into sophisticated state-of-the-art technology solutions both in the office and at the consumer's fingertips.

A record 25.6 million taxpayers filed a tax return across the world in fiscal year 2012 by visiting H&R Block retail offices, using H&R Block At Home™ online or

> *Henry's vision was to provide services to small businesses like temporary workers, plus accounting, collection and management services, and, yes, even income tax preparation.*

One of the first H&R Block advertisements placed in The Kansas City Star.

software, having their taxes prepared by a tax professional through the company's fully integrated, secure one-of-a-kind virtual tax preparation experience Block Live℠, or choosing to file with a tablet or smartphone. H&R Block provides peace of mind to taxpayers, ensuring they claim all of the credits and deductions they deserve and helping them keep more of their own money for what matters most to them.

JE Dunn Construction

JE Dunn is a $2 billion company with 20 offices across the United States and plans to expand. From building to redevelopment, JE Dunn's involvement can be seen across the Kansas City skyline.

"The only thing we build better than our buildings are our relationships," says William H. Dunn Sr., chairman emeritus of **JE Dunn Construction**. This employee-owned company, founded in 1924 by William's father, John Ernest (Ernie) Dunn, has grown to be the 10th largest building contractor in the country.

"We're certainly proud of that accomplishment," says Terry Dunn, president and CEO. "Throughout that time, we've maintained our family values and we're equally proud of that."

A prime example of the importance of those core values is that JE Dunn gives 10 percent of pretax profits to charities. In addition, employee involvement in community is encouraged.

"We've created an environment for our employees here in Kansas City, as in all locations, that encourages them to get involved in the communities where they live and work," says Terry Dunn. A long list of Dunn associates sit on local boards and the company supports more than 400 nonprofit organizations nationwide.

The philanthropic environment is transfused throughout the organization since Bill Dunn Sr. took sole control of the business in 1974. Bill Dunn states it very simply, "It's important to leave the world in better shape than when you came into it."

In keeping with the standards of the founder, Terry Dunn is quick to point out, "We can provide the direction, but it's the folks who come to work every day that make this company what it is."

JE Dunn is a $2 billion company with 20 offices across the United States and plans to expand. From building to redevelopment, JE Dunn's involvement can be seen in the Kansas City skyline, with buildings like the Kauffman Center for the Performing Arts, H&R Block World Headquarters, IRS Processing Building, Federal Reserve Bank of Kansas City, Nelson-Atkins Museum of Art, many of the hospitals through out the metro area and

Roy Inman

The Dunn family is involved in the daily operations of the construction company. Back row, from left to right: Bob Dunn, Bill Dunn Jr., Terry Dunn, Steve Dunn. Front row: Bill Dunn Sr.

Bruce Mathews

countless other notable projects throughout our great city.

"One of our recent accomplishments is winning the National Construction Safety Excellence Award in the Large Contractor category given by the Associated General Contractors of America," says Steve Dunn, chairman of the board. "This award represents not only the hard work of our field and project staff, but the dedication of the entire organization to a safe and healthy work environment for our employees, our subcontractors, our clients, and everyone who comes in contact with our work. I'm particularly proud of this award and our people who make safety a priority every day."

JE Dunn's mission is to be the best client-centered building partner, providing construction services in a professional and highly ethical manner, while exceeding client expectations.

The goal is clear, to propel JE Dunn forward, creating a culture of continuous improvement and ensuring it remains a leading-edge construction company while providing the highest level of value and satisfaction for its clients. As part of this objective, the company has recently implemented lean construction practices. Lean principles, which focus on maximizing value and eliminating waste, are essential and yield higher efficiency on all resources.

Equally important is facilitating a higher level of collaboration among all project stakeholders. JE Dunn has invested heavily in the development of a suite of technology tools to enable new levels of collaboration.

Through these initiatives and a dedication to clients, partners and employees, JE Dunn will continue to operate by its mission statement, "In Pursuit of Building Perfection," and live up to their seven pillars: integrity, collaboration, wisdom, quality, value, sustainability and safety. It's simply the JE Dunn way.

John Deere — Olathe

John Deere has grown to be the world's leading farm equipment manufacturer and supplier of turf, construction, forestry and power equipment with one of the world's most recognized corporate logos.

John Deere opened a new, world-class facility in Olathe, Kan., in September 2011. This building achieved LEED certification (Gold Level) and houses over 400 employees.

Everyone who enjoys the abundant supply of safe, healthy, and inexpensive food should be grateful for John Deere and his polished steel plow, agricultural historians are quick to point out.

"Never in history has an acre of land been moldboard plowed with less physical effort by the plowman. Never has the soil been better tilled, nor has it produced more. Today the work is performed 1,800 times faster than the person who spaded the acre, and 122 times faster than with the plow of the mid-1800s," according to documents from the Illinois Periodicals Online Project at Northern Illinois University Libraries.

Deere & Company marked its 175th anniversary in early 2012. The business began in 1837 when the founder, John Deere, moved from his home in Vermont to start a small blacksmith shop in Grand Detour, Ill.

He revolutionized agriculture when he successfully manufactured and marketed the self-scouring plow that made farming in the Midwest a productive and profitable venture. He later moved to Moline, Ill., where the company's world headquarters is now located.

After the Civil War, many farmers began settling their families and raising crops and livestock on the fertile land south and west of the Missouri River. Kansas City became a gateway to the rapidly emerging bread basket of the World. Deere & Company realized they needed a distributor to provide equipment to this rapidly developing farming area and built their first branch house in the West Bottoms area of Kansas City in 1869.

Through the years, John Deere has grown to

> *"Our roots run deep in Kansas City and we are committed to those who cultivate, harvest, transform and enrich the land."*
>
> -- John Lagemann, Senior Vice President, Sales and Marketing for the Americas and Australia/New Zealand

John Deere, one of the oldest continuous companies in Kansas City, started in the West Bottoms and has had a strong presence since 1869 in the Greater Kansas City area.

be the world's leading farm equipment manufacturer and supplier of turf, construction, forestry and power equipment. One of the world's most recognized corporate logos, the leaping deer trademark has been a symbol of quality John Deere products for more than 135 years.

The John Deere North American Agricultural Marketing Center opened in Lenexa, Kan., in March 1999. This sales and marketing center consolidated many key services such as accounting, training, marketing, communications and market research for John Deere branches and dealers in the United States and Canada.

In September 2011, Deere completed construction and opened its new LEED Certified (Gold Level) building in Olathe, Kan.. This state-of-the-art facility includes more global functions with exceptional digital communications technology. It now houses John Deere's largest global sales and marketing group of over 400 employees (and growing), which provides world-class sales and marketing support services to customers, dealers and other Deere units worldwide.

"Our roots run deep in Kansas City and we are committed to those who cultivate, harvest, transform and enrich the land," says John Lagemann, Senior Vice President, Sales and Marketing for the Americas and Australia/New Zealand. "We live and breathe our core values: integrity, quality, commitment and innovation to deliver superior products to our customers. All of us at John Deere, Olathe, are proud to be one of the cornerstones to the future success and growth of our company worldwide."

Kansas City Area Transportation Authority

Public transit provides the citizens of Kansas City access to opportunities. Business owners rely on The Metro to get their employees to work, while saving them thousands of dollars on commuting costs and reducing polluting carbon emissions.

Main St. MAX has been held up as a model Bus Rapid Transit line for other cities exploring cost-effective ways to expand and enhance their transit systems. Below, in 1956, moviegoers take the bus to the Kansas City premiere of 'Bus Stop.'

Transit has been a vital part of the Kansas City community for almost 150 years. From the Kansas City and Westport Horse and Rail Company and cable cars in the 19th century, to today's network of modern buses, public transportation has been a cornerstone in building the local economy and neighborhoods.

In December 1965, the **Kansas City Area Transportation Authority (KCATA)** was formed by the signing of a bi-state compact created by the Missouri and Kansas legislatures. Since its inception, KCATA has been governed by a 10-member Board of Commissioners, five from Missouri and five from Kansas, representing the seven-county metro. KCATA began operations in 1969.

Today, The Metro logs more than 54,000 passenger

trips every weekday. Service is provided from 4 a.m. to 1 a.m., seven days a week.

Several types of transit service are offered: MAX bus rapid transit, Metro fixed-route service, MetroFlex, AdVANtage vanpool and Share-A-Fare paratransit services.

Metro local and express services create a network of routes to provide access to employment, education, shopping and healthcare. The Metro uses both small and large buses to provide the most efficient service.

MetroFlex is a demand-response bus service that allows for front door pick-ups and drop-offs in low-density areas where traditional fixed-route service cannot operate efficiently. Vanpools provide shared transportation to people who do not have bus service in their neighborhoods. KCATA also owns and maintains the popular Harry Wiggins Trolley Track Trail on the Country Club Right-of-Way.

Streetcars served many Kansas City neighborhoods until the late 1950s.

corridor and has been recognized as a national model for its low-cost, high-results implementation.

Main Street MAX Orange Line launched in 2005. Troost Avenue MAX Green Line kicked off in 2011 and features the region's first hybrid-electric buses and other environmentally friendly features.

On the heels of these successes, public transportation is being discussed in board rooms and living rooms throughout the community. From streetcars to commuter rail and other regional enhancements, public transportation is evolving at a fast-pace, and the KCATA is ready to support and lead future efforts.

Looking forward, KCATA is poised to convert from diesel fuel to clean Compressed Natural Gas (CNG), and, soon, customers will be trip planning, tracking their bus and paying their

As an innovative agency focused on continually improving the customer experience, KCATA introduced Bus Rapid Transit (BRT) to Kansas City. MAX Bus Rapid Transit has changed the face of public transit locally, and has helped shape the evolution of BRT across the nation. The service provides faster, more frequent service, and features the latest transit technology.

MAX Bus Rapid Transit uses easy-to-identify vehicles. Its stops are well-lit, with iconic information markers and newly designed passenger shelters. Information markers feature real-time MAX arrival information so that customers may wait with greater confidence. This new way of delivering public transit resulted in a doubling of ridership in the Main Street

fares on their mobile devices. As the world of technology evolves, KCATA pledges to never stop innovating.

Public transit provides the citizens of Kansas City access to opportunities. Business owners rely on The Metro to get their employees to work, while saving thousands of dollars on commuting costs and reducing polluting carbon emissions.

Students depend on MAX to get to and from campus and around town without breaking the bank. Thousands of trips every day are taken on The Metro for critical medical care. And motorists throughout the area enjoy a less congested drive because The Metro means fewer cars each day and safer travels each night.

Whether you ride the bus or not, The Metro touches your life.

Kansas City Aviation Department

Kansas City's airports are much more than places for planes to take off and land and for people and goods to be transported. They are major international economic engines that impact individuals and companies in the region.

Bruce Mathews

When dedicating Downtown Airport, Charles Lindbergh stated that airport's central location and proximity to the business district were major assets. This holds true today by providing executives direct access to downtown.

The Kansas City Aviation Department owns and operates Kansas City International (KCI) Airport and Charles B. Wheeler Downtown Airport. The two airports have a long history of providing air transportation and contributing jobs to the region's economy. In fact, KCI Airport turned 40 and Downtown Airport turned 85 in 2012.

Downtown Airport — Location always key. Charles Lindbergh dedicated the Kansas City Municipal Airport in 1927 after his historic solo crossing of the Atlantic. He praised Kansas City, indicating that the city's central location and the airport's proximity to the business district gave the city the potential to become the air capital of the United States. Those strengths indeed became major factors in success of the city and the airport over the years.

The airport's activity grew, as did the size and range of aircraft operating there. By the 1960s, Municipal Airport could no longer accommodate the larger commercial planes and increased jet and passenger traffic. Plans for a new airport were developed and commercial air operations were later transferred to a newly built KCI Airport in November 1972. Municipal Airport's name was changed to Kansas City Downtown Airport in October 1977 and then to Charles B. Wheeler Downtown Airport in 2002.

Today, the Charles B. Wheeler Downtown Airport serves more than 80,000 aircraft per year and generates more than $280 million in annual economic impact. The airport is a 24-hour facility offering fuel, maintenance, aircraft rentals, sales and flight training. More than 200 aircraft are based at MKC, including more than 40 business jets. The Aviation Department's new Hangar Complex boasts 96 hangars, a self-serve avgas fueling, an aircraft washing area and aircraft parking aprons. Most of the airfield recently underwent a much-needed $70 million overhaul.

KCI – Catalyst for business. Since it opened in 1972, KCI Airport has served as mid-America's link to the world for millions of passengers each year. Drawing passengers, cargo and commerce from Missouri, Kansas, Iowa and Nebraska, the airport is a major catalyst in the growth and development of the region and plays a significant role in bringing new business, conventions and tourists to the area. A 2006 economic impact study found KCI to account for 60,000 jobs with a combined payroll of nearly $1.6 billion, and $5.5 billion of stimulus into the area's economy.

KCI Airport welcomes approximately 10 million passengers each year and handles 100,000 tons of cargo. All major U.S. passenger airlines serve nearly every major U.S. city plus destinations in Canada and Mexico. The three runways can accommodate up to 139 aircraft operations per hour. The airport offers Foreign Trade Zone status, Enhanced Enterprise Zone tax initiatives and low landing fees.

Diversifying the KCI portfolio. The KCI complex spans nearly 11,000 acres, most of it outside the airfield. All of this land affords great opportunity for development. The Aviation Department and its economic development partners use an approach that incorporates a mix of aeronautical and non-aeronautical tenants. Much of this focus is on the KCI Overhaul Base, KCI Intermodal BusinessCentre and the Ambassador Building at KCI.

On nearly 11,000 acres KCI Airport has room to grow and attractive grounds to welcome millions of visitors each year.

> *A 2006 economic impact study found KCI to account for 60,000 jobs with a combined payroll of nearly $1.6 billion, and $5.5 billion of stimulus into the area's economy.*

This attracts a greater number of well-paying jobs to the area and diversifies the airport's revenue stream. The resulting revenue lowers costs for airlines and can translate into lower fares for travelers.

The future. Downtown Airport's renewed aeronautical infrastructure positions the facility to grow both as a business aviation airport and a general aviation airport. The recent KCI Master Plan Update study recommended eventually replacing the airport's three aging terminals and their constricted spaces with a single, more efficient and customer-friendly passenger terminal. Groundwork is currently being laid on financial, environmental and preliminary design aspects of a new terminal.

Kansas City's airports are much more than places for planes to take off and land and for people and goods to be transported. They are major international economic engines that impact individuals and companies in the region. Much of that activity is related to aviation, but much is not. It's a perfect balance!

Kansas City Ballet

Kansas City's oldest professional performing arts organization has become a nationally renowned ballet company by presenting an eclectic repertory ranging from contemporary ballets to well known classics.

Steve Wilson

Dancer (center): Rachel Coats.

The poet Alexander Pushkin is credited with saying that "Ballet is a dance executed by the human soul."

Since **Kansas City Ballet**'s founding in 1957, there have been thousands of human souls gracefully soaring, pushing the human form to exhilarating heights and bringing air, light and loveliness to a city eager to receive their gift. Now that gift is delivered from the most stunning of all stages imaginable, the new Kauffman Center for the Performing Arts.

With 55 seasons of performances behind it, Kansas City Ballet is the oldest professional performing arts organization in Kansas City. Over this half century, Kansas City Ballet has become a nationally renowned

ballet company by presenting an eclectic repertory ranging from contemporary ballets to well known classics.

The company's spectacular holiday production of *The Nutcracker* has become an annual celebration for tens of thousands of area families.

Kansas City Ballet was founded in 1957 by Tatiana Dokoudovska with the goal of establishing a regular presence for ballet in the city. For 20 years, she nurtured the company with her time, love, talent and even her personal financial resources as artistic director, advisor and choreographer. Ms. Dokoudovska's tremendous artistic talent and unswerving drive enriched the Midwest artistically in so many ways.

Upon Madame Dokoudovska's retirement in 1980 the trustees made the commitment to build the professional company and selected Todd Bolender as artistic director. Bolender fulfilled his vision of developing a nationally recognized ensemble based on his extensive experiences as a dancer and choreographer with George Balanchine's New York City Ballet and as an international opera and ballet choreographer.

Bolender retired in 1995 to become artistic director emeritus, focusing his talents on choreography and teaching.

William Whitener was appointed artistic director in 1996 after serving in the same capacity with Canada's Royal Winnipeg Ballet and Les Ballets Jazz de Montreal, and having worked with leaders of contemporary American ballet including Robert Joffrey, Jerome Robbins and Twyla Tharp. Whitener diversified and expanded the company's repertory with popular, contemporary work.

The impact of his tenure is clear in this review of the ballet's week of performances at New York's Joyce Theater in 2008: "It was the 50-year-old Kansas City Ballet that offered the most choreographically adventurous and aesthetically diverse evening at the ballet in New York this season." — "Back Stage," April 2008, Lisa Jo Sagolla

Kansas City Ballet numbers 28 professional dancers. The artistic staff and dancers were trained at prestigious schools and training programs affiliated with such renowned companies as New York City Ballet's School of American Ballet, The Joffrey Ballet, Pacific Northwest Ballet, the Frankfurt Ballet, and the Boston, Washington, San Francisco, and Pittsburgh ballets.

In August 2011, Kansas City Ballet completed renovation of the Todd Bolender Center for Dance & Creativity, formerly the historic Union Station Power House. The new center, which also houses the Kansas

Steve Wilson

Above, Dancer: Logan Pachciarz

Left: Dancers: Catherine Russell, Charles Martin, Nadia Iozzo

City Ballet School, gives the ballet the space needed for dancers and students to rehearse, create, study, and to expand its community outreach and residency activities. The Bolender Center, with its seven studios, includes the 180-seat Michael and Ginger Frost Studio Theater as a performance venue for both the ballet and other arts organizations throughout the Kansas City area.

In October 2011, Kansas City Ballet made its debut as the resident dance company of the Kauffman Center for the Performing Arts. The Muriel Kauffman Theatre became the ballet's new stage and was quickly recognized as an exemplary performance space for dance. The ambience of the Muriel Kauffman Theatre has added immeasurably to Kansas City Ballet's performances and its country-wide reputation of being an exciting and adventurous ballet company.

KCPT

KCPT has gone from reaching 70,000 students on UHF to reaching 2.2 million people with a digital signal. Today KCPT has three digital channels with round-the-clock programs.

In 1961, Channel 19 produced educational programming for the Kansas City School District (KCSD), including this health program about the food groups.

In today's television universe of over 500 channels, it's not unusual for a new network or channel to suddenly appear. This was not the case 50 years ago. In 1961, as you knelt before the TV console, manually turning the dial, only three of the 13 clicks revealed pictures and sound.

Imagine what it must have been like when suddenly a fourth click emerged from the TV snow. In Kansas City, it happened on Wednesday, March 29, 1961, when classrooms turned the dial to watch an educational lesson telecast from the Board of Education. Channel 19 and KCSD were born.

Initial telecasts, from the ultra-modern KCSD television studios in the Board of Education Building at 12th and McGee, were only four and a half hours long. During the day, you might learn from one of 47 different educational lessons. At night, everyone could enjoy a cultural, civic and public service show.

More than 50 years have come and gone since then. A lot has changed, but a lot remains the same.

In 1971, KCSD became **KCPT** as a community licensed public television station, broadcasting PBS programming in color for the first time.

In 1978, KCPT moved into the old KCTV5 studios on 31st and Grand Avenue. In 2002, the space expanded into the old Allen Press building next door.

Executive Producer, Cultural Affairs, Randy Mason, President & CEO Kliff Kuehl and Executive Producer, Public Affairs, Nick Haines in the Production Control Room at KCPT.

Bruce Mathews

Throughout all that time, the focus on education has never wavered, but the technology has changed dramatically! Today, KCPT reaches thousands of students and teachers across the metro with innovative educational programs like "Learn 360" and "Science Matters."

KCPT has gone from reaching 70,000 students on UHF to reaching 2.2 million people with a digital signal. In fact, KCPT has three digital channels with round-the-clock programs that are informative, engaging, heart-wrenching, gut-busting, eye-popping and mind-blowing.

As always, local programming is one of the station's mainstays. From the days of the "Kansas City Strip" through "Kansas City Illustrated" and eventually "Ruckus" and "Kansas City Week In Review," the station has emphasized thoughtful, in-depth coverage of the community that goes beyond the headlines. Programs with Charles Gusewelle, such as "This Place Called Home" and "Water & Fire: A Story of the Ozarks," have been viewer favorites. And the National Emmy for "Be Good, Smile Pretty" that sits in the lobby speaks to the station's documentary-making skills.

The arts have always been a focus for KCPT, too. "Homecoming: The Kansas City Symphony Presents Joyce DiDonato" just aired nationally on PBS, and throughout the years the heartland's creative spirit has been actively celebrated on series like "Marquee," "Portfolio," "Uniquely Kansas City" and the nationally distributed "Rare Visions & Roadside Revelations."

While the viewing possibilities on KCPT have grown in size, number and quality, the mission, the core reason for existence, remains the same. Today, KCPT is a supplement for children's education with award-winning and non-commercial shows like "Sesame Street," "WordGirl" and "Sid the Science Kid."

"Our programming can broaden your horizons; take you to the heights of mountains, the depths of our oceans, the breadth of our forests and the best burger in town," Kliff Kuehl, KCPT president and CEO. "KCPT is where you can discover more about you and your extraordinary potential. If you look back 50 years, you'll see we've been doing this all along and will continue for the next 50 years."

Kansas City Southern (KCS)

KCS, headquartered in Kansas City, is a link to ports on the Gulf of Mexico, to the international Pacific port of Lazaro Cardenas and to the world.

KCS locomotives, both old and new, are staged for this picture on Kansas City Terminal Railway tracks adjacent to Union Station, beneath the Michael R. Haverty Freight House Bridge. This pedestrian bridge connects Union Station with the Crossroads Arts District and downtown Kansas City. Formerly a KCS railroad bridge, it was moved to this location in 2006 and renamed in 2012 to honor KCS' executive chairman, who was also chairman of the board of directors of Union Station Kansas City, Inc. from 2005 to 2012.

Like the Greater Kansas City Chamber of Commerce, **Kansas City Southern (KCS)** (NYSE: KSU) celebrates its 125th anniversary in 2012.

KCS was founded in 1887 by Arthur E. Stilwell, who with Edward L. Martin, built the Kansas City Suburban Belt line serving commercial and industrial districts of Kansas City.

Stilwell had a bigger dream to provide a north-south route from Kansas City to the Gulf of Mexico, and later to Mexico. His dream was considered unrealistic, as other railroads were being built on an east-west route. In 1897, the Kansas City, Pittsburg and Gulf Railroad Company (KCP&G) was completed from Kansas City to Shreveport, La., and Port Arthur, Texas (the port city named for him) realizing part of Stilwell's larger dream.

In 1900, KCP&G became The Kansas City Southern Railway Company (KCSR). KCSR acquired the Louisiana and Arkansas Railway Company in 1939, providing a route from Dallas to New Orleans and access to areas northeast of Shreveport into Minden, La., and Hope, Ark.

In 1962, KCSR president William N. Deramus III established Kansas City Southern Industries, Inc. (KCSI), as a diversified holding company and invested in many non-rail businesses, including the company known today as DST Systems, Inc.

KCSI spun-off the non-rail financial services in 2000 and the company returned to its roots. In 2002, the name was changed from KCSI to Kansas City Southern, reflecting the focus on railway transportation.

The KCS network remained largely unchanged until

the 1990s. In 1993, the MidSouth Rail Corporation was acquired, extending the line to Meridian, Miss., Counce, Tenn., Tuscaloosa and Birmingham, Ala., providing trackage rights into Gulfport, Miss., and connecting to larger eastern railroads. Today, the Meridian Speedway line from Dallas to Meridian is the premiere rail corridor between the southeast and southwest United States.

The company began working toward acquisitions, partnerships and strategic investments in 1995 that would grow KCS into Mexico, including an investment in Mexrail Inc., owner of the Texas Mexican Railway Company (Tex Mex) and its border crossing at Laredo, Texas. This set the stage for investment in Mexico, and Stilwell's 19th century vision was renewed. In 1994, the North American Free Trade Agreement formed and would significantly change shipping patterns.

In 1996, KCS and Grupo TMM bid and won the concession for the Northeast Line rail, the premiere Mexican rail corridor, and in1997, Transportacion Ferroviaria Mexicana, S.A. de C.V. (TFM) began commercial operation.

KCS invested in the Panama Canal Railway Company in 1998 and holds a 50 percent interest. The 47.6 mile line, constructed in 1855, was restored in 2001 and provides passenger and freight transportation across the isthmus, adjacent to the Canal, from Panama City to Colon.

In 2005, KCS acquired full ownership of Mexrail, Inc., and Grupo TMM's interest in TFM. In agreement with the Mexican government, KCS acquired the remaining 20 percent interest in TFM, making it a wholly-owned subsidiary of KCS. In December 2005, TFM was renamed Kansas City Southern de Mexico, S.A. de C.V. (KCSM).

Since 2005, KCS has made tremendous investments in its seamless, cross-border network, particularly changing the landscape of North America's intermodal network. From any location along the route, KCS' customers' shipments are never more than an interchange away from any market in North America.

KCS is a link to ports on the Gulf of Mexico, to the international Pacific port of Lazaro Cardenas and to the world. KCS remains headquartered in Kansas City and a proud and long-standing member of the Greater Kansas City Chamber of Commerce.

The Kansas City Star

For more than 130 years, The Kansas City Star*'s job has been to tell Kansas Citians what's going on in their town.*

Cars, trucks and horse-drawn wagons travel by The Kansas City Star *building at 18th Street and Grand around 1920.* The Star *would go on to create WDAF Radio in the '20s — an early example of media cross-ownership.*

Kansas City has lived many lives — cowtown to the continent, miller and baker to the world, hothouse of jazz and railroad nerve center. Kansas Citians have built skyscrapers and warehouses, made greeting cards and pickup trucks, built pleasant neighborhoods and spread the city far and wide. Every day they make news across two states and seven counties and countless subdivisions.

For more than 130 years, *The Kansas City Star*'s job has been to tell Kansas Citians what's going on in their town. Gathering news isn't easy, nor is preparing it for consumption, nor is delivering it to every corner of the metropolis — and now, electronically, the world. It's what a news organization does to stay in business, but for *The Star* it has also been a mission.

Through the years, *The Star* has done more than make money. It has held the powerful accountable, given voice to the voiceless and connected the community. And the partnership between *The Star* and Kansas City has

held fast. After all, *The Star* is where Kansas City learns about itself.

By the decade, here are highlights of where the city's history and *The Star* have intersected:

• The 1890s: *Star* founder William Rockhill Nelson works with others to lead the City Beautiful movement, which results in paved roads and sidewalks, better fire and police protection, and — most enduring — the city's infamous boulevard and park system.

• 1900s: Nelson acquires morning *The Kansas City Times*, dubs it "The Morning Kansas City Star," and introduces the city to its first version of a 24-hour news operation.

• 1910s: Nelson dies at his home, Oak Hall, now the site of the Nelson-Atkins Museum of Art. Nelson's will is filed, leaving everything to his wife and to his daughter, Laura Nelson Kirkwood. After their deaths, the entire estate is to be converted to cash and the proceeds turned over to art.

The Star opened its new press production and distribution facility in 2006, demonstrating its commitment to the latest print technology and to downtown redevelopment.

- 1920s: *The Star* founds WDAF radio – an early example of media cross-ownership.

- 1930s: *The Star* launches investigations into voter fraud as the shadow of Tom Pendergast and his corrupt network of cronies and politicians turns violent and, eventually, a civic embarrassment.

- 1940s: As World War II winds down, *The Star* sees unprecedented growth in profits and circulation. Roy Roberts is named its president, and like Nelson, becomes a kingmaker in his own right and a major move in Republican circles. *The Star*'s Topeka reporter, Alvin McCoy, goes on to win a Pulitzer Prize for questioning the business dealings of the Republican national chairman. Embarrassed by McCoy's journalistic success, Roberts limits the story of the prize to just four paragraphs.

- 1950s: *The Star* gives massive and detailed coverage to the devastating Great Flood of 1951, leading *The Star* to win a Pulitzer Prize.

- 1960s: *The Star*'s top editors are told to begin hiring minorities and to begin printing more positive stories about Kansas City's black community.

- 1970s: For the first time, local ownership of *The Star* and *Times* ends as Capital Cities Communications Inc., a New York-based broadcasting and publishing company, buys the two newspapers from *The Star*'s stockholders. Capital Cities commits, though, to leaving editorial control to *The Star*'s Kansas City editors, a pledge of autonomy that still holds true today following a succession of ownership changes.

- 1980s: James Hale becomes Capital Cities' first Kansas City publisher and ushers in improvements. In his 15 years, the newspaper wins three Pulitzer Prizes, expands its zoned editions, expands business news, prints more color and takes in record profits.

- 1990s: Executives cease publication of the afternoon newspaper, combining *The Star* and *The Times* into a morning newspaper with *The Star* name. *The Star* ventures into electronic news and, by 1996, is active on the Internet. Walt Disney Co. acquires Capital Cities that year and, a year later, sells *The Star* to Knight Ridder, Inc.

- 2000s to present: *The Star* diversifies its publishing and product offerings, expanding into magazines, targeted media, book publishing and more. Most significant, KansasCity.com develops into the metro area's most popular web site and a major driver of business for *The Star*. On the print side, *The Star* opens its new press production and distribution facility in 2006, demonstrating its ongoing commitment to the latest print technology and to downtown's redevelopment. The facility ushers in unprecedented options for advertisers to target their messages.

Soon after the new plant opens, The McClatchy Co., a leading publisher, acquires *The Star*. By 2012, total readership — in print and electronic — reaches record levels.

Much has changed since *The Star* published its first edition of four pages on Sept. 18, 1880, on a small flatbed press. One thing has not changed since *The Star*'s first edition: The newspaper and its city are in this together.

Adapted from the introduction to the book, "The Star & the City: For 125 Years, Kansas City's Chronicler and Crusader," *by Monroe Dodd, published by Kansas City Star Books.*

Kansas City University of Medicine and Biosciences

College of Osteopathic Medicine. KCUMB's College of Osteopathic Medicine is one of the oldest and largest of the country's 29 osteopathic medical schools.

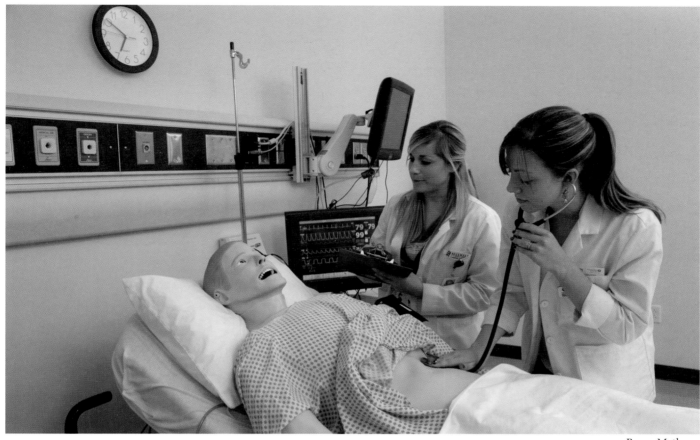

Bruce Mathews

KCUMB osteopathic medical students regularly work with high-tech patient simulators in the university's Kesselheim Center for Clinical Competence. The simulators are designed to help students integrate classroom knowledge with clinical experiences.

Kansas City University of Medicine and Biosciences (KCUMB) has been a fixture in the Kansas City community for nearly a century. About 1,100 students attend KCUMB's two colleges, the College of Osteopathic Medicine and the College of Biosciences, on the university's beautiful 21-acre campus near downtown Kansas City, Mo.

Originally founded as Kansas City College of Osteopathy and Surgery in 1916, the university has changed names four times in its history before becoming Kansas City University of Medicine and Biosciences in 2004.

The university has always been located in the historic Northeast neighborhood, one of Kansas City's oldest and most ethnically diverse neighborhoods.

KCUMB moved to its current location in the 1970s with the purchase and renovation of the original Children's Mercy Hospital building at the northwest corner of Independence Avenue and Woodland Avenue.

College of Osteopathic Medicine. KCUMB's College of Osteopathic Medicine is one of the oldest and largest of the country's 29 osteopathic medical schools. More physicians graduate annually from KCUMB than from any other medical school in Missouri.

The educational environment in the College of Osteopathic Medicine emphasizes both academic excellence and the education of well-rounded physicians who place their patients' needs above all else. As a result, the university's more than 9,600 physician graduates exemplify KCUMB's special brand of caring, compassionate medicine.

Osteopathic medical students at KCUMB learn through a patient-centered, clinical presentation-based curriculum that incorporates clinical training early in the students' first year on campus. KCUMB traditionally ranks near the top in terms of student performance on board examinations.

The university offers two dual-degree options to complement the doctor of osteopathic medicine — a master of arts in bioethics and a master of business administration in healthcare leadership, which is offered in partnership with Rockhurst University.

KCUMB's Score 1 for Health program administers free health screenings to more than 13,000 children annually and provides early clinical experiences for the university's first- and second-year osteopathic medical students.

Since 2005, KCUMB graduates have earned internships and residencies at many of the nation's most prestigious medical institutions, including Harvard University's Spaulding Rehabilitation Institute, Yale University, the Mayo Clinic and the Cleveland Clinic.

College of Biosciences. Over the past decade, KCUMB has expanded its offerings by adding master's degree programs in bioethics and biomedical sciences through the College of Biosciences. Thanks to these programs, students are able to explore the role of bioethics in research and the practice of medicine, or to learn what it's like to work toward new discoveries in a research laboratory.

Many of the more than 330 graduates of the College of Biosciences have chosen to further their educational experiences by pursuing doctoral programs in other health-related fields.

KCUMB's master of science in biomedical sciences program can provide students the skills necessary for successful and rewarding careers as research scientists in biomedical laboratories or with the solid foundation necessary to pursue doctoral programs in medicine or the life sciences.

Students choose from 12-month or 24-month tracks. The 12-month track is classroom intensive, while the 24-month track includes additional emphasis on advanced courses and allows students opportunities to conduct an original research project under the supervision of an experienced researcher.

Bruce Mathews

Approximately 1,100 students attend KCUMB on its beautiful 21-acre campus in Kansas City's historic Northeast neighborhood. KCUMB offers a doctor of osteopathic medicine degree, as well as master's-level degrees in bioethics and biomedical sciences. KCUMB will celebrate its centennial in 2016.

KCUMB is proud to offer Kansas City's only graduate-level degree in bioethics, which explores moral values as they relate to research and the practice of medicine. A full-time, one-year track is available, as well as a part-time program designed for working professionals.

Designed to accommodate students with diverse backgrounds and interests, the university's master of arts in bioethics program is ideal for those who regularly encounter ethical challenges in their work, including practicing physicians, nurses, lawyers, chaplains and other health professionals.

Kansas City Zoo

Open 12 months of the year, the Kansas City Zoo serves a metropolitan community of six counties, including urban, suburban and rural demographics, with an average of 720,000 guests visiting a year.

And to think it all started with three white rabbits and four lions.

More than 100 years ago, these strange bedfellows and a handful of other animals were the first residents of the **Kansas City Zoo**. Today, the nationally-recognized zoo is home to more than a thousand animals, ranging from black rhinos and chimpanzees to bobcats and goats.

The Kansas City Zoo's mission — to conserve and provide access to wildlife and to instill a respect for nature by entertaining and educating visitors — is timely, relevant and energizing. The advance of technology has woven education and entertainment more tightly together, while a respect for nature and conservation guide many of the Zoo's daily decisions.

Nikita, the Zoo's giant white polar bear, is a Rock Star in his Polar Bear Passage. He entertains guests year round.

From the beginning, Kansas City has supported and celebrated its zoo. In 1909, children organized letter-writing campaigns, while fundraisers, lectures and parades raised money to locate the zoo on 60 acres of natural surroundings in Swope Park. In 2011, that same community support passed a tax initiative to ensure that the zoo was well positioned to reach and surpass its goals of stimulating and inspiring all visitors, from families on Sunday-afternoon outings to students attending classes.

In 1909, a few dedicated visionaries formed the Kansas City Zoological Society that took the Zoo from concept to reality. The following year this group asked the Board of Parks and Recreation to allot $32,000 and the acreage in Swope Park to begin construction of the Kansas City Zoo. The Original Main Zoo Building opened on December 13 of that year. Animals exhibited included four lions, two timber wolves, two bison, three white rabbits, two coyotes, as well as ostriches, ducks, monkeys, pheasants and pigeons.

The first expansion took place in 1912. During the same year the Zoo became primarily self-sufficient, producing most of the animal's food from gardens within the park itself. The '40s and '50s saw a spurt of activity yet it was not until 1959 that the Zoo engaged in a partnership that continues to guide it today with the Friends of the Zoo.

In 2002 Friends of the Zoo, Inc., Kansas City, MO — a 501(c) 3, not-for-profit organization — took the reins of the Zoo's growth with a focused commitment to improving and supporting Zoo facilities, animals and educational programs.

When Randy Wisthoff left the Henry Doorly Zoo in Omaha to become the Kansas City Zoo Executive Director/CEO in 2003, he wasted no time collaborating with Zoo board members and the Kansas City mayor to spearhead a $30 million bond package that began to set the stage for the future.

Since 2007, the Zoo has invested $65 million in capital projects including a new entrance, Zoo Learning Center, the Discovery Barn, river otters, trumpeter swans, an Endangered Species Carousel, Polar Bear Passage, the African Sky Safari, Tiger Terrace and more. The original Zoo Building was also transformed into what is called the Tropics providing up-close views of primates, otters, birds and lush tropical plants.

Travel over the savannah on the African Sky Safari for the best views of the 100-acres of African wildlife including cheetahs, lions, giraffes, rhinos, hippos, chimps and more.

Many accolades have been given to the zoo. Polar Bear Passage was named the 2010 Midwest Travel Treasure by AAA. America's Best Zoo book featured the Kansas City Zoo as one of the top 60 zoos in the United States boasting the best African, Kangaroo and Chimp exhibits. The Zoo is a repeat winner of the favorite family day trip by KCParent Magazine and voted best kids' attraction by tourists visiting Kansas City.

Open 12 months of the year, the Kansas City Zoo serves a metropolitan community of six counties, including urban, suburban and rural demographics, with an average of 720,000 guests visiting a year. New attractions planned are likely to see that number balloon.

One long-awaited attraction in the Zoo's 2020 Masterplan is the new Helzberg Penguin Plaza, which will open in 2013 bringing both the cold-water and warm-water black and white friends to the Kansas City Zoo. Still to come are a new gorilla and orangutan exhibit, Predator Canyon, a giraffe feeding station, a new elephant watering hole and so much more.

Every day is a great day to visit the Kansas City Zoo — there's always a new adventure providing a lifetime of zoo memories. And to think it all started with three white rabbits and four lions.

Kansas State University Olathe

The greater Kansas City area accounts for one third of the $19 billion global animal health market, positioning K-State Olathe in an ideal location for growth.

Bruce Mathews

The first building on K-State Olathe's campus was completed using a design-build method and is a 108,000 sq.-ft, LEED Silver certified structure. The multi-use building houses classrooms, office space, meeting space, state-of-the-art laboratories and kitchens, and conference/event space.

When Kansas State University began talks with the City of Olathe and the Kansas Bioscience Authority in 2005 about establishing a campus in the greater Kansas City area, it seemed a far-off reality.

As luck would have it, K-State became aware that the University of Kansas was interested in pursuing a county-wide sales tax increase to fund the development of new campus buildings for the KU Medical Center and KU Edwards campus. This became the impetus for a mutually-beneficial treaty.

Blue and red do make purple, after all, and KU and K-State worked in partnership to support the Johnson County Education Research Triangle (JCERT) tax. The partnership agreed that, should the ballot measure pass in the 2008 general election, each of the three campuses would receive one-third of the tax proceeds — roughly $5

Since its grand opening, K-State Olathe has welcomed over 20,000 people in the facility, hosted over 800 events and 15 major conferences.

million each, annually.

The tax passed with an overwhelming margin of victory, in one of the worst economic climates in our country's recent history. It was the first local tax for higher education passed in the county, and equivalent to the seventh-largest endowment to a public university. It proved that greater Kansas City was hungry for education. With that, building began for this new member of the K-State family, on the heels of the university's 150th anniversary.

In keeping with its land grant heritage, **Kansas State University Olathe** was built on land gifted by the City of Olathe. Ninety-two acres in all were granted for the Kansas Bioscience Park in northwest Olathe, near College Boulevard and K-7, with 38 acres for the campus. The first building was the 108,000-square-foot International Animal Health and Food Safety Institute opening on April 26, 2011.

Just one year later, the third campus in Kansas State University's three-campus system has announced its first five graduate degree programs: MS degrees in Adult and Continuing Education, Veterinary Biomedical Science, Food Science, Biological and Agricultural Engineering and Horticulture, with an emphasis in Urban Food Systems.

K-State Olathe serves as a resource for the Kansas City Animal Health Corridor, which stretches from Manhattan, Kansas, to Columbia, Missouri. As a portal to core laboratories and other resources at K-State's main campus in Manhattan, the school also provides faculty in Manhattan and Salina with greater access to Kansas City-area resources. The greater Kansas City area accounts for one third of the $19 billion global animal health market, positioning K-State Olathe in an ideal location for growth.

Since its grand opening, K-State Olathe has welcomed over 20,000 people in the facility, hosted over 800 events and 15 major conferences. All 10 of the university's labs are being filled by industry and academia, including an R&D lab for Lenexa-based Ceva Biomune, the US-China Center for Animal Health, SmartVet USA, Urban Water Institute, Advanced Manufacturing Institute and K-State food science and microbiology labs.

The university is also partnering with Unified School Districts and higher education institutions in Johnson County and greater Kansas City. These initiatives promote and encourage students to get involved in the bioscience fields — and to date, over 5,000 students have attended events at K-State Olathe, as well in their schools, in the fields of animal health and food safety. Graduate-credit summer institutes for K-12 educators have also

Bruce Mathews

Sitting on 38 acres, the K-State Olathe campus is part of the Kansas Bioscience Park. The Bistro (above) is one of the many spaces available for use by academia, industry and the community.

been developed with over 40 teachers having completed the program to date.

"We've had an outstanding beginning," said Dan Richardson, CEO, K-State Olathe. "The partnerships and progress we've made are unparalleled, and we look forward to our long and thriving future here. It's a future where we'll be changing the landscape — and changing lives."

Ewing Marion Kauffman Foundation

The Foundation's mission evolves from Ewing Kauffman's vision — to help individuals attain economic independence by advancing educational achievement and entrepreneurial success.

The legacies of Ewing and Muriel Kauffman live on. The Ewing Marion Kauffman Foundation advances numerous entrepreneurship and education initiatives throughout Kansas City and across the nation, while the Muriel McBrien Kauffman Foundation shapes our community's cultural arts landscape.

Ewing Kauffman took his shot and succeeded beyond his wildest dreams. He made his mark in business and baseball, but it was his desire to give back to others that set him apart.

He started the **Ewing Marion Kauffman Foundation** to encourage others to share his curiosity about the world, learn, pursue new ideas and always believe that a group of common people working together can achieve uncommon results.

The quintessential American entrepreneur, Kauffman understood how to bring organizations to life to be productive and vital. Above all, he had a zest for life and a social awareness that was grounded in his belief in people. The Kauffman Foundation's mission evolves from his vision — to help individuals attain economic independence by advancing educational achievement and entrepreneurial success.

From the time he opened for business in 1950, operating out of the basement of his modest Kansas City home, until the day he relinquished sole control of the company in 1989, Kauffman built Marion Laboratories into a Fortune 500 company with 2,500 local associates and the area's most widely held stock. Associates remember the company earning revenues of $23 million a year in 1970, then growing to generate $23 million a day in the span of just two decades.

Kauffman stirred "The Marion Spirit" by connecting with his associates. He led associate meetings from the company's loading dock and, when the company outgrew that venue, he took the stage of the auditorium of the Baptiste Junior High School. Later, he moved to Municipal Auditorium for rousing "Marion on the Move" meetings, where he praised associates and set expectations even higher.

Kauffman liked to say that Marion Labs was built on promises. And those promises paid off for his loyal associates. When Marion Labs merged with Merrell Dow Pharmaceuticals Inc., more than 300 Marion associates became millionaires. Estimates are the company entrusted a total of $775 million to its associates.

Bruce Mathews

The entrepreneurial heritage of both Ewing Kauffman and the Kansas City region is artistically depicted in a mural created by Bryan Haynes and displayed in the Kauffman Foundation Conference Center.

Marion Labs has figured into the corporate lineage of a handful of pharmaceutical firms. And, it's estimated that more than 50 companies currently operating in the Kansas City area trace their roots to Marion Labs and its associates.

The Kauffman legacy demonstrates the impact of a single entrepreneur to make lives better with innovation, create hundreds and even thousands of jobs, and grow the economy locally, nationally, and globally.

The Kauffman Foundation honors the legacy of its extraordinary founder by taking an entrepreneur's perspective in applying resources in new ways.

In Kansas City, the Foundation supports the Ewing Marion Kauffman School, the Kauffman Scholars program, the KC STEM Alliance, and Teach for America to help young people, especially those from disadvantaged backgrounds, get a quality education and reach their full potential.

Across the country, the foundation works with educators, researchers, and others to extend the power of entrepreneurship and train the nation's next generation of entrepreneurial leaders. The foundation also works to develop and disseminate proven programs that enhance entrepreneurial skills and abilities, and improve the environment in which entrepreneurs start and grow businesses.

Kauffman research contributes to a broader, more in-depth understanding of what drives innovation, the science of startups, and economic growth in an entrepreneurial world.

In Kansas City, the foundation proudly supports important local institutions, including the Kauffman Center for the Performing Arts, the Kansas City Public Library, The Nelson-Atkins Museum of Art, the National World War I Museum and many others. And the foundation's Conference Center hosts a wide range of events and welcomes innovative thought leaders to share their insights.

Throughout his life, Ewing Kauffman brought an entrepreneurial spirit and creative style to everything he did. He energized the people around him, rallied a city, mentored fellow entrepreneurs and philanthropists, and challenged us all to do more.

KPMG LLP

KPMG LLP, the audit, tax and advisory firm, opened an office in Kansas City in 1908, ranking KPMG among the oldest and largest public accounting firms in the area.

Bruce Mathews

L to R: Dave Fowler, Kevin Kaufman, Rick Seagraves.

For Dave Fowler, the managing partner of KPMG's Kansas City office, not a day goes by that he isn't reminded of the contributions of those before him.

"We have a lot to be thankful for in terms of the partners and professionals who have built our firm and local office into what it is today," said Fowler, who has been managing the office since 2000. "And it is our job to continue that good work and strive to make this office the best that it can be."

KPMG LLP, the audit, tax and advisory firm, traces its roots to 1897 in New York City. It wasn't that long after, in 1908, that the firm opened an office in Kansas City, ranking KPMG among the oldest and largest public accounting firms in the area. The impetus to open the

Kansas City office initially was attributed to the need for local banking expertise as well as to follow the national grain trade in the Midwest.

Over the decades the office has grown to match the needs of the greater Kansas City community, where today about 300 KPMG partners and professionals maintain a commitment to providing leadership, integrity and quality to the capital markets.

In fact, Kansas City is viewed within KPMG as a priority market, one of 21, within the firm's some 85 offices in the United States.

"As a result of our predominant size and diverse client portfolio in Kansas City, from entrepreneurs to Fortune 500 companies, we have a depth of resources in

Bruce Mathews

L to R: Kevin Kaufman, Regina Croucher, Mike Mollerus, Dave Fowler, Mike Koeppen, David Seay.

our local office that is unsurpassed," says Fowler. "We are proud to provide audit services to a high percentage of the leading companies in most, if not all industries. Our knowledge of ever-changing business practices as well as audit and tax emerging issues, provides valuable assistance in company's future growth and development plans."

Kansas City KPMG local office audit leader Kevin Kaufman says the pace of business has grown dramatically in recent years. "Even the best managed organizations are recalibrating their expectations and abilities to respond quickly to shifting technologies, public policy reforms and other competitive pressures," he says. "KPMG clients are continuing to raise the bar on operational efficiencies and risk management to remain competitive in the 'new normal,' post-recession environment."

And while the office opened in 1908 to serve banking and grain, today KPMG is deep in a number of industries, including consumer markets, financial services, government, healthcare and pharmaceuticals, industrial markets, technology and media and telecom. Additionally, KPMG is committed to serving mid-market and high-growth companies at all stages of development throughout the business life cycle. These companies provide extraordinary value to the markets and customers they serve.

The other key connectivity to KPMG's past is the office's record of giving back to the community.

"Our partners and managers actively serve on many boards of nonprofit civic and charitable entities providing financial and managerial support," says Kaufman. In addition, all KPMG employees annually donate their time through "INVOLVE," the firm's national employee volunteer program, to countless local Kansas City needy organizations.

"Our office supports the United Way and a variety of other local charities and nonprofit organizations through a Community Giving Campaign, actively volunteering, making financial contributions, and being committed to making a difference in Kansas City," continues Kaufman.

Fowler adds, "Just like many of the companies that we serve, we strive to make Kansas City the best place to work and raise a family. Our investment in Kansas City runs deep, and we are very proud of our 100-year record in business."

Lathrop & Gage LLP

Lathrop & Gage has steadily grown to include 11 offices nationwide and is located in Kansas City's Crown Center district, just blocks from where the firm was founded in 1873.

Bruce Mathews

Lathrop & Gage leadership continues its tradition of active participation in The Kansas City Chamber of Commerce, including L to R: Executive Committee Member Jennifer Hannah; Chief Executive Officer Joel Voran; Marketing Partner Jay Felton; and Litigation Partner Dan Cranshaw.

Lathrop & Gage was founded on the Heartland principles of honor, service, trust and value. That commitment to unwavering client service continues today. The firm's bedrock values were exemplified by attorneys Gardiner Lathrop and John Gage, who helped shape the development of Kansas City.

Today's Lathrop & Gage was created in 1996 through the merger of the legacy firms Lathrop & Norquist and Gage & Tucker. Since that time, the firm has steadily grown to include 11 offices nationwide, from New York to Los Angeles. Located in Kansas City's Crown Center district, the firm's headquarters is just blocks from where

the firm was founded in 1873.

The firm provides the full spectrum of legal services across the intellectual property, litigation and transactional disciplines. And while the firm has tallied many courtroom successes in the past 140 years, it is most proud of its client retention history. The firm still represents its first-ever client, now known as the BNSF Railway Co., and a number of local companies have been clients for more than a century.

Lathrop & Gage has been an integral piece of the fabric of Kansas City and its business community since Lathrop and William Smith hung a shingle outside an office in the River Market.

Lathrop was the son of a nationally known educator and the first president of the University of Missouri. Lathrop was a graduate of the University of Missouri, Yale and Harvard Law School. He was a leader in the community serving as a United States commissioner, president of the Kansas City Bar Association, president of the Board of Curators of the University of Missouri and president of the School Board of Kansas City. He was also a board member of The Lathrop School, which was named for his father and stood where the Folly Theater stands today.

As a prominent attorney and community leader, Lathrop delivered the commencement address at Kansas City's Central High School in 1903. The ceremony included a prescient moment when Lathrop presented a diploma to an 18-year-old John Gage. The ambitious Gage went on to the University of Kansas and entered the legal profession upon graduation. He opened the firm of Gage & Hillix in the Bryant Building at 11th & Grand in 1930.

A decade later, when Tom "Boss" Pendergast's political machine collapsed under his conviction for income tax evasion, Gage displayed his steadfast commitment to his community by running for mayor on

Missouri Valley Special Collections,
Kansas City Public Library

Gardiner Lathrop

the Citizens Association ticket, which was made up of reform-minded leaders from both Democratic and Republican parties.

Gage actively engaged the women voters of Kansas City with the slogan "WANTED: 75,000 women with pioneer courage…let us keep faith with those who blazed the trail." His six-year tenure was widely praised for the reforms he enacted in the post-Pendergast era.

The firm's tradition of leadership in government at the local, state, even federal levels has continued uninterrupted as the firm counts four mayors, one U.S. senator, one U.S. representative and three governors among its alumni.

Community involvement includes active participation in the Kansas City Chamber of Commerce. Attorney Bert Bates served as the chamber's chair and was a member of the board of directors for nearly three decades. Former Gage & Tucker Managing Partner John Kreamer was voted The Chamber's "Mr. Kansas City" in 1983. The firm is also home to several Centurions and numerous other chamber leaders.

While Lathrop & Gage has grown to have a national presence, it remains firmly rooted in Kansas City and provides each of clients with the value that comes from a Kansas City heritage of hard work and sensible solutions.

Lockton Inc.

Lockton is the world's ninth largest insurance broker and the world's largest privately owned, independent insurance brokerage firm.

More than 40 years have passed since Jack Lockton began working from his Kansas City apartment cold-calling companies and selling surety bonds and insurance.

That spark of entrepreneurial energy transformed Lockton Insurance into **Lockton, Inc.** Today, it's the world's ninth largest insurance broker and the world's largest privately owned, independent insurance brokerage firm. The global company has more than 4,450 associates with offices in the United States, Europe, Latin America, the Middle East and Asia. Through Lockton Global, a partnership of independent brokers, the company provides innovative risk management and employee benefit services anywhere in the world.

Today, the company stands beside clients in many different industries that are facing the challenges of these modern times, whether it's data and privacy risks or navigating healthcare reform for employee benefits.

For the first 10 years, Lockton was dedicated to the construction industry. In fact, Lockton started his career as an underwriter for a surety bond company before he started his insurance brokerage firm. The company developed its core values and philosophies by focusing on the construction industry, a business that values partnerships, innovation, a sense of urgency, and strong loss prevention and claims management services.

In 1987, Lockton expanded its service offering to include employee benefits and financial services. This entity now provides professional consultative and brokerage services to nearly 3,000 clients nationwide. Mirroring the success of the Property and Casualty operation, this division is one of the most successful and fastest-growing benefit groups in the country.

Lockton's success flows from its commitment "to provide the most uncommon results and service in a most common business." While the company has experienced remarkable growth, its flat organizational model and short lines of communication remain. David Lockton, chairman and brother of Jack Lockton, and the leaders of the operating companies have day-to-day responsibilities regarding client relationships and new business opportunities. They bring a strong sense of clients' needs to the decisions made regarding the operation and future of the company.

Lockton Companies is headquartered in Kansas City, with offices in the heart of the Country Club Plaza.

"Our horizon is a quarter of a century, not a quarter of a year," said David Lockton,

This philosophy has allowed Lockton to lead the industry with annual client retention of 95 percent and associate retention of 90 percent. Business is managed for consistent and orderly growth, and the company boosts of a fiercely competitive and aggressive sales organization.

Rick Kahle, (left), President of Lockton Benefits in Kansas City; Ron Lockton, President of Lockton's Property Casualty Operations in Kansas City. Right, David Lockton, Lockton Chairman.

Lockton's unwavering commitment to private ownership means that each associate has a single-minded focus on serving clients. Independence from Wall Street keeps Lockton focused on client needs, not the demands of analysts or stock price.

Lockton's principles are simply to be committed to the highest standards of excellence in everything and to practice the Golden Rule. While sustaining a highly ethical, moral and caring culture, the company believes its associates are their most valuable assets and provides them the opportunity and support to grow, improve and achieve their ultimate potential.

The company has put together a team which demonstrates a passion for delivering unparalleled service — internally and externally. Exemplary associate performance is recognized and substantially rewarded.

Relationships with each client and carrier are respected, valued and nurtured. The goal is always to make a recognizable difference to the clients' businesses through innovative solutions to their insurance needs. The company prides itself on being proactive in sustaining a meaningful corporate, social and civic responsibility.

Jack Lockton, who passed away in 2004, has a legacy that is engrained in Lockton's culture. His spirit lives on through Lockton's associates and the Lockton's culture, which is based on his philosophies of client and community service, working hard and supporting associates. He started the company as a privately held business, and the family plans for it to remain independent and a part of the Kansas City community.

The John A. Marshall Company

JAMCO is a family owned and operated business with a proud history as the oldest and largest office furnishings dealership serving the Kansas City and Wichita markets.

When the **John A. Marshall Company** (JAMCO) started as an office furniture and supply store in Kansas City in 1923, an office chair was just an office chair. Now, the office chair can be a work of art.

Office furnishings, styles and functions may have changed, but the company's commitment to service and quality has not.

JAMCO is a family owned and operated business with a proud history as the oldest and largest office furnishings dealership serving the Kansas City and Wichita markets. No longer in the supply business, the company's focus is solely furniture, flooring, and architectural products. What began as a family tradition in 1923 continues stronger than ever today with the fourth generation of the Marshall family leading the company into the 21st century.

Truly a family-owned enterprise, history has seen four generations of the Marshall family in the business. Founder John A. Marshall and son John S. (Jack) Marshall have passed away. But other generations have stepped forward. Grandson John E. Marshall is CEO; a second grandson, William C. Marshall, is currently Partner; great-grandson Stephen K. Marshall is Partner/Vice President. Mark J. Donnelly is Chairman of the Board.

In the early years, JAMCO was located at 110 W. 9th Street in downtown Kansas City after a move from its original location at 924 1/2 Baltimore, which is now a parking facility for Boatmen's First National Bank. The building went through many updates and remodeling, but when a new company, Office Pavilion, was formed in 1987 by JAMCO with partner Mark Donnelly, it soon became evident that a move must be made to a larger space. A facility was secured at 10930 Lackman Road in Lenexa, Kansas. After extensive remodeling and upgrading, the move to the new 57,500 square foot headquarters took place in April 1996. More warehouse expansions quickly followed, and in total the building now spans 84,500 square feet.

In 2003, the company took over Goldsmith's Inc., the Herman Miller dealer in Wichita. This acquisition opened the company up to a new market and an additional client base in a multitude of market segments, from aviation to higher education institutions, as well as local government agencies, corporate businesses and healthcare facilities. John A. Marshall Company leased an office space inside the Bank of America building at 100 North Broadway in downtown Wichita to house the office/showroom, separate from the warehouse facility.

Executive boardroom outfitted with a Geiger Caucus conference table, Keilhauer Vanilla seating, all set on top of Atmosphere carpet from Tandus Flooring.

> *JAMCO is a family owned and operated business with a proud history as the oldest and largest office furnishings dealership serving the Kansas City and Wichita markets.*

Following the successful takeover of Goldsmith's Inc., JAMCO determined it was time to branch out from furnishings and venture into the world of commercial flooring.

In 2006, JAMCO purchased FDC Contract, the leading commercial flooring dealer in the Kansas City metropolitan area. It was a great marriage of companies, because where there is furniture, there is always flooring.

The addition of FDC Contract also provided a more streamlined sales approach with customers. Instead of dealing with multiple vendors for an interiors project, they could simply turn to JAMCO and bundle it together in one purchase, through one point of contact.

In 2011, the company completed a small interiors renovation project to bring itself more in line with the current furniture designs and applications that are shaping the new landscape of the corporate office world. New designs and applications include such innovations as lower dividing walls, shared storage, collaborative areas, wireless presentation capabilities, increased natural light penetration and roller shades instead of traditional mini blinds. Many more are on the horizon and generations of Marshalls will be there, making sure their clients are introduced to them all.

Missouri Gas Energy (MGE)

Celebrating its 150th anniversary in 2017, MGE has over 500,000 customers in 155 communities throughout western Missouri.

In 1867, the famous architect Frank Lloyd Wright was born, Nebraska became the U.S.'s 37th state and Alaska was purchased for $7.2 million. But it was an historical event closer to home that was to mean more to Kansas Citians and Missourians. It was the formation of a company that would bring light into their homes for their children to read by, energy to allow stoves to cook their dinners and heat in the winter to make their homes warm.

That was the year that Kansas City Gas Light & Coke Company was formed, which was the genesis of today's **Missouri Gas Energy (MGE)**. Before pipeline technology was developed to deliver natural gas from wellheads to distant cities, gas was manufactured primarily from coal in a process that produced "coal gas" for lighting, cooking and heating.

In 1895, the Kansas City Gas Light & Coke Company was reorganized and named the Kansas City Gas Company. In 1897, the company merged with its chief competitor, the Missouri Gas Company, and became the Kansas City Missouri Gas Company, though it was still commonly called by its former name, Kansas City Gas Company.

In 1873, natural gas was discovered in southeast Kansas and the entrepreneurial atmosphere might have been described as similar to the gold rush of the West. Many small companies organized to build pipelines to deliver natural gas to nearby urban areas. Each had to receive the approval of the city council to provide service, also known as a franchise agreement, which is still done today. During these times, companies were gobbled up, merged and merged again.

Bruce Matthews

Missouri Gas Energy corporate headquarters at 3420 Broadway in Kansas City, Mo. MGE also has offices in St. Joseph, Lee's Summit, Warrensburg, Joplin, Republic, Neosho and Monett.

Although the Kansas City Gas Company was the first business on the Missouri side to provide natural gas service to the city, it was delayed due to the multiple business interests competing for the city franchise rights.

The winner of this competition was a businessman named Hugh J. McGowan, who later became president of the company. McGowan was a farm boy from Liberty, Mo., who became a successful businessman and politician. McGowan and then Kansas City, Missouri, Mayor Jay H. Neff didn't agree on the details of the proposed franchise agreement and a bitter political and legal fight ensued. The conflict was finally settled after Mayor Neff left office and a franchise agreement was awarded to the company in 1906.

By 1924, an Ohioan named Henry L. Doherty entered the scene and began buying natural gas distribution and pipeline operations throughout Missouri, Kansas, Oklahoma and Nebraska. He was to become the new owner of the Kansas City Gas Company and the Wyandotte County Gas Company in 1924. In 1925, Doherty consolidated his gas operations in these four states to form The Gas Service Company.

From 1925 to 1983, The Gas Service Company served Kansas City and over 250 other communities throughout Missouri, Kansas, Nebraska and Oklahoma. In 1983, Kansas Power & Light (KPL) bought The Gas Service Company. This marked the first of several successive changes in ownership. In 1992, KPL merged with the Kansas Gas & Electric company to become Western Resources (now known as Westar Energy).

In 1994, Western Resources sold its Missouri natural gas assets to the Southern Union Company headquartered at the time in Austin, Texas. Southern Union began operating this newly formed division as Missouri Gas Energy. In 2012, Southern Union, along with Missouri Gas Energy, was sold to Energy Transfer Equity, a diversified natural gas pipeline company headquartered in Dallas.

MGE

The Kansas City Gas Company's Plaza Office at 4714 Broadway in Kansas City, Mo. The company's main headquarters was in the Scarritt Building at 819 Walnut in downtown Kansas City, Mo.

Today, MGE has over 500,000 customers in 155 communities throughout western Missouri. Celebrating its 150th anniversary in 2017, MGE looks forward to providing many more years of warmth, comfort, and efficiency of natural gas service to homes and businesses in Kansas City. It stands ready to meet the challenges of the next generation by providing natural gas service for use in space and water heating, cooking, clothes drying and as an alternative fuel for transportation.

MRIGlobal

MRIGlobal has contributed to the advancement of science and technology, especially in core business areas of national security and defense, life sciences, energy and environment, agriculture and food safety, and engineering and infrastructure.

In the early years, MRIGlobal's research made a revolutionary breakthrough for farmers by creating a better fertilizer that increased crop yields. Since that time, from developing instant coffee to robots, **MRIGlobal**'s imprint can be found on many aspects of our lives.

As one of the nation's leading independent research and development organizations, MRIGlobal has adapted to each decade's challenges. The company is providing ways to protect the world from biological terrorism and to keep our food supplies safer. And, when a cure for cancer finally emerges, it will be due in no small part to MRIGlobal's research efforts.

In 1944, as World War II was ending, Americans were in awe and respectful of what technology had done to end the greatest global struggle in history. Kansas City's most prominent civic leaders imagined an institute that could serve the region by advancing science and technology to grow and protect society. They organized a not-for-profit institute called Midwest Research Institute with a charter "to conduct scientific research for the benefit…of humankind."

The vision was enormous and audacious. At the time, Kansas City was widely characterized as a farming community, with fewer than 500 chemists and engineers in the region. With J.C. Nichols as the first chairman of the board, the Institute began recruiting scientific talent to Kansas City.

Michael F. Helmstetter, Ph.D., President and Chief Executive Officer

The first project was for the Spencer Chemical Co., working on ammonium nitrate for fertilizer. When the compound encountered moisture, it clumped and caked and became unusable. In a collaborative cross-disciplinary approach, geologists and chemists at the Institute found a way to coat the compound crystals, lubricating them, allowing them to remain free-flowing in the fields, ultimately increasing crop production.

From that first project, the Institute quickly embarked on an array of projects in agriculture, energy, engineering and health care. Clients came from government agencies, academic institutions, and industry. By 1951, the Institute was performing work internationally.

Work in a chemistry lab in the 1950s at MRIGlobal's Volker Boulevard office

Early MRIGlobal innovations supported devices, practices, and services that are now common in everyday life — instant coffee and drip coffee makers, the Crock-Pot® and quick-cooking rice, for example. The scientific endeavors also encompassed work on spacesuits for NASA, air quality testing for the EPA, developing robots, and projects for safer highways.

Along the way, MRIGlobal earned a distinguished reputation for innovation, technical excellence and scientific leadership. MRIGlobal contributed to the advancement of science and technology, especially in core business areas of national security and defense, life sciences, energy and environment, agriculture and food safety, and engineering and infrastructure.

Today, prominent civic, science, university, and industry leaders remain involved, serving on the board of directors and as trustees. MRIGlobal has grown, operating in nine states and Washington, D.C., with more than 3,300 staff. In addition to its own laboratories, MRIGlobal manages and operates laboratories for the U.S. Department of Energy (DOE) and supports the U.S. Department of Defense.

MRIGlobal manages the National Renewable Energy Laboratory (NREL) in Golden, CO, for the DOE, a role it has held since NREL's inception in 1977. NREL is the only federal laboratory dedicated to the research, development, commercialization and deployment of renewable energy and energy efficiency technologies.

In 2011, the Institute adopted the name MRIGlobal. "Our name now reflects the broad impact of our work, spreading well beyond the founders' initial vision," said Michael F. Helmstetter, Ph.D., President and Chief Executive Officer.

In addition to its scientific contributions, MRIGlobal is a generous and respected corporate citizen, giving of its time and resources to advance the communities in which it works. MRIGlobal was a founding sponsor of Science Pioneers, and has more than 50 years of commitment to encouraging education in science, technology, engineering, arts and mathematics.

MRIGlobal also co-founded the Kansas City Area Life Sciences Institute, and continues to support the region's scientific and economic development through the Animal Health Corridor, the Greater Kansas City Chamber of Commerce, the KC Economic Development Corp., Kansas City Area Development Corporation, The Civic Council of Greater Kansas City, and dozens of other organizations. In addition, MRIGlobal has informally adopted the Paseo Academy of Fine and Performing Arts, sponsoring its FIRST Robotics team and providing support in staff coaches, mentors and tutors as well as a variety of scholarships, clubs, and special events for students.

"We're proud of our long history and deep roots in Kansas City," Helmstetter said. "We look forward to continued involvement in our community, as well as to our next generation of innovations and advancements for a better world."

Oppenheimer & Co.

Continuing the firm's key role in developing the regional economy, Oppenheimer & Co.'s Investment Bankers have been involved in financing many of the Kansas City area's most significant projects

Bruce Mathews

Oppenheimer professionals, seated left to right: Jack Holland, Kristie Svejda, Michael Short, Greg Schaff; standing left to right: Elliott Hollub, Brynn Dexter, Brad Max, Joanne Huey, Matthew Webster.

As the oldest continuing member of the chamber, **Oppenheimer & Co.** traces its roots to the founding of B.C. Christopher & Co. on Sept. 3, 1878, in Kansas City, Mo.. Originally established as a grain trading firm, Christopher became one of the nation's largest operators of grain elevators. The firm entered the securities industry in the 1940s and became a member the New York Stock Exchange in 1955.

In 1990, B.C. Christopher was acquired by Fahnestock & Co., a firm founded in 1881 by William

The grain trading firm founded in 1878 at the confluence of the Missouri and Kaw rivers has become an investment firm with a global reach appropriate for the 21st Century.

Fahnestock, whose father, Harris C. Fahnestock, had been financial adviser to Abraham Lincoln during the Civil War. Through the Great Depression and beyond World War II, Fahnestock flourished and grew as a result of a number of acquisitions, including the purchase of B.C. Christopher.

Fahnestock's Kansas City representatives continued the tradition, established at Christopher, of being a dynamic part of the growth of Greater Kansas City and the Midwest. The firm's retail brokerage, institutional sales, investment banking, bond underwriting and public finance departments served

OPPENHEIMER

clients throughout the region and beyond.

Another milestone occurred in 2003 when Fahnestock acquired Oppenheimer & Co., an international investment banking and wealth management firm founded in 1950. While the combined firm assumed the Oppenheimer name, the B.C. Christopher legacy continued throughout the Midwest and Southwest and was enhanced by the international reach of Oppenheimer.

With offices throughout the United States and in Europe, Asia, South America and the Middle East, the grain trading firm founded in 1878 at the confluence of the Missouri and Kaw rivers had become an investment firm with a global reach appropriate for the 21st Century.

Continuing the firm's key role in developing the regional economy, Oppenheimer & Co.'s Investment Bankers have been involved in financing many of the Kansas City area's most significant projects, including: Kansas City International Airport, Sprint Arena, Truman Sports Complex, Kansas Turnpike, Kansas Speedway, Nebraska Furniture Mart, Livestrong Sporting Park, Kauffman Center, American Royal, The Country Club Plaza, Zona Rosa and the NNSA National Security Campus.

Oppenheimer's experienced financial advisers continue to provide sound advice and wealth management to governments, institutions, individuals and families throughout Greater Kansas City. To reach us at the Country Club Plaza, call 816-932-7000. To reach our Leawood offices, call 913-383-5100. Or visit our web site at www.opco.com.

Benjamin Campbell Christopher, founder of B.C. Christopher, one of the nation's largest operators of grain elevators, and predecessor to Oppenheimer & Co., the oldest continuing member of the chamber.

Park University

Founded in 1875, Park University's mission, then, as it is today, is to provide a quality higher education experience that encourages learners to think critically, communicate effectively, demonstrate a global perspective and engage in lifelong learning and service to others.

From its perch high on the bluff overlooking the Missouri River in Parkville, Mo., **Park University**'s flagship campus stands as a beacon of learning serving a local, national and international audience.

"We are very proud to be the only Kansas City headquartered, non-profit educational institution with a truly national physical presence on 40 campus centers in 21 states providing face-to-face class instruction," says President Michael Droge. "Park also has amazing online undergraduate and graduate degree programs that connect Park with thousands of national and internationally located learners."

Founded in 1875 by Colonel George S. Park and John A. McAfee, Park University today enrolls more than 22,000 students annually. The mission then, as it is today, is to provide a quality higher education experience that encourages learners to think critically, communicate effectively, demonstrate a global perspective and engage in lifelong learning and service to others.

The founders' original concept called for students to receive tuition and board for almost no cost in exchange for working up to half a day at the college constructing buildings, planting and harvesting crops, cooking and cleaning — nearly any task necessary to maintain the school.

Inclusion was always a core element of Park's philosophy — the first graduating class of three women and four men included one American Indian.

Today, the main campus in Parkville, as well as the campus centers in downtown Kansas City and Independence, Mo., serve the broader Kansas City area. Each year, about 4,000 Park students who enroll are Missouri residents, many from the Kansas City area.

Academic degree programs offered at Park University include 11 associate degrees, 49 bachelor's degrees and seven master's level degrees. The largest employer in Parkville, Park University employs nearly 400

full-time staff and 123 full-time faculty, and is accredited by the Higher Learning Commission, a member of the North Central Association of Colleges and Schools.

U.S. News and World Report ranked Park University as the seventh most affordable private university/college in the nation in 2011 and in June 2012 the U.S. Department of Education ranked Park highest in lowest net price for all non-Bible/religious college/university in the West North Central states of the Midwest region.

Park is proud to be both affordable and provide a quality education. In 2011 and 2012, Park University

was among the 300 colleges and universities across the country and one of only seven in Missouri to be named to the Colleges of Distinction list.

Park's International Center for Music occupies a niche in the Kansas City community as a boutique, world-class conservatory. The music faculty and students are recognized nationally and internationally for their talent, which is nurtured by the European apprenticeship approach to instruction, a methodology found regionally only at Park University. The program works with the Kauffman Center for the Performing Arts, the Kansas City Symphony and other area arts organizations to offer musical events in the Greater Kansas City area and is a major contributor to the cultural life of the Kansas City community.

With a long history of serving the unique needs of our military, Park's programs assist military students, wounded warriors, and veterans to navigate opportunities and challenges with education, employment, finances, relationships, post-traumatic stress disorder and traumatic brain injury. Annually, more than half of Park's students are military service members or their family members, making Park the sixth-largest provider of college credit to the military in the nation.

Since the first international student landed at Park in 1880, the university has grown to host more than 700 international students from more than 100 countries each year. Nearly 30 percent of the Parkville campus annual student population is international.

Park's notable and successful legacy is securely linked with the foundational elements of "Park's Promise" to students, alumni, and friends to "serve those who serve their community and country with personalized, globally-relevant education for life."

Polsinelli Shughart

*A Kansas City-based national law firm built on a commitment
to putting clients' interests first*

Bruce Mathews; background image courtesy Wilborn & Associates

*Jim Polsinelli was ahead of his time founding one of the first law firms on the Country Club Plaza. Today,
Polsinelli Shughart's reach is coast to coast with more than 630 lawyers in 16 cities.*

The history and transformation of Polsinelli Shughart can be marked in many ways — from its growth to more than 630 attorneys, to an unwavering focus on helping clients succeed and an ongoing dedication to civic involvement in Kansas City, Mo., the firm's headquarters.

Firm Evolution. The evolution of the firm's Kansas City office began when 28-year-old Jim Polsinelli started a law firm on the Country Club Plaza with two other lawyers in 1972. The Polsinelli firm, which had its own entrance to the wildly popular Harry Starker's restaurant and bar, was adjacent to a busy movie theater.

Polsinelli remembers, "We always knew when they had a popular movie because there would be more popcorn than usual strewn throughout the steps."

Polsinelli added attorneys in phases and eventually used satellite space in other buildings. In 1991, the firm moved to its current location at 700 W. 47th Street, still on the Country Club Plaza.

Shareholders elected Russ Welsh chairman in 1998, a position he holds to this day. At that time the firm had 90 attorneys, and it has been under his leadership that numerous mergers, acquisitions and key lateral hires have transformed the firm into one of the fastest-growing law firms in the United States.

The firm's roots are in corporate law, and the Business Department, led by Frank Ross, Jr., remains its largest. Among the major growth initiatives were the additions of 10 financial services attorneys led by Dan Flanigan, who joined the firm in 1999; the merger with

Bruce Mathews

The future of Polsinelli Shughart includes attorneys (left to right) Vedrana Balta, Kraig Kohring, Chase Simmons, Eric Wu and Brook Bailey. Seated are (left to right) Kelly Sullivan and Anthony Springfield.

the 32-lawyer St. Louis-based Suelthaus PC in 2003; a new Washington, D.C., office in 2005; opening of a Chicago office in 2006; and a Wilmington, Del., office in 2008.

On Feb. 1, 2009, another major milestone occurred. The 300-attorney Polsinelli firm merged with the 180-lawyer Shughart Thomson & Kilroy, P.C., a Kansas City-based, regional law firm that traces its roots to 1939. The firm's growth was due, in large part, to the success of its premiere trial attorneys including Jack Kilroy, Sr., Tom Kokoruda and Larry Ward, all three Fellows in the American College of Trial Lawyers.

The merger brought the combined firm to Denver, Phoenix, St. Joseph and Springfield. Since 2009, the firm has continued its dramatic growth with the addition of offices in Dallas and Los Angeles.

Across the state of Missouri, Polsinelli provides clients strong support in St. Louis, the firm's second largest office, where the firm has 110 attorneys. Mergers and recruiting of lateral attorneys have grown the firm's Chicago and Phoenix offices to more than 60 attorneys each and expanded the Denver office to over 50 attorneys. These offices are thriving and strategically important, helping to support many of the firm's national clients.

Kansas City remains the firm's largest office with more than 250 attorneys locally. The firm's commitment to Kansas City and to its County Club Plaza roots will culminate in its signature headquarters. In the fall of 2013, the firm will move to a new 253,000-square-foot office building. The overall project, called Plaza Vista, revitalizes the west side of the Plaza with a boutique hotel and retail space.

Central to the firm's growth has been strategic alignment with Polsinelli Shughart founders' vision of a law firm providing clients with quality, service and value. The growth pleases founder Polsinelli, "Though when we first started out we said we were never going to get any larger than 25 attorneys, times do change."

Focused on Clients' Success. Polsinelli Shughart attorneys work to leverage cross-disciplinary strengths within industry areas, coupled with a deep understanding of their clients' businesses.

The firm's ongoing growth has further enhanced capabilities in well-established national practices in health care, financial services, real estate, life sciences and technology, energy, and commercial litigation.

Inc. Magazine ranked Polsinelli Shughart as the nation's fastest growing full-service law firm in 2012.

American Health Lawyers Association ranked the firm's health care practice seventh largest in 2012, and *Midwest Real Estate News* ranked Polsinelli Shughart's Real Estate Practice among the Best of the Best for 2012 based on total number of successfully completed transactions. Large additions in Chicago and Denver benefited the practice which partners with major national health care clients to address a comprehensive range of transactional, regulatory, and business issues.

Civic Commitment and Charitable Efforts. In addition to founding and leading a highly successful law firm, Jim Polsinelli has also been involved in a number of civic causes that bettered the way of life for Kansas Citians. Most notably, as former chair of the Kansas City Area Transportation Authority, he led the construction of an exercise trail around Mill Creek Park and the famous Plaza Neptune Fountain.

Always a proponent of education, Polsinelli was the first lay chairman of the Rockhurst High School Board of Trustees, a member of the Board of Trustees for Rockhurst University and president of the UMKC Law Foundation.

Polsinelli Shughart Chairman Welsh is the incoming chair of the Greater Kansas City Chamber of Commerce. He also is chairman of the board of directors for Starlight Theatre, a board member of the United Way of Greater Kansas City, a board member of the Community Blood Center, and a former member of the Kansas City Public Improvement Advisory Committee. He also is a member of the Civic Council of Greater Kansas City.

Prior to the merger, the Shughart Thompson & Kilroy Symposiums, attended by 12,000 people over

Bruce Mathews

The firm's offices have relocated or expanded to new spaces in Chicago, Denver, Dallas, New York, Phoenix, St. Louis and Wilmington. In Kansas City, attorneys, including Chairman Russ Welsh (pictured), are scheduled to move into the new Plaza Vista building on the west side of the Plaza.

Founder Jim Polsinelli, Chairman Russ Welsh and Shareholder Jack Kilroy, Jr. make history as they sign the steel beam at the "topping out ceremony" for Plaza Vista on June 20, 2012. Attorneys from the existing Plaza and downtown offices will move in to the firm's headquarters in the fall of 2013 and will bring a new vitality and energy to one of Kansas City's most important neighborhoods.

the years, were a series of popular forums focused on a planning agenda for Kansas City for the 21st century. Topics included education, revitalization of downtown and encouraging collaboration across the state line.

In 2012, the firm renewed its commitment to an informed public policy discourse by sponsoring a Public Policy Speakers series in conjunction with The Greater Kansas City Chamber of Commerce.

Polsinelli Shughart recognizes the important role of charitable contributions and pro bono client assistance. Over the years Polsinelli Shughart attorneys have chaired numerous civic and charitable organizations such as the American Red Cross, the March of Dimes and the Greater Kansas City Sports Commission, to name just a few.

Firm attorneys have also helped create important annual fundraisers such as "Treads and Threads" and the "Tour de BBQ," both benefitting the University of Kansas Cancer Center, as well as helping found important organizations such as the KCNext Technology Council. In addition to maintaining a commitment to pro bono client representation, Polsinelli Shughart supports an internal program called Volunteers Investing Service in our Neighborhoods (VISION), which encourages employees to volunteer their time at local food banks, community kitchens and shelters.

"Our attorneys' strong business perspective has helped our clients meet their goals. I am very proud to have been a part of the phenomenal success story of Polsinelli Shughart," said Welsh, the firm's chairman for the past 14 years.

Quality Hill Apartments

The motto for the renovation was "Preserve, Protect and Progress." It's hard to argue with the results. Quality Hill Apartments has been recognized both locally and nationally for the exceptional renovation.

Bruce Mathews

The historic Coates House, Located at 10th and Broadway is one of 21 buildings managed by CRES Management, L.L.C. The award winning Quality Hill Apartments offers their residents homes in a prime downtown location.

Located in Kansas City's most enduring historic neighborhood, **Quality Hill Apartments and Condominiums** is steeped in the city's charm and colorful past. The ground the development sits on is entrenched in history. Union soldiers lived in cavalry barracks on the grounds in 1897, and U.S. presidents frequently graced the Coates House Hotel.

Quality Hill Apartments and Condominiums is professionally managed by C.R.E.S. Management, L.L.C. The 382-unit property is situated on the west side of downtown and stretches over four city blocks, providing a beautiful community for Kansas City residents seeking a more urban lifestyle. The property consists of 21 residential mid-rise buildings, 11 of which are listed on the National Historic Register, and includes a YMCA Fitness Center.

The information center for Quality Hill Apartments is located at 1003 Broadway Blvd in The Coates House. The Coates House was formally known as the Coates House Hotel and is notable for the worst fire disaster in

Kansas City's history. The building was designed in 1857 by Kersey Coates, a prominent civic leader, who developed Quality Hill and founded the Kansas City Board of Trade.

The hotel didn't officially open its doors until 1868, after it had served as part of the Union Garrison Camp during the Civil War. The Coates House Hotel was considered one of the most prestigious hotels in Kansas City. Presidents Grover Cleveland,

Bruce Mathews

William McKinley and Theodore Roosevelt were among the distinguished guests that stayed at the hotel. The renovation of The Coates House was a major component in restoring the property to its Old World charm.

C.R.E.S. Management L.L.C. became part of the exciting adventure to revitalize downtown Kansas City when it acquired the property in February 2008. The acquisition of the property coincided with the 150th anniversary of the Quality Hill neighborhood and renovations, and rehabilitation projects stayed true to the character that set Quality Hill apart.

The motto for the renovation was "Preserve, Protect and Progress." It's hard to argue with the results. Quality Hill Apartments has been recognized both locally and nationally for the exceptional renovation. The Apartment Association of Kansas City voted Quality Hill Apartments "Property of the Year," and Multifamily Executive Magazine awarded the renovation "Project of the Year."

Today a beautifully restored information and amenity center occupy the space where the lobby once was. Quality Hill residents can now enjoy a game room, business center with complimentary Wi-Fi, a library and a lounge to socialize and meet their fellow downtowners.

A bronze plaque of designer Kersey Coates — on loan from the Historic Kansas City Foundation — sits among the fine furnishings and wonderful decor as a tribute to the building's original designer.

There were no "small" details when renovating the apartments themselves. Timeless materials such as brick, glass and tile blend seamlessly with the rich, organic warmth of renewable, natural woods, trims, and textures. The property is now a must-see thanks to updates such as new appliances, countertops and cabinetry.

C.R.E.S. Management, L.L.C., is honored to be the management company for Quality Hill Apartments. C.R.E.S. is a Kansas City-based firm with more than 30 years of expertise in the acquisition, development, renovation and management of multi-family properties. A well-known and respected leader in the real estate industry, C.R.E.S. owns and operates seven other properties in Kansas City as well as in communities in Indiana, Georgia and Texas.

The company strives to develop and renovate distinctive communities and to create homes for every lifestyle. Quality Hill's careful planning and attention to detail have made it a success story in the ongoing revitalization of the downtown core.

The Roasterie

Keeping the quality always at the highest standard, The Roasterie imports only 100-percent Arabica Specialty Grade coffees from more than 30 different producing countries.

Bruce Mathews

The O'Neill family and The Roasterie lead team on board the company DC-3 plane; a symbol of adventure and vision that represents The Roasterie brand.

On Nov. 22, 1978, as a high school foreign exchange student in Costa Rica, Danny O'Neill picked his first batch of coffee beans in the mountainous, coffee-growing region around the Poás volcano. Right then and there, he fell in love with the country, the people and the coffee — especially the coffee. Quality and customer service start with the company's vision, which is to "serve discerning customers by sourcing and roasting the world's finest coffee".

Fifteen years later, on Nov. 4, 1993, O'Neill founded **The Roasterie** in his basement in one of Kansas City's great neighborhoods, Brookside. His simple but bold mission is to "create extraordinary coffee experiences" by adopting these rules to live by: buy the best beans in the world, to roast them the best way known to man (air-roasting), and to deliver them as fast as humanly possible.

> *The aviation imagery also makes reference to seeking out the best coffee from anywhere in the world and refers to Kansas City's aviation history.*

In 2005, The Roasterie Café opened in Brookside at 6223 Brookside Blvd. Soon after, KC Magazine recognized the café as the "Best Coffee Shop" in Kansas City. Building on its success in Brookside, The Roasterie opened a second café at 4511 W. 119th St., Leawood, Kan. in 2010. The Roasterie Factory & Retail Store is located at 1204 W 27th St., Kansas City, and is a must-see destination for locals and visitors with free daily tours that include education on coffee, the air-roasting process, and much coffee sampling. This location was recently updated as part of a facility expansion that doubled the production capacity of the factory, added an event space, and mounted a real life DC-3 plane on top of the building.

With O'Neill's roots in farmer-friendly rural Iowa, it just made sense that he would partner directly with farmers and pay above market values to get the best of

Bruce Mathews

Carla O'Neill, General Manager of the three Roasterie Cafes, pictured here at the original Brookside location in Kansas City, MO.

the best coffee beans. His emphasis on direct trade and environmental responsibility has made The Roasterie a model for sustainable business practices in both the Kansas City community and the coffee industry.

Removing the middleman from the equation was just the beginning of The Roasterie's innovative history. Beans are roasted using a convection air-roasting method, instead of the more traditional drum-roasting method, to ensure superior consistency and a more flavorful, smoother cup of coffee.

To emphasize the air-roasting method, The Roasterie initiated a rebranding in 2010. The company's identity and packaging includes a DC-3 airplane, which has come to symbolize The Roasterie's belief in air-roasting. The aviation imagery also makes reference to seeking out the best coffee from anywhere in the world and refers to Kansas City's aviation history.

Keeping the quality always at the highest standard, The Roasterie imports only 100-percent Arabica Specialty Grade coffees from more than 30 different producing countries. Each coffee bean purchased by The Roasterie

has been picked by hand, and such attention to detail has paid off. Since January 2010, nine of The Roasterie's coffees have received a ranking of 90 or higher on CoffeeReview.com, the premier international coffee-buying guide.

The only thing that is as strong as The Roasterie's taste for great coffee is its passion for giving back to the communities that it loves. That's why it donates its products, time and resources to more than 150 local charities each year. In addition to the community events and sponsorships, The Roasterie sells dozens of custom-made blends where 10 percent of the proceeds are given back to local charities or non-profit organizations.

The Roasterie is the region's largest coffee roaster and producer that services espresso bars, coffeehouses, fine restaurants, high-end grocers, offices and retail accounts. Hundreds of different types of coffee and teas are available online at www.theroasterie.com, as well as merchandise. To ensure freshness, the company only roasts what is ordered, when it's ordered and offers same-day shipment.

Saint Luke's Health System

As a strong, locally owned and operated, spiritually based organization, Saint Luke's has a unique commitment to caring for patients and families.

From one small hospital to a system of 11, **Saint Luke's** has been at the heart of Kansas City since 1882, when All Saints Hospital, the predecessor to Saint Luke's Hospital, was founded. From the beginning, Saint Luke's has been known for innovation, quality, and compassion.

That innovation has helped Saint Luke's grow to become a nationally recognized health system with more than 1,300 licensed beds in 2011. As a strong, locally owned and operated, spiritually based organization, Saint Luke's has a unique commitment to caring for patients and families.

Saint Luke's Hospital opened at its current location near 44th and Wornall Road in 1923. The fire-proof, brick-and-terracotta structure faced Mill Creek and included state-of-the-art features for the time, including electrically operated dumbwaiters and a solarium on each floor.

The first century of Saint Luke's began in 1882, when the Rev. Henry David Jardine, an Episcopal priest, convened a meeting of businessmen in a small wooden church to discuss the need for better hospital care. The result was All Saints Hospital.

After 11 years, All Saints closed. It reopened a year later as Saint Luke's Hospital of Kansas City, and the first bishop of the new Episcopal Diocese of West Missouri assumed sponsorship. Today the diocese maintains that oversight, with the bishop serving as chairman of the hospital's board of directors.

From its beginning, Saint Luke's has focused on education, training future physicians and nurses. Saint Luke's College has educated more than 3,500 nurses over the years since 1903. Saint Luke's is primary teaching hospital of the University of Missouri-Kansas City School of Medicine.

Saint Luke's is known for its innovative care. In 1981, Saint Luke's opened the nation's first heart hospital, Saint Luke's Mid America Heart Institute. Today, it is recognized as one of the nation's finest cardiac facilities, earning worldwide acclaim for outcomes, innovation, and research.

Following the Heart Institute model, Saint Luke's created Saint Luke's Neuroscience Institute, a leader in the reversal of ischemic strokes.

Saint Luke's also offers comprehensive obstetric services and is a regional leader in cancer care, kidney and liver transplant and more.

Major expansions completed in 2010 and 2011 included new facilities for the Heart Institute, Ellen Hockaday Center for Women's Care, and Muriel I. Kauffman Women's Heart Center. A new home for the Neuroscience Institute opens in 2013.

Today Saint Luke's Hospital is one of the region's largest, with 600 beds and a medical staff of 600 physicians representing 60 specialties.

The hospital grows right along with Kansas City. From 1882 until 1989, Saint Luke's was just one facility.

In October 2011, Saint Luke's Hospital completed a major expansion featuring a new facility for Saint Luke's Mid America Heart Institute, the nation's first heart hospital. It includes spacious rooms equipped with the latest medical technology, comfortable accommodations for visitors, and hybrid surgery suites for increased collaborative care.

Now the health system includes 11 hospitals and 9,500 employees.

Expansion began in 1989 with the construction of Saint Luke's North Hospital-Barry Road in Platte County and the addition of Spelman Memorial Hospital, now called Saint Luke's North Hospital-Smithville.

Today the health system also includes:

- Saint Luke's East Hospital in Lee's Summit. East has doubled in size since its opening in 2005.

- Saint Luke's South Hospital in Overland Park, which opened in 1998 and is one of the busiest hospitals in Johnson County.

- Crittenton Children's Center, founded in 1896, specializing in caring for the emotional health of children and families.

- Saint Luke's Home Care, which includes Kansas City's oldest hospice, founded in 1975.

- Cabot Westside Medical & Dental Center, founded in 1906 to care for Kansas City's immigrant families, now providing bilingual/Spanish care and education.

- Saint Luke's also includes Wright Memorial Hospital in Trenton, Mo., Hedrick Medical Center in Chillicothe, Mo., Anderson County Hospital in Garnett, Kan., and Cushing Memorial Hospital in Leavenworth, Kan.

From its humble beginnings, Saint Luke's has grown to become one of the region's largest employers. But despite this rapid growth, Saint Luke's has maintained its vision of delivering exceptional care. From honors like the Malcolm Baldrige National Quality Award to leading the region in patient satisfaction, Saint Luke's has always been dedicated to quality. The health system is also consistently recognized among the best places to work in Kansas City.

Sprint

With its relentless drive to continually set new standards of excellence, Sprint has been a game-changing force in creating advanced network capabilities, groundbreaking Internet Protocol (IP) and wireless applications and unprecedented mobility solutions.

In 1999, Sprint firmly planted its roots in the Kansas City area with the completion of a 200-acre campus headquarters in Overland Park. Large enough to have its own ZIP code and providing nearly 4 million square feet of office space, the campus features walking trails, restorative prairie grass, 6,000 trees and an 8-acre lake.

When times get tough, the tough get going. Sprint's founder, Cleyson LeRoy (C.L.) Brown, was a dreamer who refused to let adversity stop him. As the 19th century was coming to a close, he lost an arm in a farming accident. Far from being discouraged, his response was to start a local telephone company in nearby Abilene, Kan., and personally build it into a wide-ranging corporation with operating companies across many states. The legacy of Brown's aspiring spirit and unflagging determination has carried forward to this day.

Brown's story reminds us that bold innovation and cutting-edge technology sometimes begin with very deep and storied roots.

Bold innovation has always been the cornerstone of Sprint's foundation. And, considering the company was created before Henry T. Ford unveiled the Model T or the first airplane flight by the Wright brothers, one can't help but recognize Sprint for pioneering and shepherding that innovation through more than a century of technology evolution. In fact, in 2012, Sprint ranked as one of America's top 100 companies for issued patents.

Today, Sprint is a nimble, Fortune 100, industry-leading wireless company offering a comprehensive range of wireless and wireline communications services to consumers, businesses and government users. Widely

Cleyson LeRoy (C.L.) Brown began the Sprint legacy by starting a local telephone company in nearby Abilene, Kan. in 1899.

recognized for developing, engineering and deploying innovative technologies, Sprint offers industry-leading mobile data services, leading prepaid brands, instant national and international push-to-talk capabilities and a global tier 1 internet backbone.

Sprint's enduring mission of providing a simple, enriching and productive customer experience has never been more important to the company, its employees and the communities it serves. In 2012, the American Customer Satisfaction Index rated Sprint number one among all national carriers in customer satisfaction and most improved, across all 47 industries studied, during the last four years.

Decades ago, Sprint represented the combined achievements of many legendary predecessors, including United Telecommunications, US Sprint and Centel.

Each embraced the same bold approach that Sprint's founder Brown showed in 1899, when the Brown Telephone Company successfully went toe-to-toe with the Bell monopoly in Abilene. By the mid-1970s, the company's aggressive growth strategies had firmly established it as the nation's largest independent local telephone provider.

When long distance opened to competition in the 1980s, Sprint immediately seized the opportunity. By 1986, Sprint led all United States telecom companies by completing the first nationwide, 100 percent digital, fiber-optic network. At the same time, the company was a pioneer in data communications, establishing the world's third largest commercial packet data network in 1980.

Sprint charged into the 1990s with pacesetting moves for both consumers and businesses. The company that gave America pin-drop clarity also became a global leader in voice and data services.

A new kind of telecom company emerged in 1993 when Sprint and Centel merged to become a unique provider of local, wireless and long distance services. Sprint took its wireless strategy a big step further in the late '90s by building the only nationwide Personal Communications Services (PCS) network in the United States in 1996.

In 1999, Sprint firmly planted its roots in the Kansas City area with the completion of a 200-acre campus headquarters in Overland Park. Large enough to have its own ZIP code and providing nearly 4 million square feet of office space, the campus features walking trails, restorative prairie grass, 6,000 trees and an 8-acre lake. Sustainable efforts such as recycling, promoting "greener" transportation and using wind-powered electricity have all made the Sprint Campus one of the most environmentally-responsible campuses in the country.

Sprint continued to innovate with a number of industry firsts in 2002, including becoming the first carrier to complete a 3G wireless network upgrade, launch GPS-enabled devices, mobile streaming video, over-the-air downloads and the first camera phone in the United States.

In 2005, Sprint merged with Nextel, a leader in walkie-talkie technology using the Integrated Digital Enhanced Network (iDEN) network platform. Today, this important push-to-talk service has evolved into a code division multiple access (CDMA) technology-based service called Sprint Direct Connect. Launched in 2011, this service provides broadband data capabilities, familiar

By1986, Sprint led all United States telecom companies by completing the first nationwide, 100 percent digital, fiber-optic network.

Sprint

push-to-talk features, rugged and reliable handsets and nationwide coverage.

In 2008, Sprint was the first national U.S. wireless carrier to launch WiMAX, a 4G wireless technology, and a game-changer in wireless technology for the United States.

But improved call quality and faster data speeds were only one proverbial cog in the ever-turning wheel of technology when it came to providing a quality customer experience. In 2008, Sprint also began offering the industry's first unlimited plan for voice, text and data — Simply Everything.

It then followed with more industry innovations around simplicity and value like unlimited data plans and Ready Now, the industry's first one-on-one customized smartphone set-up and education process at the retail store.

Today, wireless is arguably the most important industry in the world. Globally, there are more mobile phones in use today than televisions, personal computers and automobiles – combined. Sprint has continued to offer solutions to help its customers live less stressful lives with the first mobile payment solution in 2010. In 2012 it launched the first mobile security and safety applications in the industry.

In 2012, Sprint embarked upon a major upgrade to its network and began a build-out of a next-generation network, using Long Term Evolution (LTE) technology.

Just as C.L. Brown was committed to important causes of his day, Sprint also realizes it has a corporate social responsibility to the communities where people work and live.

Sprint has been at the forefront of recycling efforts in

Kansas City-based employees volunteered 21,000 hours in 2011 to various local non-profit organizations.

the wireless industry and has launched four eco-friendly devices since its first device in 2009, which was made of corn-based bio-plastic with a solar-charging battery cover. In 2011, Sprint was ranked third in Newsweek's environmental ranking of America's largest corporations, the highest among U.S. telecom companies, for its efforts to reduce its carbon footprint and energy costs from virtually every aspect of its business.

Through the years, Sprint's commitment to its hometown has never wavered and the 7,000 people that live, work and play in the Kansas City community share that commitment. Kansas City-based employees volunteered 21,000 hours in 2011 to various local non-profit organizations.

Through the Sprint Foundation, corporate and employee giving, non-profit sponsorships and memberships, Sprint contributed $3.5 million to local Kansas City philanthropic initiatives and partnerships in 2011. The company also sponsors many arts, cultural and athletic institutions, including the Kansas City Chiefs, the Kansas City Royals, Sporting Kansas City, Starlight Theatre and the Sprint Center.

With its relentless drive to continually set new standards of excellence, Sprint has been a game-changing force in creating advanced network capabilities, groundbreaking Internet Protocol (IP) and wireless applications and unprecedented mobility solutions.

Sprint values its employees, customers and supports the environment and community. History has shown that the concepts of simplicity, value and commitment to creating the best possible customer experience continue to ring true for Sprint.

Swope Community Enterprises

Since 1969, Swope Community Enterprises has been dedicated to improving the health of their neighbors and surrounding neighborhoods.

Left, Dr. Tinka Barnes reviews a patient's medical history at Swope Health South, which opened its doors in December 2010 and provides much-needed medical services to South Kansas City. Right, E. Frank Ellis, Chairman, Swope Community Enterprises. Below, SCB constructed the Twin Elms Senior Housing Complex to accommodate the needs of low-to moderate-income senior residents. This tax credit senior housing development has been recognized for its art deco design and amenities.

E. Frank Ellis and his dedicated board were not going to sit back and watch the working poor of Kansas City fall through the cracks of the health care system.

In 1969, with seed money from the Lyndon Johnson Administration's Model Cities program, a clinic opened in the basement of Metropolitan Missionary Baptist Church. That first year, with a budget of $100,000 and 20 employees, Swope Community Enterprises (SCE) served 2,000 patients. This was the genesis for the integral public safety net provider now known today as **Swope Health Services (SHS).**

Since 1969, both Swope Community Enterprises and Swope Health Services have been dedicated to improving the health of their neighbors and surrounding neighborhoods. The operating budget for SHS is now $40 million with 500 employees, serving some 40,000 patients.

But treating the physical body wasn't enough.

Mental illness and drug and alcohol dependency were crippling the inner city's core. In 1980, a comprehensive mental health center was added to SHS so that the behavioral and chemical issues that impacted the lives of their patients could be addressed.

From this beginning emerged comprehensive ambulatory services that include psychiatric and psychological outpatient services, day treatment services, residential treatment services, specialized services for

With more than 155,000 square feet of retail space and an investment of more than $35 million dollars, The Shops on Blue Parkway offer first-rate services and products to Kansas City residents.

children and adolescents and substance abuse treatment and prevention services.

Now, primary care and mental health staff were able to work together to develop and deliver a pioneering holistic model that embraced both the physical and mental health needs of their patients. But the model was not yet complete for SCE leaders, who identified another gap in care: the health of the environments in which their patients lived. What good did it do their substance abuse patients if, once treated, they returned to a neighborhood plagued with crack houses and gang violence?

This realization led to the development of Swope Community Builders (SCB), a nonprofit community development corporation dedicated to transforming the physical, economic and social landscape of deteriorating urban areas in Kansas City. Since 1991, SCB has provided a broad spectrum of community building services including affordable housing and commercial development, neighborhood planning, community

The Shops on Blue Parkway have been recognized with a Cornerstone Award from the Economic Development Corporation of Kansas City for its contribution to the city's economic growth.

organizing and community relations programs.

In addition to transforming the physical landscape of several urban neighborhoods, SCB and its staff have been recognized nationally as a catalyst for strengthening civic investment, building social networks and enhancing economic opportunities within neighborhoods. Through private and public partnerships, the organization successfully stretches limited resources to provide solutions for struggling neighborhoods.

Through the years, these SCE affiliates have grown in scope and influence. Today, SHS serves more than 40,000 patients annually at 11 medical, dental, and behavioral health/residential treatment centers located throughout the greater metropolitan area including Kansas City, Independence, Kansas City North, South Kansas City and Wyandotte County, Kansas. Its main facility, Swope Health Central, was built on land reclaimed from a blighted flood plain in a neighborhood ignored by development for 40 years, and acts as an economic catalyst for ongoing development in the Brush Creek

Today, SHS serves more than 40,000 patients annually at 11 medical, dental, and behavioral health/residential treatment centers located throughout the greater metropolitan area

corridor.

To date, SCB has invested more than $200 million in infrastructure improvements along Brush Creek, one of Kansas City, Missouri's most critical corridors, including several office projects such as the award-winning Blue Parkway Office Building, and the H&R Block Service Center, the first Fortune 500 Company to invest in Kansas City's urban core. SCB staff has also completed more than 550 housing units and 162,000 square feet of commercial retail development.

Most recently, SCB opened the East Village Apartments located at 950 Holmes Street of Kansas City, Missouri. This is the first project launched by SCB to redevelop the East Village area in Downtown Kansas City, Missouri. The project, which is part of the East Village redevelopment plan, has transformed a former parking lot into a 50-unit apartment building that provides quality

Swope Community Builders opened East Village Apartments, located at 950 Holmes Street, in November 2011. The project transformed a parking lot into a 50-unit, high-quality apartment complex for low and mid-income families.

EAST VILLAGE APARTMENTS

Developer	Swope Community Builders
Owner	Swope Community Builders MI LP
Architect	Pendulum Studio
Civil Engineer/Surveyor	Taliaferro & Browne, Inc.
MEP Engineer	BGR Consulting Engineers
Structural Engineer	DuBois Consultants, Inc.
Construction Manager	JE Dunn Construction
Project Manager	Radford Management Services
Financing	US Bank CDC
	Missouri Housing Development Commission
City Leadership	Mark Funkhouser, Mayor
	Sharon Sanders Brooks, Chair of Housing Comm

Deb Hermann	Bill Skaggs
Ed Ford	Russ Johnson
Melba Curls	Jan Marcason
Beth Gottstein	Terry Riley
Cathy Jolly	John Sharp
Cindy Circo	

Acting City Manager, Troy Schulte
Assistant City Manager, Bob Langenkamp
Housing Director, Shirley Winn
Planned Industrial Expansion Authority
The KC EDC TIF Commission

Pendulum studio

For Leasing Information ca
816-861-407(

Managed by: DALMAR

SWOPE COMMUNITY BUILDERS℠
Member Swope Community Enterprises

The East Village project is a key component of downtown Kansas City, Mo.'s revitalization. Swope Community Builders is working to ensure that the quality of life for all urban core residents will be enhanced through the $4.5 billion invested in the city's renaissance.

housing for low and mid-income families.

With an eye toward adding services for the elderly in both Kansas and Missouri, SCE has just this year added a new affiliate to its family of companies, Kansas City Home Care, Inc., founded by gerontologist Cheryl Smith. As a care manager for the elderly and the disabled, Cheryl was unimpressed with the quality of home care being provided to her clients. Out of necessity to provide excellent service to her clients, Smith opened the doors of Kansas City Home Care in 1989. Now the area industry leader, Kansas City Home Care specializes in providing excellent home care services with a focus on quality and reliability.

"By combining the services of all of our entities," said E. Frank Ellis, "we're able to accomplish our

vision, which is to see 'self-empowered, healthy people in healthy communities.' Our diverse staff works in a team-based, problem-solving environment where they're encouraged to reach their full potential. We also actively involve members of the community, and we value their participation in solving problems."

SCE has built a reputation for honest, trustworthy, morally responsible actions that support mutually beneficial relationships. The very nature of this organization involves their staff daily in service to the community. From health care to community development and urban planning, Swope Community Enterprises is actively improving Kansas City one person, one family, one neighborhood at a time.

The Harry S. Truman Library and Museum

The library houses Truman's presidential papers, as well as those related to his career in the United States Senate and Jackson County government. The collection also includes the papers of numerous cabinet members, political associates and family members, along with nearly 40,000 artifacts.

Bruce Mathews

As evidence of the enduring legacy of President Truman, his presidential library frequently is the site for national and international media events, including veterans ceremonies, public programs by top state & Federal officials, even the outgoing message to the world by former U.N. Secretary-General Kofi Annan.

Following nearly eight years as president of the United States, Harry S. Truman returned to his hometown of Independence, Mo., in January 1953. He and wife Bess settled into the same stately Victorian Era home at 219 Delaware St. that they had occupied for more than 25 years before Truman became the nation's 33rd president.

Once he returned to Independence, Truman decided to place his presidential library within a few blocks of his home, on property donated by the city of Independence. Meanwhile, the former president was provided office space at the Federal Reserve building in downtown Kansas City.

Groundbreaking for the new **Harry S. Truman Library and Museum** took place on Truman's birthday,

May 8, 1955, and construction began immediately. The first phase of the new presidential library, only the second such facility in a new federal system operated by the National Archives and Records Administration, was financed with $1.7 million raised by a private organization.

The library was dedicated on July 6, 1957, with U.S. Supreme Chief Court Justice Earl Warren providing a dedication address. Former President Herbert Hoover and former First Lady Eleanor Roosevelt were among the VIPs in attendance.

The new library would eventually house Truman's presidential papers, as well as those related to his career in the United States Senate and Jackson County government. The collection now includes the papers of numerous cabinet members, political associates and family members, along with nearly 40,000 artifacts.

Researchers began using the new library in 1959, and school groups, civic organizations and tourists visited the library in ever-increasing numbers. In the early years, researchers and visitors often were greeted by the former president himself.

Over the years, the library has been expanded several times, most recently in 2010. The exhibits are now highly interactive and reflect the latest in museum technology. In addition, millions of people throughout the world conduct research and enjoy virtual visits to the Truman Library by logging on to its website, www.trumanlibrary.org.

The same year the library was dedicated, a private not-for-profit organization was incorporated in Missouri to "encourage, foster and assist the growth and development of the Harry S. Truman Library as a national center for study and research."

This organization was the Harry S. Truman Library Institute for National and International Affairs, and it was modeled on the University of Kansas Endowment Fund, another not-for-profit supporting a public entity. Early members of the institute's board included Truman, former Secretary of State Dean Acheson and former Presidential Advisor Averell Harriman.

Photos by Bruce Mathews

Since its opening in 1957, the museum has welcomed more than a half a million visitors. Pulitzer Prize-winning author David McCullough has said that "you can understand more about our nation by spending a day...at the Truman Library than anywhere else in the country."

For more than five decades, the institute has supported research and publishing activities, exhibits and public programs. Many individuals, corporations and foundations in the Kansas City region, across the nation, and in foreign countries have generously contributed to the institute's mission.

There are now 13 presidential libraries in the system of the National Archives and Records Administration, but none provide visitors with the historical scope and depth as the exhibits at the Harry S. Truman Library and Museum. In a recent article, the Dallas Morning News stated that the Truman facility is "America's best Presidential Museum."

Truman Medical Centers (TMC)

As the primary teaching hospital for the University of Missouri-Kansas City School of Medicine, TMC is particularly distinguished for its expertise in management of chronic diseases, women's health, orthopaedics, family medicine and trauma services.

At **Truman Medical Centers** (TMC), care is given to those with the best insurance and those with none at all.

TMC's mission is simple: to provide accessible, state-of-the-art health care to the community — Jackson County and Kansas City, Mo. — regardless of one's ability to pay.

Employing more than 4,200 people, TMC is a vital component of Kansas City's health care system, providing two acute care hospitals and a comprehensive adult mental health facility, in addition to primary care clinics and other outreach services.

TMC admits nearly 20,000 patients and handles more than 320,000 medical outpatient visits and 220,000 mental health visits annually. TMC's emergency room treats more than 100,000 patients annually.

As the primary teaching hospital for the University of Missouri-Kansas City School of Medicine, TMC is particularly distinguished for its expertise in management of chronic diseases, women's health, orthopaedics, family medicine and trauma services.

Last year, TMC provided nearly $130 million in uncompensated primary, specialty and inpatient care to the uninsured and many other lower-income people. The medical center serves a diverse group of vulnerable populations and provides critically important services that might otherwise be absent.

While shouldering this responsibility, TMC holds itself highly accountable for providing the highest possible standards of care. "We are tremendously proud of the quality of care and services our patients receive. It is the result of the innovation, teamwork, compassion and

TMC

TMC Hospital Hill, located on the southern edge of Kansas City's downtown area, is a vital part of the region's healthcare delivery system, with a strong tradition of clinical excellence.

attention to detail that is at the heart of the TMC culture," says John W. Bluford, TMC president and CEO.

TMC's distinguished service record includes delivering more than one-third of all babies born in Jackson County; offering a combined capacity of nearly 600 beds, including 92 inpatient mental health beds and 188 long-term care beds, and, providing 30 on-site language interpreters in Spanish, Somali and Arabic. In addition, TMC provides translation services for 150 languages through CyraCom, a translation service for healthcare.

In the last several years, TMC has been nationally recognized as:

- Healthcare's Most Wired, 2011 and 2012 by Hospitals & Health Networks Magazine

TMC

Located in the rolling hills of Eastern Jackson County, TMC Lakewood is a full-service medical campus featuring a spacious community hospital as well as a long-term care facility.

- One of Kansas City's Top Ten Companies by KC Business magazine, 2009 and 2012
- One of the top three healthiest employers by the Kansas City Business Journal, 2011 and 2012.
- A top provider of outpatient mental health care with the 2009 National Association of Public Hospitals and Health Systems' (NAPH) President's Award for Vulnerable Populations
- Quality Oncology Practice Initiative Certification Program: TMC Hospital Hill Outpatient Oncology Care Certification
- A National Center of Excellence in Women's Health by the Department of Health and Human Services
- A Level III Patient-Centered Medical Home by the National Committee for Quality Assurance (NCQA)

Truman Medical Centers' corporate vision of "leading the way to a healthy community" is reflected in several innovative programs.

"While our mission, of course, is to care for the sick, we strive to help those in our community live in a healthy

TMC was voted one of Kansas City's Top Ten Companies by KC Business magazine in 2009 and 2012.

manner, so they are less likely to get sick," says Bluford.

The Healthy Harvest Produce Market and the Healthy Harvest Mobile Market bring good nutrition to areas of Kansas City's urban core considered "food deserts." The produce market is open every Wednesday, April through October, on the TMC Hospital Hill campus. The Mobile Market is on the road every Tuesday and Thursday. Both offer fresh fruits and vegetables at lower-than-retail prices.

TMC and the Kansas City Chiefs are in a long-term partnership to improve the health of the Kansas City community through health fairs and high-energy educational events.

By taking care of the soul as well as the body, the Truman Center for the Healing Arts program has grown to include several venues within our system and features more than 400 pieces of permanent and long-term loaned art, as well as monthly musical concerts at both TMC campuses.

For more information about TMC, please visit *tmcmed.org*.

UMB Financial Corporation

What began as a storefront bank with first-day deposits of $1,100 in 1913 has grown to become a diversified financial services holding company with multi-billion dollar assets.

The story of **UMB Financial Corporation** and its founders — the Kemper family — is a success story in the best tradition of American free enterprise. What began as a storefront bank with first-day deposits of $1,100 in 1913 has grown to become a diversified financial services holding company with multi-billion dollar assets.

Looking forward to celebrating 100 successful years in 2013, UMB Financial Corporation has grown to be recognized among the nation's most respected financial institutions. Additionally, the Kemper family strongly maintains its century-old commitment to the historic preservation and persistent growth of the Kansas City community.

As UMB expands its footprint across the United States, it is creating and investing in leading-edge technology within the financial industry, ensuring it services future generations of tech-savvy customers. Before diving into where UMB plans to head in the next 100 years, it's important to know the rich history behind how it all started.

The Beginning. The first UMB Bank was chartered as City Center Bank during World War I by William Thorton Kemper — the first to establish the Kemper name in what would be generations of Kemper bankers in the Midwest.

R. Crosby Kemper Sr. became president of the bank in 1919, making his mark by vigorously growing the bank under his unique leadership style and innovative ideas for providing banking services. He actively solicited business

In 1931, the bank offered a new modern banking service, the Automobile Deposit Window, thought to be the first drive-up bank in the nation.

in the community at the close of regular business hours each day. An extrovert at heart, Kemper Sr. would get out in the lobby and visit with customers. He could also be found walking around downtown greeting and visiting with anyone and everyone on the block.

While many banks would simply open their doors and wait for customers to approach them, he proactively recruited his customers. These tactics worked, and the bank steadily grew by establishing the need for a trust department, bond department and correspondent banking services.

In 1931, the bank added a "drive-up" window, which is believed to be the first in the country. Through the 1930s, the bank expanded again and became City National Bank and Trust Company, moving its headquarters to the heart of Kansas City's downtown financial center. This building at 928 Grand Blvd. is still owned by the bank today. In 1945, an international department was added to service customer needs in the field of international commerce and travel.

Seeing the bank through several challenging economic cycles, such as the Great Depression and World War II, R. Crosby Kemper Sr. undoubtedly made his mark among the generations of Kemper bankers to come.

Expansion and Innovation. Another generation of Kempers, R. Crosby Kemper Jr., became the bank president in 1959 and guided it to become the first regional bank to install its own computer processing center in 1960. By 1971, "United" was added to the holding company Missouri Bancshares to create a common corporate identity in urban markets and throughout the state, and "UMB" was born.

R. Crosby Kemper Jr. was a steadfast leader through arguably the widest range of industry and economic change in UMB history. Regarded as the newest "expansion driver" of the company, his legacy was marked by boom and bust cycles through the '70s, '80s, '90s and early 2000s. Whether it was the oil crisis of the 1970s, the rise and fall of the dot-com era, millennium uncertainty or post-September 11 tragedies, UMB maintained a slow and steady rise.

Even as other banks stumbled during the 1980s, Kemper's cautious habits kept the bank strong. A new 255,800-square-foot UMB headquarters building began construction in 1984 on the lot bounded by Grand Avenue, 11th and Walnut streets

As federal banking regulations changed throughout the 1980s, UMB ventured into interstate banking with a series of acquisitions well into the 1990s. During this time, the bank expanded to southern Illinois, St. Louis, Colorado, and areas throughout Kansas.

In 1994, the bank's name was changed to UMB Financial Corporation, better suiting the multi-bank holding company offering a growing product line throughout the states of Missouri, Illinois, Colorado and Kansas. Further expansion continued into the mid-1990s with the addition of bank locations in Oklahoma and an increase in ATMs to include popular convenience stores as well as new grocery stores throughout the footprint.

In 1999, UMB opened a 200,000-square-foot technology center in downtown Kansas City, consolidating under one roof its internal operations and management information functions. It also launched eScout, a business-to-business e-commerce network that connects small and midsize businesses in a virtual marketplace.

A Company of Firsts. UMB made Midwest banking history in 1995 by becoming one of the first banks to offer an online banking product. Customers now had the

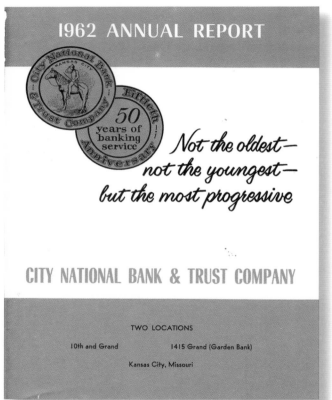

City National Bank & Trust Company, 1962 Annual Report. The bank celebrated its 50th Anniversary in 1962. UMB will commemorate 100 years in 2013.

(Left to Right) UMB Financial Corporation executives Mariner Kemper, chairman and CEO; Peter J. deSilva, president and chief operating officer and Mike Hagedorn, vice chairman, chief financial officer and chief administrative officer.

chance to pay bills, reconcile accounts and transfer funds between accounts all from their own computers.

Continuing to blaze trails in financial services technology, UMB was the first bank in the United States to create a Web Electronic Data Interchange (EDI) service for its commercial customers, which made business communication and document exchange easier than ever before. Familiar with making firsts, UMB also became the first bank in the country to engage in a successful public test of its most common deposit transaction systems for "Year 2000" readiness.

The New Millennium. UMB introduced a new home equity loan product in 2002; received a gold award in Ingram's Best of Business Kansas City listing as "Best

Bank," as well as placed second in Kansas City Business Journal's Top 25 Commercial Lending Banks ranking.

An end of an era came in 2002, when UMB Bank's time and temperature line shut down. The telephone number, 816-844 and any combination of four numbers, was a local institution for 58 years. In honor of UMB's 90th anniversary, R. Crosby Kemper III opened trading on the NASDAQ Stock Market on April 23, 2003.

After 54 years of leadership, R. Crosby Kemper Jr. retired as senior chairman from the company and its board of directors in October 2004. Upon his retirement, UMB Financial Corporation had $7 billion in assets and operations in Missouri, Illinois, Colorado, Kansas, Oklahoma and Nebraska.

UMB LEED-certified banking center in Prairie Village, KS.

In 2004, Mariner Kemper took the lead as chairman and CEO of UMB Financial Corporation and Peter deSilva was named president and chief operating officer. The following year Michael Hagedorn joined UMB as executive vice president and chief financial officer. Under their leadership, UMB has weathered the economic storms that rocked the financial services industry from 2008 and into the present day.

A lot can happen in 100 years: booms, recessions, inventions, reinventions and more. The last 100 years

> *What started as a small, one-man operation has turned into a steadfast banking model that is still upheld by the company's leadership nearly a century later.*

have made UMB who they are today. What started as a small, one-man operation has turned into a steadfast banking model that is still upheld by the company's leadership nearly a century later.

While UMB continues to thrive and build its business across the United States, the company remains faithfully dedicated to its genuine interest in making Kansas City better than it has ever been and a memorable place where families will continue to grow and prosper for generations to come.

UMKC

The vision, the commitment and the resolve of the Depression-era founders lives on today at a great university immersed in the life, the hopes and the dreams of a great city.

In the midst of the Great Depression, Kansas City focused on solutions that would build up the community. They created a university the city could call its own.

At the onset of the Great Depression — when many Americans were overcome with shock and despair — the people of Kansas City demonstrated uncommon foresight and resolve.

Recognizing that education would be a critical factor in reversing the economic collapse, civic leaders focused on a bold concept: a university that Kansas City could call its own. Their vision was for an institution of higher learning that would both meet national and international standards, and also be a truly local partner and cornerstone for the community's growth and development for generations to come.

In 1929, local leaders chartered the University of Kansas City (UKC). The first class of 264 students met on opening day, Oct. 2, 1933.

UKC quickly became the focal point of higher education for the community. By 1960, pre-existing Kansas City-based law, dental and pharmacy schools, and a music conservatory, had merged into the burgeoning university as it grew into the role of primary educator for the city's professional workforce.

A vision born of resolve in the face of adversity had become a successful reality.

UKC becomes UMKC. Over the years, UKC added programs and increased its enrollment. Despite the growth, however, UKC lacked sizeable endowments to provide financial stability, and merged with the University of Missouri in 1963, becoming the University of Missouri-Kansas City (UMKC).

Today, housing and classroom expansion barely keep

pace with enrollment. UMKC has grown from 12,000 students in 2000 to over 16,000 welcomed in August 2012. The majority of our students are from the Kansas City area, and 60 percent of our graduates stay in the city to live and work.

UMKC has grown in stature as well. The university attracts tens of millions of dollars annually in research funding. UMKC's accomplished faculty and students regularly earn scholarly awards of national stature. Conservatory Music Composition Professor Zhou Long composed the Pulitzer Prize-winning opera "Madame White Snake." Numerous other UMKC faculty and students have earned Guggenheim, Fulbright and other prestigious scholarships and fellowships.

The Henry W. Bloch School of Management is widely recognized as one of the top business schools in the world, and its world-class expertise in entrepreneurship is key to Kansas City's goal to become "America's Most Entrepreneurial City".

In 2012, the school was ranked No. 1 in the world for innovation management research. The MBA entrepreneurship focus was selected as a national model program. Both the graduate and undergraduate entrepreneurship programs were ranked in the top 25 by the Princeton Review. The Master of Public Administration Nonprofit Management emphasis area at the Bloch School was ranked No. 15 in the nation for 2013 by US News and World Report.

The new student union building is the hub for an active and vibrant campus lifestyle encompassing academics, activism, performing arts, Division I intercollegiate sports, and more.

> *UMKC's accomplished faculty and students regularly earn scholarly awards of national stature.*

Serving the Community. As an urban-serving university, UMKC has always recognized that community involvement is a vital aspect of our mission. The medical faculty practice in the city's hospitals, and their research studies provide access for local patients to clinical trials on the cutting edge of modern medicine.

The dental school's clinic provides care to underserved populations. The School of Education has a national reputation as a leader in culturally responsive teaching, an approach that adjusts teaching methods to fit the diverse backgrounds of students. Programs ranging from music and dance to engineering and science conduct regular outreach programs to the young people of the community.

The vision, the commitment and the resolve of the Depression-era founders lives on today at a great university immersed in the life, the hopes and the dreams of a great city. This is the University of Missouri-Kansas City — where arts and ideas flourish, where medical and entrepreneurial innovations are born, and where young minds tap their potential. This is Kansas City's university.

Union Station

The station draws tourists from all over the world who marvel at the Grand Hall's 95-foot ceiling, three 3,500-pound chandeliers and the 6-foot-wide clock hanging in the station's central arch.

There is no place in Kansas City — or in any city — quite like **Union Station**. This magnificently restored train station now houses not only Amtrak services, but an innovative science museum. It was called "the gateway of the west" by President Woodrow Wilson at its opening in 1914.

Today, it is Kansas City's most prominent destination for civic, cultural and entertainment activities.

Union Station will celebrate its 100th anniversary in October 2014. As one of Kansas City's oldest and most iconic buildings, Union Station is now home to many important organizations, such as the Greater Kansas City Chamber of Commerce. It continues to serve as Kansas City's civic center and the central gathering place for inspiring community and cultural events.

The Building of Union Station Kansas City.
To create this one-of-a-kind train station, architect Jarvis Hunt drew inspiration from ancient Greek and Roman design at a time when efforts were being made to beautify the urban environment with green parks, gracious boulevards and noble architecture.

When Hunt designed Union Station, he believed

that the beautiful buildings could bring about social change. Hunt also designed railroad stations in Oakland, Calif., Jolliet, Ill. and Dallas. But it is Kansas City's Union Station, one of Hunt's finest designs, that was the capstone of his career.

Following three years of construction to create this historic monument, Union Station opened on Oct. 30, 1914. The grand opening created tremendous fanfare and the greatest crowd that ever gathered at one time in Kansas City for an event of this nature.

Union Station encompasses a 17-acre site and includes 850,000 square feet inside the building, which originally featured 900 rooms. In its prime as a working train station, the building accommodated tens of thousands of passengers every year.

At its peak during World War II, an estimated 1 million travelers passed through the station. The north waiting room could hold 10,000 people and the complex included restaurants, a cigar store, barber shop, railroad offices, the nation's largest railway express building and a powerhouse providing steam and power.

Following a steep decline in train travel during the 1950-60s, Union Station began to experience its own decline as well. In 1972, Union Station was placed on the National Register of Historic Places, yet few people were coming through the Station at that time. By 1989, no tenants remained at Union Station, as Amtrak had moved to a building on Main Street.

The Station sat empty and neglected for many years, barely escaping demolition on several occasions.

Restoring this Historic Landmark. After several years of being embroiled in a lawsuit with Trizec Corporation, a Canadian firm originally given the task of redeveloping the property, the city finally was able to establish the Union Station Assistance Corporation in 1994 and renovation began. The Kansas City Museum decided to house Science City inside of Union Station as a primary public attraction.

In 1996, a historic bi-state initiative was passed by voters in four counties — three in Missouri and one in Kansas. This was the only bi-state tax ever funded in the United States. This short-term tax provided $118 million in funding to restore Union Station and provide the shell to build Science City. An additional $100 million in private donations and $40 million in federal funding secured the additional money necessary to fund the station's renovation, which was completed in 1999.

On Nov.10, 1999, Union Station re-opened with great anticipation after being closed for 16 years. Its beautifully patterned marble floors had been returned to their original luster. The spectacular 95-foot high ceiling was cleaned and repainted to its original red, blue and gold hues. The clock, the chandelier and the oak leaf plaster ornamentation were all restored to the way they were on opening day in 1914.

Union Station Today. After nearly 100 years, Union Station continues to serve its essential purpose as a popular and thriving destination for the surrounding community. The meticulously restored facility is open to the public for viewing at no charge.

In 2001, Science City opened at Union Station, with the dream of becoming a world-class science museum.

A Feb. 20, 2012, Kansas City Star article reported that, "This will be a big year for Science City. A 'floating' orb to demonstrate planetary science opens next month, soon to be followed by an activity room devoted to the basic principles of engineering, a bigger version of last year's inventors' extravaganza called the Maker Faire, and a new exhibit designed by budding scientists at Olathe North High School."

Today, through Science City, Union Station is the community's connection point for science and technology, offering students greater learning opportunities for science, technology, engineering and math (STEM) education through Science City, and helping students network with and learn from the business community through a variety of annual STEM-related events.

As Kansas City's science center, Science City continues to advance by continuing to add new interactive exhibits, and a large variety of programs and offerings for students. This is thanks to key investments from Burns & McDonnell and other corporations and foundations.

Union Station's traditional office space is fully leased to key civic and business organizations that are a central part of connecting our community. As a result, Union Station has become the meeting place among the critical business and entrepreneurial organizations working to advance new business growth in our community.

Other Union Station's attractions include:

- A showcase for the Smithsonian Institution and other high-profile traveling museum exhibits;
- The state-of-the-art Arvin Gottlieb Planetarium, offering digital planetary shows in a 360 degree dome;
- A model railroad train exhibit and the KC Rail Experience.
- An entertainment district that includes the H & R Block City Stage for live theater and the region's largest screen (5-story high) movie theater, upgraded in 2012 to a 3-D digital theater experience;
- Harvey's and Pierpont restaurants, Parisi's Artisan Coffee and Rocky Mountain Chocolate Factory; and The Science City Adventure Store and The Kansas City Store.

Union Station's restoration helped to stimulate more than $600 million in private economic development in a seven-block area surrounding the station. In 2006, a central connection happened when a former railroad bridge that crossed the river was moved to connect Union Station with the Crossroads District and downtown Kansas City.

Known today as the Michael R. Haverty Freight House Bridge, this pedestrian walkway is a central connector for Kansas Citians and tourists to get to and from downtown and to spur business growth between the

two areas.

The station draws tourists from all over the world who marvel at the Grand Hall's 95-foot ceiling, three 3,500-pound chandeliers and the 6-foot-wide clock hanging in the station's central arch. And just like in 1914, passengers can catch the trains at Union Station's Amtrak stop, as Union Station continues to be one of the few large operating train stations in America.

Union Station Kansas City, Inc., operates the Kansas City Museum at Corinthian Hall in Kansas City's historic northeast neighborhood. Union Station houses the permanent collections and archives for Union Station Kansas City, Inc., and the Kansas City Museum.

As a nonprofit organization, Union Station's operating costs are funded by revenues earned through commercial space leases and facility rental, admission to the station's attractions and exhibits, individual and family memberships, private donations and grants. Union Station receives no tax dollars, and all operating costs are covered by revenues earned from these sources.

Keeping the building maintained and operating annually costs more than $3 million. Union Station members are key partners in supporting the history, preservation, maintenance and daily operations of this magnificent building. To learn more about Union Station, call 816-460-2020 or visit www.unionstation.org.

The University of Kansas Hospital

*Since 1998, patient volume has doubled to about 27,000 patients,
and the hospital has had major recent expansions to accommodate patient demand.*

The **University of Kansas Hospital** was founded in 1906, but it was the hospital's rebirth in 1998 that propelled it to be one of the best academic medical centers in the country.

That was the year the Kansas Legislature removed the hospital from the University of Kansas system and put it under an independent public authority. The change allowed the hospital to focus exclusively on patient care.

Since 1998, The University of Kansas Hospital has received no state or local tax money (aside from Medicare and Medicaid). The hospital lives off its own revenue, its own credit and its own plan for the future.

The results have been spectacular.

In a 2012 study of the 101 top academic medical centers in the country (conducted by University HealthSystem Consortium), The University of Kansas Hospital ranked third in the nation for patient quality and safety.

"It is gratifying for our team of physicians, nurses and other healthcare professionals to be recognized for their outstanding patient outcomes. We are delighted to be honored, but we do not focus our organization on winning awards. Our focus has been and always will be on our patients," said Bob Page, president and chief executive officer of The University of Kansas Hospital.

Other honors include being named to 10 of the 12 *U.S. News & World Report* 2012-13 Best Hospital lists. The hospital was honored in Cancer (#37), Cardiology & Heart

The University of Kansas Hospital

Surgery (#24), Diabetes & Endocrinology (#38), Ear, Nose & Throat (#20), Gastroenterology (#20), Geriatrics (#17), Nephrology (#15), Neurology & Neurosurgery (#22), Pulmonology (#15) and Urology (#45). The magazine also named The University of Kansas Hospital as the best adult hospital in the Kansas City metropolitan area and the best adult hospital in Kansas.

The high ranking for clinical cancer care is even more significant when coupled with the 2012 announcement that The University of Kansas Cancer Center became a National Cancer Institute-designated facility. The cancer center combines leading-edge research of the University of Kansas Medical Center, the University of Kansas and other leading regional research centers with clinical care from The University of Kansas Hospital. Additionally, clinical trials are offered throughout Kansas and the Kansas City area by the Midwest Cancer Alliance.

The hospital has the largest cancer program in the region and includes the area's only adult blood and marrow transplant program. Its 2011 partnership with Kansas City Cancer Center established an array of leading neighborhood cancer centers in both Kansas and Missouri.

The University of Kansas Hospital's heart program has been on the *U.S. News & World Report* list for six years and has received many other national honors. Cardiologists, heart surgeons and staff work together to create new knowledge in heart care in such diverse areas as GPS technology, hybrid minimally invasive procedures and even yoga.

Sports medicine is another growing strength. The University of Kansas Hospital is the official healthcare provider for Kansas Speedway, Sprint Center, the Kansas City Royals and the Kansas City Chiefs. In 2013, the growing program will have a clinic open to the public on the grounds of the Chiefs practice facility.

The hospital has the area's only nationally verified Level I Trauma Center, the highest national level epilepsy center, and a major solid organ transplant program for liver, kidney and pancreas.

All of this has resulted in remarkable growth for the hospital. Since 1998, patient volume has doubled to about 27,000 patients, and the hospital has had major recent expansions to accommodate patient demand.

It's a success story that began with the freedom to focus and invest in the best patient care, and the story gets better every year.

Bob Page, President and Chief Executive Officer, left, and Bob Honse, Chairman of the Board.

ACKNOWLEDGMENTS

The wide variety of libraries and other historical resources in and near Kansas City matches the richness of the area's history, which is rich, indeed. Those institutions are staffed by knowledgeable and helpful people who do an excellent job preserving, organizing and improving their collections.

At the State Historical Society of Missouri Research Center — Kansas City (formerly the Western Historical Manuscript Collection — Kansas City), David Boutros early in this project made invaluable suggestions about sources for the history of business and the economy in Kansas City. He and Manuscript Specialist Nancy Piepenbring kept their good humor intact during my last-minute combing for illustrations.

In the matter of illustrations, no one could have exceeded the calm and careful work of Jeremy Drouin at the Missouri Valley Special Collections of the Kansas City Public Library, who put up with a bombardment of my eleventh-hour image requests.

Frank Lenk at the Mid-America Regional Council spared time to help me understand the more recent functioning of the area's economy.

Also, I'm grateful for their help to Lisa Keys of the Kansas State Historical Society, Melanie Mattes at the Greater Kansas City Chamber of Commerce, Mindi Love at the Johnson County Museum, and also to Kansas Citians Bruce Mathews and Anita Gorman for their aid in my search for images. Derek Donovan and Jo Ann Groves of *The Kansas City Star* helped me greatly in searching the newspaper's holdings and acquiring items for publication in this volume.

The Mid-America Regional Council, U.S. Bureau of Labor Statistics, U.S. Bureau of Economic Analysis and the U.S. Bureau of the Census have shared much of their data online, a great help.

SOURCES

Here is a selection of sources that provide good overviews for various periods and people in Kansas City business history.

"A Century of Growth," supplement to *The Kansas City Business Journal*, December 10, 1999.

City of the Future: A Narrative History of Kansas City, 1850-1950 by Henry Haskell and Richard Fowler, F. Glenn Publishing Company, 1950.

"The Commercial Club of Kansas City, 1887-1993," paper by Betty Gibson. A. Theodore Brown papers, State Historical Society of Missouri Research Center – Kansas City.

"Economic Base of Greater Kansas City (Preliminary Draft of Text September 27, 1949)" by Jeannette Terrell and Patricia Zimmer. Paper prepared for the Economic Research Department of the Federal Reserve Bank of Kansas City, September 27, 1949.

"The Industrial Development of Kansas City" by Philip Neff and Robert M. Williams. Federal Reserve Bank of Kansas City, 1954

J.C. Nichols and the Shaping of Kansas City: Innovation in Planned Residential Communities by William S. Worley. University of Missouri Press, 1990.

Kansas City and the Railroads: Community Policy in the Growth of a Regional Metropolis by Charles N. Glaab. University Press of Kansas, 1993 (first published in 1963).

Kansas City: An American Story by Rick Montgomery and Shirl Kasper. Kansas City Star Books, 2007.

Kansas City: Rise of a Regional Metropolis by William S. Worley. Heritage Media Corporation, 2002.

"KC: 100 Years of Business" by Lawrence Larsen and Frederick Sploetstoser, supplement to *The Kansas City Business Journal*, 1989.

K.C.: A History of Kansas City, Missouri, by A. Theodore Brown and Lyle W. Dorsett. Pruett Publishing Company, 1978.

Kansas City, Missouri: An Architectural History, 1826-1990 by George Ehrlich. University of Missouri Press, 1992.

Kansas City, Missouri: Its History and Its People, 1808-1908 by Carrie W. Whitney. Reprinted by Brookhaven

Press, 2005 (originally published in 1908).

Minute Books of the Commercial Club of Kansas City. Archives of the Greater Kansas City Chamber of Commerce.

Pendergast! by Lawrence H. Larsen and Nancy J. Hulston. University of Missouri Press, 1997.

Numerous presentations made as part of the Midcontinent Perspectives Lecture Series from 1974 to 1994, sponsored by the Midwest Research Institute.

Numerous presentations made as part of the Charles N. Kimball Lecture Series, sponsored by the State

Historical Society of Missouri Research Center – Kansas City.

Various issues of these publications:

The Kansas Citian, publication of the Greater Kansas City Chamber of Commerce.

The Kansas City Journal

The Kansas City Star

The Kansas City Times

ILLUSTRATION CREDITS

Files of *The Kansas City Star*: 5, 6, 13, 18 (right), 19, 21 (center left and bottom), 24, 26, 28, 32, 40 (bottom), 42, 43, 48-49, 50, 51 (top), 52 (center left), 55 (top and center left), 56 (top left), 58-59, 60, 61 (bottom), 67, 70-71, 73 (bottom), 75, 76 (bottom), 78, 79, 81, 82 (top), 85, 86, 87, 90 (top), 91 (top right), 92-93, 96 (top left and right), 98, 100, 101, 103, 104 (bottom left), 105, 106 (top), 108 (bottom right), 109 (top), 110, 111, 114, 115, 116 (bottom), 118, 119 (bottom right), 121, 122, 123, 124-125, 126 (bottom), 128, 129 (lower left), 132, 133, 134, 135, 136, 137, 138, 139, 142-143, 144, 145 (bottom), 146, 147, 148, 149, 150, 151, 152, 153, 154, 155, 156-157, 158, 159, 160, 161, 162, 163, 164, 165, 166-167, 168, 169, 170-171, 172, 173, 174-175, 176, 177, 178, 179, 180-181, 182, 183, 184, 185, 186, 187.

Missouri Valley Special Collections, Kansas City Public Library: 8, 11, 12-13, 16-17, 18 (left), 21 (top right), 22-23, 25, 29, 30 (top left), 33, 34, 35, 36-37, 40 (top), 44-45, 46 (top), 47, 53, 54, 56 (top right), 65, 66, 68, 69, 72, 73 (top), 84, 88 (top and center), 89, 102, 108 (top right), 119 (top and bottom left), 120, 129 (top right), 130-131, 140.

Greater Kansas City Chamber of Commerce: 82 (left center), 83 (bottom right), 91 (lower left), 96 (lower left), 104 (top left), 106 (bottom), 107, 108 (top left), 109 (bottom), 127 (bottom left), 129 (top left).

Kansas City Museum/Union Station Kansas City Collections, Kansas City MO: 1, 2, 15, 41, 51 (center right), 55 (top right), 64.

State Historical Society of Missouri Research Center – Kansas City: 4, 82 (bottom right), 83 (top left, top right and bottom left), 86, 90 (bottom), 99 (top), 141.

Library of Congress: 30-31, 38-39, 46 (bottom), 52 (top), 56 (center left), 57, 61 (top), 62-63.

Jackson County (Mo.) Historical Society Archives: 99 (bottom), 112-113, 116 (top), 117.

Wyandotte County Historical Society: 94-95, 97.

Kansas State Historical Society: 10, 14, 52 (center right).

Courtesy Johnson County Museum: 96 (lower right), 127 (top and bottom center).

Wilborn & Associates: 76 (top), 145 (top).

DeGolyer Library, Southern Methodist University, Dallas, Texas, Ag1982.0086: 27.

Overland Park Historical Society: 126 (top).

Art © T.H. Benton and R.P. Benton Testamentary Trusts/ UMB Bank Trustee/Licensed by VAGA, New York, NY: 80.